Contents Table

Section 1: Introduction to Pega Systems and BPM

Section 2: Getting Started with Pega Platform

Section 3: Designing and Building Applications

Section 4: Advanced Application Development Techniques

Section 5: Automation and Integrations

Section 6: Security and Compliance

Section 7: Performance Optimization and Troubleshooting

Section 8: Monitoring and Reporting

Section 9: Advanced Administration and Management

Section 10: Case Studies and Real-World Applications

Section 11: Future Trends and Innovations

Section 12: Learning and Certification Paths

Appendices

Welcome & What You'll Learn

Welcome to *Pega Systems: The Science Behind Process Automation*. This book serves as your comprehensive guide to understanding and leveraging Pega Systems for streamlining business operations through Business Process Management (BPM) software. Whether you are a seasoned developer, a business analyst, or a technology enthusiast looking to expand your knowledge, this guide will provide you with an in-depth look at Pega's capabilities and their role in modern business automation.

Why This Book Matters

In today's competitive business landscape, efficiency, agility, and precision are more important than ever. Pega Systems has emerged as a leading platform for BPM, providing a robust set of tools for automating complex workflows and enhancing enterprise productivity. By reading this book, you will gain the knowledge to build, manage, and optimize Pega applications that can transform business processes and drive meaningful results.

What You Will Learn

In this book, you will journey through foundational concepts to advanced practices in Pega development and application. Here's what you can expect to learn:

- **Understanding the Foundations of Pega Systems and BPM**: Develop a strong grasp of the basics of Business Process Management and how Pega Systems fits into the broader landscape of process automation. You will become familiar with key terminologies, concepts, and the strategic benefits that Pega offers to modern enterprises.
- **Getting Started with the Pega Platform**: Learn about the architecture and environment setup of the Pega platform, including user interface navigation and understanding essential components. This section will lay the groundwork for effectively using Pega Studio and understanding case management basics.
- **Designing and Building Applications**: Master the process of creating your first Pega application, designing case lifecycles, implementing workflows, building data models, and configuring user interfaces. You will also explore how to integrate business rules, leverage visual modeling tools, and create seamless user experiences.
- **Advanced Development Techniques**: Enhance your skill set by delving into complex case types, decision rules, reusable components, SLA implementation, dynamic user interfaces, and building mobile-compatible applications.
- **Automation and Integrations**: Discover how to integrate Pega with external systems, manage APIs and web services, and incorporate robotic process automation (RPA) and AI capabilities into your applications.
- **Security and Compliance**: Understand the importance of securing Pega applications, implementing user authentication, role-based access control, data privacy measures, and monitoring potential threats.
- **Performance Optimization and Troubleshooting**: Equip yourself with best practices for optimizing application performance, using tuning tools, managing system metrics, and troubleshooting common application issues.
- **Monitoring and Reporting**: Learn how to create monitoring dashboards, use reporting tools, design custom reports, and leverage real-time analytics to drive better decision-making.
- **Advanced Administration and Management**: Gain insights into application version management, configuration for optimal performance, environment migration, and Pega's deployment and DevOps practices.

- **Real-World Case Studies**: Read about successful implementations in industries like banking, healthcare, supply chain, customer service, and telecommunications, with lessons learned from actual deployments.
- **Future Trends and Innovations**: Explore the future of BPM and how emerging technologies will shape the next generation of Pega solutions and support agile transformations.
- **Learning and Certification Paths**: Find guidance on Pega training, certification pathways, tips for exams, and resources to further your learning journey. You'll also discover the best ways to engage with the Pega community for support and growth.

How to Use This Book

This book is structured to guide you step-by-step, from understanding the fundamental concepts of Pega to applying advanced techniques and exploring real-world scenarios. You can read it sequentially for a comprehensive learning experience or jump to specific sections that align with your current needs and expertise.

Whether your goal is to develop powerful Pega applications, improve your business processes, or advance your career with Pega certifications, this book is your roadmap. Dive in and start your journey to mastering Pega Systems and unlocking the potential of process automation for your organization.

Let's get started!

Section 1:
Introduction to Pega Systems and BPM

Welcome to Process Automation with Pega

Pega Systems has long been recognized as a pioneer in the field of Business Process Management (BPM), providing comprehensive tools for automating and optimizing business operations. This chapter serves as your introduction to the core principles of process automation and highlights why Pega is an essential tool for enterprises looking to enhance efficiency, streamline workflows, and improve overall business outcomes.

The Importance of Process Automation in Modern Business

In an era where speed, accuracy, and adaptability define success, process automation stands as a critical strategy for businesses to maintain their competitive edge. Automating routine and complex processes reduces manual work, minimizes errors, and allows businesses to scale their operations efficiently. It also supports agility, enabling companies to respond swiftly to market changes and customer demands.

Pega Systems offers a robust solution that integrates process automation seamlessly with business operations, helping organizations achieve these goals. From simplifying customer service interactions to managing intricate back-end workflows, Pega's capabilities ensure that businesses can maintain high standards of performance and productivity.

A First Look at Pega Systems

At its core, Pega Systems is designed to facilitate the creation of dynamic, adaptive, and efficient business applications. It combines BPM with artificial intelligence (AI) and robotic process automation (RPA) to offer a powerful platform for orchestrating business processes. This comprehensive approach supports everything from workflow design and case management to real-time decision-making and predictive analytics.

Pega's platform enables non-technical and technical users alike to build and modify applications without extensive coding knowledge. This low-code approach accelerates development timelines and empowers teams to innovate and iterate solutions more rapidly.

Key Benefits of Using Pega for Automation

Implementing Pega for process automation yields significant advantages, including:

- **End-to-End Automation**: Pega allows for the automation of entire processes, ensuring consistency and efficiency from start to finish.
- **Scalability**: Whether managing a handful of workflows or overseeing large-scale enterprise operations, Pega's architecture supports scalability to accommodate growth.
- **Intelligent Process Management**: By integrating AI and RPA, Pega enhances decision-making capabilities and enables intelligent task automation, which can anticipate needs and optimize workflows.
- **Customizable Solutions**: The platform offers a wide range of tools and templates that can be adapted to meet the unique needs of different industries and business objectives.
- **Enhanced User Experience**: Pega's interface is designed to be user-friendly, making it accessible for teams across various departments and skill levels to navigate and use effectively.

An Overview of What's to Come

This chapter sets the stage for a deeper exploration into the features, tools, and strategies that make Pega an invaluable resource for business process management. In the following sections of this book, you will learn about:

- **Foundational Concepts**: The history and essential terminologies of BPM and Pega.
- **Getting Started**: Setting up your Pega environment and becoming familiar with its architecture and core components.
- **Building Applications**: Creating your first application, designing workflows, and developing data models.
- **Advanced Techniques**: Implementing complex case types, decision rules, and mobile-compatible applications.
- **Integration and Automation**: Leveraging Pega's RPA and API management capabilities to connect with external systems and enhance automation.
- **Security and Compliance**: Ensuring data privacy, managing user authentication, and aligning with regulatory standards.
- **Performance Optimization**: Best practices for maintaining and optimizing system performance.
- **Real-World Applications**: Case studies demonstrating Pega's effectiveness in various industries.
- **Future Trends**: Insights into how Pega is evolving to meet the challenges of tomorrow's business landscape.

With this foundation in place, you're now ready to dive deeper into Pega Systems and BPM. Let's explore the dynamic world of process automation and discover how Pega can transform your business operations for the better.

Understanding Business Process Management (BPM)

Business Process Management (BPM) stands at the core of operational efficiency and strategic business transformation. It is a systematic approach aimed at optimizing, managing, and automating the processes that drive an organization's day-to-day activities. This chapter delves into the principles, objectives, and significance of BPM, setting the stage for understanding how Pega Systems leverages BPM to create powerful, automated business solutions.

What is Business Process Management (BPM)?

BPM is the practice of designing, executing, monitoring, and continuously improving business processes. It involves analyzing current workflows, identifying inefficiencies, and implementing solutions that enhance productivity and quality. Unlike traditional process management, BPM is holistic, focusing on aligning processes with organizational goals and ensuring agility in response to changing business needs.

BPM encompasses the full lifecycle of processes, including:

- **Design**: Outlining the process steps, roles, and rules.
- **Modeling**: Creating representations of processes to visualize potential changes.
- **Execution**: Implementing process models through automation or manual operation.
- **Monitoring**: Keeping track of process performance using key metrics.
- **Optimization**: Refining processes for better efficiency and effectiveness.

Key Objectives of BPM

BPM is implemented to achieve several strategic objectives that drive long-term success:

1. **Increased Efficiency**: Streamlining workflows to minimize waste, reduce manual effort, and improve resource utilization.
2. **Enhanced Productivity**: Enabling teams to focus on higher-value tasks by automating routine processes.
3. **Consistency and Quality**: Standardizing processes to ensure uniform outputs and reduce errors.
4. **Agility**: Providing the flexibility to adapt processes quickly in response to market changes, technological advancements, or customer demands.
5. **Compliance and Risk Management**: Ensuring processes meet regulatory standards and mitigate potential risks.

The Evolution of BPM Practices

The concept of BPM has evolved significantly over the years, shifting from traditional, document-based approaches to more dynamic, technology-driven strategies. Initially, BPM was a manual process improvement effort, often involving extensive documentation and incremental changes. Today, advancements in technology and software have transformed BPM into a comprehensive and automated practice that integrates with various enterprise tools and systems.

Modern BPM approaches emphasize:

- **Digital Transformation**: Leveraging software and platforms to automate complex processes and reduce human intervention.
- **Integration with AI**: Using artificial intelligence to analyze data, predict outcomes, and make real-time decisions.
- **Cloud Computing**: Enabling processes to be more accessible, scalable, and collaborative across teams and geographies.

How BPM Differs from Workflow Automation

While BPM and workflow automation share similarities, they serve different purposes. Workflow automation focuses on automating specific tasks or activities within a process. It typically follows a linear path and is limited to predefined steps. BPM, on the other hand, encompasses a broader approach that covers the entire process lifecycle and includes the flexibility to adapt and optimize processes continuously.

Key Differences Include:

- **Scope**: Workflow automation is task-focused, while BPM takes a process-oriented view.
- **Adaptability**: BPM involves continuous monitoring and improvement, whereas workflow automation often operates as a static set of tasks.
- **Complexity**: BPM solutions handle complex, cross-departmental processes, while workflow automation can be applied to simpler, standalone tasks.

The Role of BPM in Business Strategy

BPM plays an integral role in aligning business processes with organizational strategy. By breaking down silos and promoting cross-functional collaboration, BPM helps businesses create cohesive, customer-centric experiences. Effective BPM leads to:

- **Improved Customer Satisfaction**: Faster and more consistent service delivery.
- **Operational Resilience**: The ability to withstand disruptions through adaptable processes.
- **Strategic Growth**: Freeing up resources to focus on innovation and expansion.

Preparing for BPM Implementation

Implementing BPM requires a strategic approach that starts with mapping out existing processes and identifying key pain points. Successful BPM implementation often includes:

1. **Stakeholder Engagement**: Ensuring buy-in from all relevant teams and departments.
2. **Process Analysis**: Conducting a thorough review of current workflows to spot inefficiencies.
3. **Technology Selection**: Choosing the right BPM platform, such as Pega Systems, that supports the needs and scale of the business.
4. **Continuous Improvement Culture**: Fostering an environment where process optimization is an ongoing effort rather than a one-time project.

Why Pega Systems Stands Out in BPM

Pega Systems is a leading BPM platform that provides a range of tools designed for process automation, case management, and workflow optimization. What makes Pega unique is its ability to combine BPM capabilities with AI, RPA, and advanced integration functionalities. This combination enables organizations to manage complex processes more efficiently while maintaining the flexibility to adapt and scale as needed.

With Pega's low-code environment, businesses can design and modify processes with ease, making it accessible to both developers and non-technical users. The platform supports end-to-end process automation, ensuring seamless connectivity between various systems and teams.

The Role of Pega Systems in Modern Enterprises

In today's fast-paced, technology-driven business environment, enterprises need tools that support agility, efficiency, and scalability. Pega Systems has become a cornerstone in the realm of Business Process Management (BPM) and digital transformation, empowering organizations to streamline their operations and foster innovation. This chapter explores how Pega Systems fits into the landscape of modern enterprises and why it is a valuable asset for businesses seeking process automation and operational excellence.

Understanding Pega Systems' Unique Value Proposition

Pega Systems offers a unified platform that integrates BPM, customer relationship management (CRM), artificial intelligence (AI), and robotic process automation (RPA) to help organizations build robust applications without extensive coding. This low-code approach enables businesses to design, deploy, and adapt applications quickly, significantly reducing development timelines and fostering rapid innovation.

Key features that make Pega stand out include:

- **End-to-End Process Automation**: Pega supports comprehensive process automation, from task initiation to completion, ensuring consistency and reducing manual intervention.
- **Scalability**: The platform is built to support enterprises of all sizes, allowing them to scale their operations seamlessly as their needs evolve.
- **Flexibility**: Pega's architecture supports integration with existing enterprise systems, enabling businesses to extend the platform's capabilities while leveraging their current IT investments.
- **AI-Driven Decision-Making**: The platform integrates AI and machine learning to deliver intelligent, data-driven insights that optimize business processes in real-time.
- **User-Centric Design**: Pega's user interface is designed to be intuitive, making it accessible to non-technical users while providing advanced functionality for experienced developers.

The Strategic Role of Pega in Modern Enterprises

The role of Pega Systems in modern enterprises can be broken down into several strategic areas that directly contribute to an organization's growth and competitive advantage.

1. **Enhancing Customer Experience** Enterprises today prioritize customer experience as a key differentiator. Pega's CRM capabilities enable organizations to deliver personalized, consistent, and efficient service across various channels. By automating customer interactions and utilizing AI-driven insights, businesses can better understand customer needs, predict behavior, and proactively address issues, ultimately improving customer satisfaction and loyalty.
2. **Streamlining Business Operations** Pega Systems excels in simplifying complex workflows and processes that span multiple departments. Through its case management and workflow automation features, Pega helps organizations reduce bottlenecks, minimize errors, and enhance cross-functional collaboration. This streamlined approach leads to increased operational efficiency and higher productivity.
3. **Driving Digital Transformation** As businesses embrace digital transformation, they require platforms that support seamless integration and modernization. Pega's low-code and no-code environment allows enterprises to digitize and automate their processes quickly. This capability is particularly valuable for organizations looking to move away from legacy systems that hinder their ability to innovate and adapt.
4. **Supporting Agile and Adaptive Operations** Modern enterprises need to be agile to respond to rapidly changing market conditions. Pega's platform is designed to be adaptable, supporting the continuous improvement of processes through its iterative development approach. This agility empowers businesses to pivot quickly, test new strategies, and implement changes without significant downtime.

5. **Ensuring Compliance and Security** Regulatory compliance and data security are paramount in today's business landscape. Pega Systems provides robust features for user authentication, role-based access control (RBAC), and data privacy, helping organizations adhere to regulations and industry standards. This focus on security ensures that sensitive information is protected, reducing the risk of data breaches and compliance issues.

Real-World Applications of Pega in Enterprises

Pega Systems has proven its effectiveness in a variety of industries, each benefiting from its tailored solutions:

- **Financial Services**: Banks and financial institutions use Pega to automate loan processing, enhance fraud detection, and streamline customer onboarding.
- **Healthcare**: Healthcare providers leverage Pega for patient engagement, claims processing, and improving care coordination.
- **Telecommunications**: Companies in the telecom sector utilize Pega to manage service requests, automate support tasks, and improve network operations.
- **Insurance**: Pega supports policy management, claims automation, and customer service enhancements within the insurance industry.

These examples underscore Pega's ability to handle diverse and complex business processes, demonstrating why it is a preferred choice for many leading enterprises.

How Pega Aligns with Modern Business Goals

Modern businesses aim to maximize efficiency, foster innovation, and deliver exceptional customer experiences while maintaining a focus on cost reduction and scalability. Pega Systems aligns with these goals by:

- **Reducing Time to Market**: Pega's low-code environment accelerates the development and deployment of new applications.
- **Enabling Data-Driven Decisions**: The integration of AI and advanced analytics helps enterprises make informed decisions that align with their strategic goals.
- **Facilitating Seamless Collaboration**: Pega's collaborative design capabilities allow cross-functional teams to work together more effectively, ensuring that business and IT goals are aligned.
- **Supporting Sustainability Initiatives**: By optimizing processes and reducing redundancies, Pega helps organizations minimize waste and support sustainability efforts.

In the following chapter, we will explore the key concepts and terminology that form the foundation of Pega Systems, providing you with the essential knowledge needed to navigate and utilize this powerful platform effectively.

Key Concepts and Terminology in Pega

Understanding the fundamental concepts and terminology used within Pega Systems is essential for mastering the platform and building efficient, automated business applications. This chapter introduces key terms and concepts that form the backbone of Pega's framework, allowing you to navigate its environment with confidence and develop robust solutions.

1. Case Management

Case management is a core concept in Pega, where a "case" represents a business transaction or process that needs to be completed. Cases encompass multiple stages and steps, and Pega's case management capabilities enable the modeling and management of complex processes from start to finish.

- **Stages**: High-level groupings that represent major phases of a case.
- **Steps**: Individual tasks or actions within a stage that drive the case forward.
- **Subcases**: Smaller, related cases that form part of a larger case.

2. Rules and Rule-Based Architecture

Pega's rule-based architecture is one of its defining features. **Rules** are building blocks in Pega that define how a system behaves. Unlike traditional programming logic, Pega organizes and reuses rules for greater flexibility and maintainability.

- **RuleSet**: A collection of rules grouped together for versioning and deployment.
- **Rule Types**: Include decision rules, data transforms, activities, and user interface components.
- **Inheritance**: Pega uses pattern and directed inheritance to share and reuse rules across different layers of applications.

3. Case Types and Case Designer

Case types are blueprints for how a specific business process is managed in Pega. The **Case Designer** tool in Pega Studio allows users to define the lifecycle of a case by mapping out its stages, steps, and transitions.

- **Primary Stage**: The main path a case follows from start to finish.
- **Alternate Stage**: Handles exceptions or alternative paths that a case might take.

4. Data Pages and Data Models

Data pages are structures in Pega that load and store data for use across cases and applications. They ensure that data is accessed efficiently and consistently.

- **Single-Page Data Page**: Holds data for one instance of an object.
- **List Data Page**: Contains a list of data objects, such as a collection of customer records.
- **Properties**: Define the structure of data models, acting as fields or attributes within cases and rules.

5. Flow Rules and Flow Shapes

Flow rules are diagrams that outline the sequence of actions or steps within a case. **Flow shapes** are the visual elements used in these diagrams, representing decision points, subprocesses, assignments, and integrations.

- **Assignment Shape**: Marks where user interaction is required.
- **Decision Shape**: Represents a conditional step that evaluates criteria before proceeding.

6. Worklist and Workbasket

A **worklist** is a personalized list of tasks assigned to a user, while a **workbasket** is a shared list of tasks accessible to a group of users or roles. These help manage workloads and distribute tasks effectively within an organization.

7. User Interfaces (UIs) and Sections

Pega's user interface components are built using **sections**, which define how data is presented to users. Sections can be nested and reused to create comprehensive views.

- **Harness**: A type of rule that organizes sections and layouts to create user screens.
- **Portals**: Interfaces through which users interact with Pega applications, such as user portals for customer service agents or manager dashboards.

8. Decision Tables and Decision Trees

Pega incorporates powerful tools for decision-making, such as **decision tables** and **decision trees**. These rules allow for conditional logic that can automate complex business policies.

- **Decision Table**: Uses a tabular format to evaluate conditions and return results.
- **Decision Tree**: Visualizes decision paths through branching conditions.

9. Declarative Rules

Declarative rules automate data changes and calculations without requiring user intervention. They include rules like **constraints**, **declare expressions**, and **declare triggers**, ensuring that data stays consistent throughout the application.

10. Data Transforms

Data transforms are used to manipulate and map data between various sources. They can be invoked to prepare data for use within cases, initialize properties, or transform data from one format to another.

11. SLA (Service Level Agreement)

SLAs define the deadlines and urgency levels associated with tasks in Pega. They help manage expectations by specifying when tasks should be completed and alerting users if deadlines are at risk.

- **Goal**: The desired completion time for a task.
- **Deadline**: The time by which a task must be completed to avoid breaching SLA terms.
- **Escalation**: The process that occurs if a task goes beyond its deadline, such as sending notifications or reassigning tasks.

12. Integration and Connectors

Pega facilitates seamless integration with external systems through **connectors**. These are pre-configured tools that allow applications to communicate with databases, web services, and other enterprise systems.

- **SOAP and REST Connectors**: Support integration with external APIs.
- **Connect-Database**: Used to connect directly to external databases.

Conclusion: These core concepts and terminologies are the building blocks of Pega Systems. Understanding these elements will provide you with a solid foundation to explore more complex aspects of Pega application development and process automation.

A Brief History of Pega Systems

Pega Systems, now a leader in Business Process Management (BPM) and Customer Relationship Management (CRM) solutions, started with a vision of transforming the way businesses handle complex processes. Understanding the history of Pega provides valuable insights into its evolution, growth, and the strategic innovations that have shaped its development over the years.

The Founding of Pega Systems

Pega Systems was founded in 1983 by Alan Trefler, who remains an influential leader as the company's CEO. Trefler's background in computer science and championship-level chess played a crucial role in his approach to business automation. He recognized the need for a platform that could combine business logic with adaptable processes, allowing organizations to automate tasks efficiently while accommodating change.

Initially, Pega's focus was on streamlining decision-making processes in financial services, but its capabilities soon expanded to other industries as well. The company's early success was marked by its ability to deliver robust solutions that reduced operational inefficiencies and improved customer experiences.

Key Milestones in Pega's Growth

Pega Systems' journey from a niche software company to a global BPM and CRM leader includes several significant milestones:

1. **1990s – Early Growth and Expansion**: In its early years, Pega made strides in automating complex business processes, securing its foothold in the financial sector. The platform's ability to adapt rules and automate workflows attracted major clients looking for scalable and flexible solutions.
2. **2000s – Diversification and Global Reach**: The early 2000s saw Pega Systems expanding beyond financial services and into healthcare, insurance, and telecommunications. This period marked the introduction of Pega's unique rule-based architecture, which differentiated it from competitors by allowing greater customization and easier application management. The company went public in 1996, raising capital that fueled its growth and product innovation.
3. **2010s – Embracing Low-Code Development and AI**: One of the pivotal moments for Pega was its shift toward a low-code development approach. This move democratized application development, enabling non-technical users to create and modify applications using visual tools. Pega also integrated artificial intelligence and machine learning into its platform, enhancing its decision-making capabilities and predictive analytics.
   During this decade, Pega launched its Pega Infinity™ platform, which combined BPM, CRM, and AI to offer end-to-end automation and customer engagement solutions. This move solidified Pega's reputation as a pioneer in intelligent process automation.
4. **2020s – Continuous Innovation and Future-Oriented Solutions**: The current era of Pega Systems is defined by its focus on hyperautomation and digital transformation. With the introduction of cloud-native solutions and enhanced integration capabilities, Pega supports enterprises in adapting to rapidly changing markets. The company continues to innovate by incorporating advanced robotic process automation (RPA) and expanding its capabilities in customer engagement and intelligent automation.

Strategic Acquisitions and Partnerships

To bolster its product offerings and expand its technological reach, Pega has made strategic acquisitions over the years. These acquisitions have brought in specialized technology and expertise, further enhancing Pega's platform:

- **Chordiant Software**: In 2010, Pega acquired Chordiant Software, a leading provider of customer experience software, which helped Pega strengthen its CRM capabilities and customer-centric approach.
- **OpenSpan**: In 2016, the acquisition of OpenSpan allowed Pega to integrate robotic desktop automation (RDA) and RPA, enabling more comprehensive automation solutions and empowering users to optimize both front and back-office operations.

Partnerships with cloud providers, system integrators, and technology vendors have also been instrumental in extending Pega's reach and enhancing its solutions. Collaborations with major industry players have allowed Pega to offer seamless integrations and adapt to diverse IT environments.

Pega's Core Philosophy and Mission

Pega Systems has always adhered to a mission of simplifying complex processes and empowering organizations to deliver exceptional customer experiences. This philosophy is reflected in the platform's core strengths:

- **Unified Architecture**: Pega's architecture supports seamless collaboration between business users and IT teams, fostering a unified approach to application development and process management.
- **Flexibility and Adaptability**: The rule-based design ensures that Pega applications can be easily modified to meet evolving business needs without extensive redevelopment.
- **Scalability**: Pega's solutions are built to grow with enterprises, enabling them to scale operations without sacrificing efficiency or performance.

The Impact of Pega Systems Today

Today, Pega Systems is recognized as a leader in BPM, CRM, and automation, with a client base spanning various industries, including financial services, healthcare, insurance, and government. The platform's ability to integrate with existing technologies and offer a comprehensive suite of tools for automation, decision management, and customer engagement has solidified its position as a preferred choice for enterprises seeking digital transformation.

Pega's influence is evident in its continued commitment to innovation, investment in AI and machine learning, and emphasis on low-code development. These attributes make Pega an indispensable tool for organizations looking to streamline operations and foster a culture of continuous improvement.

Advantages of Using Pega for Business Operations

Pega Systems has gained widespread recognition for its robust, flexible, and scalable platform that empowers organizations to streamline their business operations effectively. This chapter outlines the key advantages of using Pega, emphasizing how it enhances productivity, supports innovation, and helps enterprises achieve strategic goals.

1. Comprehensive Process Automation

One of the standout features of Pega is its ability to automate end-to-end processes, reducing the need for manual intervention and ensuring consistency throughout. Pega's case management and workflow automation capabilities allow businesses to:

- **Minimize human error** by automating repetitive and rule-based tasks.
- **Accelerate task completion** with streamlined workflows that follow predefined logic.
- **Enhance efficiency** through a centralized approach that unites multiple departments under a single process flow.

With Pega, organizations can seamlessly automate complex processes that involve decision-making, data collection, and task routing, ensuring comprehensive operational control.

2. Scalability and Adaptability

Pega is built to scale alongside an organization, making it suitable for enterprises of all sizes. The platform's architecture supports growth by allowing new features and capabilities to be added without disrupting existing processes. This adaptability ensures that as a business evolves, Pega can accommodate changes, including shifts in business models, market demands, and regulatory requirements.

- **Modular Design**: Pega's modular architecture means organizations can start with a specific process or department and expand to other areas as needed.
- **Flexible Customization**: Businesses can easily modify applications and workflows to align with changing operational goals without extensive redevelopment.

3. Low-Code Development Environment

Pega's low-code development platform is designed to empower both technical and non-technical users to create, customize, and deploy applications with minimal coding knowledge. This democratizes application development and:

- **Reduces development timelines** by enabling rapid prototyping and iteration.
- **Lowers dependency on IT teams**, allowing business users to implement changes quickly.
- **Fosters collaboration** between IT and business units, ensuring that applications are built to meet user needs effectively.

The intuitive drag-and-drop interface in Pega Studio allows users to build processes, design user interfaces, and configure rules without requiring extensive programming skills.

4. Integration Capabilities

Modern enterprises often operate using a diverse set of applications and systems. Pega's powerful integration capabilities enable organizations to connect their existing software and data sources seamlessly. Pega supports integrations through:

- **REST and SOAP APIs** for communication with external services.

- **Connectors and adapters** that facilitate data exchange between legacy systems and modern applications.
- **Real-time data synchronization**, ensuring that applications have the most up-to-date information available.

These integrations not only extend Pega's functionality but also help maintain consistency across business operations, reducing data silos and promoting unified workflows.

5. Enhanced Decision-Making with AI and Machine Learning

Pega incorporates artificial intelligence (AI) and machine learning (ML) to enhance decision-making and automate complex tasks intelligently. By leveraging these technologies, businesses can:

- **Predict customer behavior** and tailor interactions accordingly.
- **Optimize workflow routing** based on real-time data analysis and insights.
- **Identify process bottlenecks** and recommend adjustments for improved efficiency.

Pega's AI-driven capabilities also provide predictive analytics, helping organizations foresee challenges and make informed, data-backed decisions.

6. Improved Customer Experience

A significant advantage of using Pega is its focus on customer-centric process management. The platform is designed to deliver personalized, timely, and effective customer interactions. Businesses can leverage Pega's CRM features to:

- **Deliver consistent multi-channel support**, ensuring seamless experiences across different customer touchpoints.
- **Automate customer service workflows**, reducing response times and enhancing satisfaction.
- **Leverage case management** to track and resolve customer issues comprehensively.

This focus on customer engagement not only boosts client retention but also strengthens brand loyalty and trust.

7. Compliance and Regulatory Support

Meeting industry regulations and maintaining data privacy are critical for many organizations. Pega's built-in compliance features help businesses align with legal and regulatory requirements by:

- **Ensuring secure data handling** through robust encryption and access control.
- **Providing detailed audit trails** for transparent record-keeping and reporting.
- **Supporting governance policies**, making it easier for enterprises to implement consistent security and compliance measures across operations.

These features give organizations peace of mind, knowing that their operations meet industry standards and safeguard sensitive information.

8. Real-Time Monitoring and Reporting

Pega's platform includes comprehensive monitoring and reporting tools that provide real-time insights into process performance. This visibility helps organizations:

- **Track key performance indicators (KPIs)** to ensure alignment with business objectives.
- **Identify potential issues** before they impact the business, allowing for proactive management.
- **Generate customizable reports** that can be shared across departments to facilitate informed decision-making.

Real-time analytics empower teams to stay agile and adapt processes as needed to optimize performance and achieve better outcomes.

9. Cost Efficiency

While investing in a BPM platform can represent a significant upfront cost, Pega's automation capabilities often lead to substantial long-term savings. By reducing manual workloads, improving process efficiency, and minimizing errors, businesses can:

- **Lower operational costs** through reduced overhead and resource allocation.
- **Enhance productivity**, leading to increased output without proportional increases in costs.
- **Streamline project timelines**, cutting down time spent on development and deployment.

Pega's return on investment (ROI) is seen through improved operational efficiencies and better resource management.

These advantages make Pega Systems an indispensable tool for organizations looking to optimize their business operations, drive efficiency, and maintain a competitive edge.

Section 2:
Getting Started with Pega Platform

Overview of the Pega Platform Architecture

The Pega platform is renowned for its powerful architecture that supports dynamic case management, comprehensive process automation, and seamless integration with various systems. To harness the full potential of Pega, understanding its underlying architecture is essential. This chapter provides a detailed overview of the Pega platform's architecture, outlining the main components and how they interact to deliver an efficient, scalable, and secure environment for building enterprise applications.

1. The Layered Structure of Pega

The Pega platform is built on a layered architecture designed to promote reusability, scalability, and efficient development. These layers enable organizations to structure their applications in a modular way that facilitates maintenance and future enhancements.

- **Enterprise Layer**: This topmost layer contains shared components and assets that are common across the enterprise. It allows for centralized control and management of reusable assets, including business rules, data models, and integrations.
- **Framework Layer**: The framework layer consists of application components that provide industry-specific functionality. These frameworks can be customized to meet unique business needs while still adhering to best practices.
- **Implementation Layer**: This layer is where specific business applications are developed and configured. It builds upon the reusable elements of the enterprise and framework layers to create tailored solutions for specific use cases.

2. Core Architectural Components

Pega's architecture is composed of several core components that interact to deliver its robust functionality. These include:

- **Rules Engine**: At the heart of Pega lies its rule-based architecture, which allows users to define business rules that drive application behavior. The rules engine processes these rules dynamically to control workflows, user interfaces, decision logic, and more.
- **Case Management Engine**: Pega's case management engine supports the creation and handling of cases, facilitating complex workflows that may span multiple stages, steps, and actors. This component is key for orchestrating processes and maintaining data consistency.
- **Database Management**: Pega uses a relational database to store application data, user information, and process states. This backend database can be configured for high availability and performance to meet enterprise-level demands.
- **User Interface Layer**: Pega's UI layer is designed to support responsive, user-friendly interfaces. Using Pega's low-code design tools, users can create dynamic sections and harnesses that ensure a seamless user experience across devices.
- **Integration Services**: Pega's integration services facilitate connectivity with external systems, enabling data exchange through REST, SOAP, and other protocols. This component ensures that Pega applications can work in harmony with existing enterprise software.

3. The Role of PegaRULES Database

The **PegaRULES database** is an integral part of the platform, managing the storage of rules, case data, and work items. It supports the rule-based architecture by handling versioning and inheritance, allowing for precise control over rule execution and modifications.

- **Rule Resolution**: The PegaRULES database utilizes rule resolution to determine which rules should be applied in specific contexts. This system ensures that the most relevant and current rules are executed, even as applications evolve over time.
- **Version Control**: By storing different versions of rules and case types, the database allows developers to manage changes without affecting the stability of running applications.

4. The Pega Runtime Environment

The Pega platform operates within a runtime environment that interprets and executes the rules and case logic defined by developers. This environment supports scalability and high performance, making it suitable for handling enterprise-level workloads.

- **Pega Application Server**: Pega applications run on application servers that execute Java code and manage communication between the user interface, case management engine, and database.
- **Java and JVM**: Pega leverages Java as its underlying programming language, ensuring platform compatibility and robust performance across different environments. The Java Virtual Machine (JVM) facilitates cross-platform operation and optimizes execution speed.

5. Deployment Options

Pega offers flexible deployment options to suit various business needs, including on-premises, cloud, and hybrid configurations.

- **On-Premises Deployment**: Ideal for organizations that require complete control over their infrastructure and data.
- **Pega Cloud**: A fully managed cloud solution that offers the advantages of scalability, maintenance-free operations, and high availability. Pega Cloud is designed to provide rapid deployments with minimal overhead.
- **Hybrid Deployment**: Combines on-premises and cloud capabilities, allowing businesses to manage sensitive data on-site while leveraging cloud features for non-sensitive operations.

6. Security Features

Security is a critical component of Pega's architecture. The platform is equipped with robust security mechanisms that protect data, manage user authentication, and control access.

- **Role-Based Access Control (RBAC)**: Pega's RBAC ensures that users only have access to functions and data relevant to their roles.
- **Authentication Services**: Pega supports multiple authentication methods, including single sign-on (SSO) and multi-factor authentication (MFA).
- **Data Encryption**: Pega's architecture includes data encryption options for secure data handling and compliance with industry regulations.

7. Architectural Benefits for Businesses

The architecture of the Pega platform offers several benefits that make it an attractive solution for businesses:

- **Scalability**: Pega's modular and layered design supports scaling from small departmental applications to large, complex enterprise solutions.
- **Flexibility**: The platform's architecture allows businesses to adapt their applications easily as requirements change.

- **Reusability**: Components developed in the enterprise and framework layers can be reused across different applications, reducing development time and cost.
- **High Availability and Performance**: Pega's architecture is built to ensure that applications are available and performant, even under heavy load.

Understanding the architecture of Pega provides a solid foundation for delving deeper into the platform's functionalities.

Setting Up Your Pega Environment

Getting started with Pega requires setting up an environment that supports the development, testing, and deployment of Pega applications. A well-configured Pega environment ensures that teams can collaborate effectively, applications run smoothly, and processes are optimized from the beginning. This chapter guides you through the essential steps for setting up your Pega environment, from system requirements to best practices for configuration.

1. System Requirements and Preparation

Before diving into the setup, it is crucial to understand the basic hardware and software requirements for a Pega environment. Ensuring that your system meets these specifications will contribute to a stable and efficient platform.

- **Hardware Requirements**:
  - **CPU**: Multi-core processor for handling simultaneous operations.
  - **Memory (RAM)**: At least 16 GB for development environments; 32 GB or more for larger-scale or production environments.
  - **Storage**: SSDs with sufficient space for the Pega installation and related data, with a minimum of 100 GB recommended.
- **Software Requirements**:
  - **Operating System**: Pega can be run on various operating systems, including Windows, Linux, and macOS.
  - **Java Development Kit (JDK)**: Ensure the appropriate version of Java is installed (e.g., JDK 11).
  - **Database**: Supported databases include PostgreSQL, Oracle, Microsoft SQL Server, and more, depending on the scale and purpose of the environment.
  - **Application Server**: Pega supports servers such as Apache Tomcat, IBM WebSphere, and Red Hat JBoss EAP.

2. Installing the Pega Platform

The installation process for Pega varies slightly depending on the deployment model (e.g., on-premises or cloud). Below are the general steps for setting up an on-premises Pega environment:

- **Download the Installation Package**:
  - Access the Pega Community website or your organization's Pega licensing portal to download the installation package that matches your operating system and application server.
- **Configure the Application Server**:
  - Ensure your chosen application server is properly configured to support the Pega deployment. This step may involve setting memory allocation parameters and deploying the necessary Java libraries.
- **Database Setup**:
  - Create a new database schema to host the PegaRULES and PegaDATA tables. Run the setup scripts provided with the installation package to initialize the database structure.
- **Deploy the Pega WAR/EAR File**:
  - Deploy the provided Pega WAR or EAR file to your application server. This action typically involves copying the file to the server's deployment directory and restarting the server.
- **Run the Installation Wizard**:
  - Access the Pega installation wizard through a web browser to complete the setup process. This wizard will guide you through the configuration options, including database connectivity and initial settings.

3. Configuring Initial Environment Settings

Once Pega is installed, configure the initial settings to tailor the environment to your needs:

- **Admin User Setup**:
    - Create administrative user accounts with full access to manage and configure the platform.
- **Security Configurations**:
    - Implement security settings such as password policies, user authentication methods, and role-based access control (RBAC).
- **Global Resource Settings**:
    - Define global resources, such as email servers and file repositories, to facilitate integrations and workflow automations.

4. Setting Up Development and Testing Environments

To support efficient development and testing, consider creating separate environments for development, testing, and production:

- **Development Environment**:
    - A sandbox where developers can build and test new features without impacting the live environment. This setup often mirrors the production environment to ensure compatibility.
- **Testing Environment**:
    - An environment configured for quality assurance (QA) and user acceptance testing (UAT). It should include test data and mimic real-world use cases to validate performance and functionality.
- **Production Environment**:
    - The live system used by end-users. This environment should be optimized for stability, performance, and security, with minimal changes applied directly.

5. Configuring Pega Dev Studio

Pega Dev Studio is the primary interface for building applications in Pega. To set up Dev Studio for your development environment:

- **Accessing Dev Studio**:
    - Log in to Pega using your administrative credentials and switch to Dev Studio.
- **Customizing the Workspace**:
    - Personalize the Dev Studio interface to include relevant toolbars, views, and components that align with your development needs.
- **Enabling Collaborative Development**:
    - Implement version control and enable branching to allow multiple developers to work simultaneously on different parts of an application.

6. Best Practices for Environment Setup

To ensure optimal performance and efficiency, follow these best practices when setting up your Pega environment:

- **Load Balancing and Scalability**:
    - Implement load balancing to distribute incoming requests evenly across multiple servers. This setup enhances performance and ensures high availability.
- **Backup and Recovery Plans**:
    - Establish regular backup schedules and create a disaster recovery plan to safeguard data and minimize downtime in case of system failures.
- **Monitoring and Maintenance**:

- Configure monitoring tools and set up performance alerts to keep track of system health and respond promptly to any issues.

7. Post-Installation Checklist

After completing the installation and initial setup, verify that the environment is fully functional by reviewing this checklist:

- Ensure that the application server and database connections are active and error-free.
- Confirm that Dev Studio is accessible and responsive.
- Validate that core Pega components, such as case management and rule configuration, are working correctly.
- Test user authentication and access control settings to ensure compliance with security protocols.

Setting up your Pega environment correctly is the first step toward successful application development and process automation.

Navigating the Pega User Interface

The user interface (UI) of Pega is designed to streamline application development and process management by providing intuitive navigation and easy access to essential tools. Familiarity with the Pega UI is vital for maximizing productivity and making the most of the platform's powerful features. This chapter guides you through the main components of the Pega UI, offering a detailed overview of its layout and essential functionalities.

1. Logging into Pega

The first step in interacting with the Pega platform is accessing the user interface through a web browser. Upon logging in with your credentials, you'll be taken to the **Pega Portal**, which serves as the central hub for managing applications, cases, and configurations.

- **Login Page**: Typically configured by the system administrator with the necessary authentication protocols, including single sign-on (SSO) or multi-factor authentication (MFA) for enhanced security.

2. Overview of the Pega Portal

The Pega Portal provides an organized workspace where users can access different tools based on their roles and permissions. The primary areas of the portal include:

- **Navigation Menu**: Located on the left-hand side, the navigation menu provides quick access to essential modules such as **Dev Studio**, **App Studio**, **Admin Studio**, and **Prediction Studio**.
- **Header Toolbar**: Found at the top of the screen, this toolbar includes quick links, search functions, and user profile settings.
- **Dashboard**: The main workspace that displays widgets and panels customized to show relevant information, such as open cases, application performance, and recent activities.

3. Understanding the Different Studios

Pega offers a set of specialized studios that cater to different aspects of application development and management:

- **Dev Studio**:
    - Primary workspace for developers and technical users.
    - Used for creating and managing rules, configuring advanced logic, and integrating systems.
    - Provides access to rule forms, flow diagrams, and configuration panels.
- **App Studio**:
    - Geared towards business users and low-code developers.
    - Simplifies the development process with visual tools for creating cases, workflows, and user interfaces.
    - Supports agile development practices through collaborative features.
- **Admin Studio**:
    - Focuses on administrative tasks, such as managing users, monitoring system performance, and configuring application settings.
    - Includes tools for viewing logs, running diagnostic checks, and handling security configurations.
- **Prediction Studio**:
    - Dedicated to building and managing predictive models and AI-driven decision strategies.
    - Enables data scientists and analysts to create machine learning models that integrate with business processes.

4. Key Components of Dev Studio

Dev Studio is the most feature-rich environment within Pega, providing access to the full suite of development tools. Here are its main components:

- **Explorer Panel**: Located on the left side of Dev Studio, this panel includes various explorers such as **Case Explorer**, **Data Explorer**, and **App Explorer**. These explorers help navigate cases, data types, and application structures.
- **Work Area**: The central part of Dev Studio where rule forms, flow diagrams, and configurations are displayed and edited.
- **Properties Panel**: Displays the attributes and properties of selected elements, allowing developers to modify details without navigating away from the main workspace.
- **Run Toolbar**: Provides tools for testing and previewing applications, including **Run** and **Trace** options for debugging.

5. Navigating App Studio for Business Users

App Studio simplifies application design by using a drag-and-drop interface and step-by-step guides. Key elements include:

- **Case Lifecycle View**: Visual representation of the stages and steps involved in a case type. Users can modify the workflow by dragging elements and configuring their properties.
- **UI Design Tools**: Intuitive tools for designing forms, sections, and layouts without the need for extensive coding.
- **Data Integration Panel**: Allows business users to integrate external data sources by configuring data pages and connectors.

6. Customizing the Dashboard

The **Dashboard** is customizable, allowing users to tailor their workspace to display the most relevant information. Users can add widgets, such as:

- **Case Widgets**: Display the status of open cases and tasks.
- **Performance Widgets**: Show key performance indicators (KPIs) and metrics.
- **Reports Panel**: Provides quick access to frequently used reports and analytics.

Customizing the dashboard ensures that users have an overview of their tasks, cases, and metrics, enhancing productivity and decision-making.

7. Searching and Navigating Rules

Pega's powerful search functionality allows users to locate rules, cases, and data efficiently:

- **Unified Search Bar**: Found in the header toolbar, the search bar can be used to find rules by name, type, or keywords.
- **Advanced Search**: Offers filters to narrow down search results, such as rule type, version, and modification date.
- **Rule History and Audit**: Users can track changes and access previous versions of a rule for review and compliance.

8. User Profile and Settings

The **User Profile** section, accessible from the header toolbar, allows users to:

- Update personal settings, such as language preferences and display themes.
- Manage session settings, including idle timeout and notifications.
- Access help resources and documentation.

9. Best Practices for Efficient Navigation

To maximize efficiency when navigating the Pega UI, follow these best practices:

- **Use Shortcuts**: Familiarize yourself with keyboard shortcuts for common actions, such as opening the search bar or switching between studios.
- **Bookmark Important Rules**: Save frequently accessed rules and cases for quick navigation.
- **Organize Worklists**: Customize worklists to prioritize tasks and maintain focus on critical work items.
- **Leverage Contextual Help**: Use the built-in help and tooltips to better understand unfamiliar sections and tools within the UI.

By mastering the Pega user interface, users can work more efficiently, develop applications faster, and maintain better oversight of their business processes.

Essential Components of a Pega Application

Understanding the essential components of a Pega application is fundamental for building effective and scalable solutions. Each component plays a unique role in ensuring the smooth execution of business processes and the creation of applications that align with user and organizational needs. This chapter breaks down the main elements that make up a Pega application and explains their significance in the development lifecycle.

1. Case Types

Case types are the backbone of Pega applications, representing business processes that need to be managed and tracked. A case type defines the stages and steps that a case goes through from initiation to completion.

- **Stages**: High-level groupings that divide a case into logical phases. Stages provide a visual overview of a case's lifecycle, making it easier to understand the flow of work.
- **Steps**: Specific tasks or actions that need to be completed within a stage. These can include assignments, data collection, or automated system actions.
- **Alternate Stages**: Paths that handle exceptions or special situations, ensuring that the case management process remains flexible and adaptable.

2. Rules

Pega's **rules** are reusable elements that dictate the behavior of an application. Rules determine how data is processed, how users interact with the system, and how decisions are made.

- **Rule Types**:
  - **Process Rules**: Define the sequence of actions within a workflow, such as flow rules and flow actions.
  - **Decision Rules**: Include decision tables, decision trees, and when conditions to guide logic based on specific criteria.
  - **UI Rules**: Control how user interfaces are structured, including sections, harnesses, and layouts.
  - **Data Rules**: Manage data structures and mapping, including data transforms and properties.
- **Rule Resolution**: A unique feature in Pega that ensures the correct rule version is executed based on factors such as class hierarchy, availability, and inheritance.

3. Data Types and Data Pages

Data types define the structure and format of data used within an application. They are essential for maintaining consistency and ensuring that data is organized effectively.

- **Data Pages**: Serve as a mechanism for loading and caching data within an application. Data pages can be configured to pull data from external sources or databases, ensuring that information is always up-to-date.
- **Properties**: Individual data fields that store specific pieces of information, such as customer names or order numbers. Properties are associated with data types to create comprehensive data models.

4. User Interface (UI) Components

The user experience is critical in any application, and Pega's UI components help build intuitive and responsive interfaces:

- **Sections**: Reusable building blocks that define how data is displayed to users. Sections can be nested and customized to create complex layouts.

- **Harnesses**: Frameworks that organize the overall structure of a page or screen, allowing for the combination of different sections.
- **Dynamic Layouts**: Enable the creation of responsive designs that adapt to different screen sizes and devices, improving usability.

5. Flow Rules

Flow rules define the sequence and structure of a case's workflow. They map out the logical path a case follows from start to finish, including decision points and subprocesses.

- **Flow Shapes**: Visual elements used within flow rules to represent tasks, decisions, assignments, and integrations.
- **Connectors**: Indicate the paths between flow shapes, guiding the case through different routes based on conditions and outcomes.

6. Activities

Activities are rules used to execute complex operations that cannot be performed through simpler rules or data transforms. They are often used to interact with external systems, manipulate data, or control advanced processing logic.

- **Steps in Activities**: Each activity consists of multiple steps that perform individual actions, such as calling another rule, setting a property, or looping through data.
- **Parameters**: Activities can accept input parameters to control their behavior dynamically, providing flexibility in how they are used.

7. Reports and Reporting Capabilities

Pega's reporting tools allow users to create detailed, real-time reports that track the performance of applications and cases:

- **Report Definitions**: Rules that specify the data source, filters, and columns for reports. They enable users to extract insights from application data.
- **Summary and List Reports**: Different types of reports that present aggregated data or detailed lists based on specified criteria.
- **Dashboard Widgets**: Customizable components that display report data on user dashboards, helping monitor key metrics and performance indicators.

8. Integrations and Connectors

Integrating with external systems is a crucial aspect of modern business applications. Pega offers various tools for seamless integration:

- **Connect Rules**: Include Connect-REST, Connect-SOAP, and Connect-Database for interacting with external APIs and databases.
- **Data Integrations**: Allow data from external systems to be accessed and displayed in Pega applications through data pages and connectors.

9. Security Components

Security in Pega is managed through various components that ensure user authentication, authorization, and data protection:

- **Access Groups and Roles**: Define user permissions and control which parts of the application users can access.
- **Privileges**: Specific permissions that are assigned to rules, restricting their use to authorized users.

- **Authentication Services**: Integrations with identity providers for single sign-on (SSO) and multi-factor authentication (MFA).

10. Case Management Features

Pega's **case management** capabilities go beyond defining case types and workflows:

- **Subcases**: Related cases that function as part of a larger parent case, enabling the breakdown of complex processes into manageable units.
- **Parallel Processing**: Allows cases to proceed through multiple steps simultaneously, increasing efficiency and reducing wait times.
- **Service-Level Agreements (SLAs)**: Define time goals for task completion, helping manage expectations and trigger escalations if deadlines are not met.

By understanding these essential components, you can effectively navigate and build robust applications within the Pega platform.

Introduction to Pega Studio

Pega Studio is the comprehensive suite of development environments that cater to different stages of the application development lifecycle within Pega Systems. Each studio is designed to support specific user roles, from business analysts and developers to system administrators and data scientists. Understanding the capabilities and features of Pega Studio is essential for harnessing its full potential and efficiently building business applications.

1. Overview of Pega Studio

Pega Studio encompasses multiple specialized environments, each with a focus on different aspects of application development and management:

- **App Studio**: Designed for business users and low-code developers. App Studio simplifies the process of building applications through an intuitive drag-and-drop interface, making it ideal for modeling case lifecycles, workflows, and user interfaces.
- **Dev Studio**: The most powerful and comprehensive of the studios, Dev Studio is tailored for technical developers who need full control over application rules, logic, and configurations. It provides access to advanced features like integrations, data modeling, and custom coding.
- **Admin Studio**: Geared towards system administrators, Admin Studio provides tools for monitoring application performance, managing user access, and configuring system settings. It is essential for maintaining and troubleshooting Pega environments.
- **Prediction Studio**: Focused on data scientists and business analysts who work with AI and machine learning. Prediction Studio enables users to build predictive models and decision strategies that enhance process automation and decision-making within applications.

2. The Purpose and Use of Each Studio

Each studio has distinct roles and capabilities, contributing to different parts of the application development and deployment cycle:

- **App Studio**:
    - Ideal for rapidly prototyping applications with minimal technical knowledge.
    - Allows users to create case types, stages, and user interfaces using visual tools.
    - Includes collaborative features that support agile development practices.
- **Dev Studio**:
    - Provides granular control over application development, including rule configuration, complex logic, and custom UI components.
    - Supports integration with external systems and enables the development of custom data transformations and activities.
    - Essential for developers who need to implement advanced functionalities and ensure that applications align with business requirements.
- **Admin Studio**:
    - Offers monitoring and management tools that ensure system health and performance.
    - Includes features for viewing and analyzing logs, setting up alert thresholds, and managing background processes.
    - Used to configure user authentication, role-based access, and other security settings.
- **Prediction Studio**:
    - Enables the creation and management of machine learning models and AI-driven decision strategies.
    - Provides tools for testing and optimizing predictive models to ensure they contribute effectively to process automation.
    - Supports integration of these models with case types and workflows to automate decision-making and enhance user experiences.

3. Navigating Pega Studio

Each studio within Pega Studio has a unique interface tailored to its function, but they share some common navigation features:

- **Navigation Pane**: Found on the left side of the screen, it provides quick access to different tools and sections relevant to the current studio.
- **Work Area**: The main space where users build, edit, and configure application components.
- **Header Toolbar**: Includes quick-access buttons for running applications, switching between studios, and accessing help resources.
- **Explorer Panels**: In Dev Studio, multiple explorer panels (such as App Explorer, Case Explorer, and Data Explorer) help users navigate application components, rules, and case structures efficiently.

4. Key Features of App Studio

App Studio's design prioritizes ease of use, allowing non-technical users to build and modify applications efficiently. Some key features include:

- **Case Lifecycle Management**: Visual tools for defining case stages and steps, enabling a clear representation of process flows.
- **UI Designer**: Drag-and-drop interface for designing user forms and sections.
- **Data Management**: Simple data modeling capabilities that allow users to define data types and integrate with data sources.
- **Preview and Test**: Instant preview options to test the application's behavior and appearance without leaving the studio.

5. Advanced Capabilities in Dev Studio

Dev Studio caters to developers who need comprehensive control over Pega applications. Its advanced capabilities include:

- **Rule Management**: Create and manage various types of rules, such as decision tables, flow actions, and activities.
- **Integration Tools**: Connectors and services for integrating with external systems, including REST and SOAP APIs.
- **Custom Scripting**: The ability to write custom code for unique application requirements, enhancing flexibility.
- **Debugging and Tracing**: Built-in tools for troubleshooting, such as the tracer tool, which tracks rule execution in real-time to identify issues.

6. Administrative Tools in Admin Studio

Admin Studio provides administrators with the tools needed to maintain system stability and security:

- **Performance Monitoring**: Real-time dashboards and reports that display system performance metrics.
- **User Management**: Options for adding, modifying, and managing user roles and access levels.
- **System Alerts**: Configurable alerts that notify administrators of potential issues, such as slow response times or integration failures.

7. AI and Predictive Modeling in Prediction Studio

Prediction Studio enables organizations to leverage machine learning for smarter process automation:

- **Model Building**: Create predictive models using historical data and pre-built templates.

- **Decision Strategies**: Design decision trees and logic flows that integrate predictive models into case types and workflows.
- **Testing and Simulation**: Simulate decision strategies to evaluate their performance and refine them for better outcomes.

8. Best Practices for Using Pega Studio

To maximize efficiency when using Pega Studio, consider the following best practices:

- **Use App Studio for Initial Prototypes**: Begin development in App Studio to quickly build the foundation of an application. Transition to Dev Studio for more complex configurations.
- **Leverage Collaboration Features**: Encourage cross-functional teams to collaborate in App Studio, aligning business needs with technical capabilities.
- **Monitor Performance Regularly**: Use Admin Studio to track system health and address potential issues proactively.
- **Test Predictive Models Thoroughly**: Ensure that AI models created in Prediction Studio are accurate and contribute positively to automation goals.

This overview of Pega Studio sets the stage for deeper exploration into how each studio contributes to successful application development.

Understanding Case Management Basics

Case management is a cornerstone of the Pega platform, enabling organizations to automate complex business processes while maintaining a flexible and adaptable framework. By understanding the fundamental principles of case management, you can effectively design and manage processes that align with your business goals and improve overall efficiency. This chapter will explore the essentials of case management in Pega, covering its core components, benefits, and how to leverage them in your applications.

1. What is Case Management?

At its core, **case management** refers to the structured approach to handling work that progresses through a series of stages and steps to reach a defined outcome. In Pega, a case is more than a simple transaction; it encapsulates a complete process or workflow that may involve multiple tasks, data, and participants.

Key Characteristics of a Case:

- **Life Cycle Management**: A case is designed to move through defined stages that represent the major phases of the process.
- **Dynamic Behavior**: Cases can adapt to changing conditions, allowing for alternative paths and exception handling.
- **Data-Driven Decisions**: Cases incorporate decision-making capabilities that determine the next steps based on the data at hand.

2. Components of Case Management

To effectively manage cases in Pega, it's essential to understand the components that make up a case structure:

- **Case Types**: Case types are the templates that define the life cycle of a case. They outline the stages, steps, and rules that govern the flow of work.
- **Stages**: Stages are the high-level phases in a case life cycle. They provide a visual representation of the process and help organize the steps required to move from initiation to resolution.
- **Steps**: Each stage contains steps that represent specific tasks or actions to be completed. Steps can involve user assignments, data collection, or automated processes.
- **Subcases**: These are smaller, related cases that support the main case. Subcases help break down complex processes into manageable parts, promoting better organization and efficiency.

3. The Case Life Cycle

The **case life cycle** is a visual framework that outlines how a case moves from start to finish. It provides a clear representation of the workflow and helps ensure that all necessary steps are accounted for.

- **Primary Stages**: These represent the main path a case follows, detailing the typical steps needed to reach a resolution.
- **Alternate Stages**: Handle exceptions, alternative paths, or special conditions that may arise during the case's progression.
- **Transitions**: Define how a case moves from one stage or step to the next, often based on user actions or system conditions.

4. Key Concepts in Pega Case Management

Several key concepts underpin Pega's approach to case management:

- **Case Context**: The data and information associated with a specific case, including properties, case history, and related subcases.
- **Assignments**: Tasks assigned to users or teams for action. Assignments are pivotal in driving the case forward and ensuring tasks are completed.
- **Routing**: The process of directing assignments to the appropriate user or team based on predefined conditions, such as skills, availability, or workload.
- **Service-Level Agreements (SLAs)**: Time-bound goals attached to assignments or cases to ensure timely completion. SLAs can trigger escalations if deadlines are not met, helping maintain process efficiency.

5. Benefits of Case Management in Pega

Implementing case management in Pega offers several advantages:

- **Enhanced Process Visibility**: The case life cycle provides a clear, visual representation of each stage, making it easier to track progress and identify bottlenecks.
- **Flexibility and Adaptability**: Pega's case management allows for real-time adjustments and decision-making, accommodating changing business needs.
- **Increased Efficiency**: Automating workflows and incorporating decision logic reduce manual efforts and accelerate task completion.
- **Collaboration and Coordination**: Cases can involve multiple users, teams, or departments, fostering collaboration through shared tasks and communication.

6. Building a Simple Case Type

To create a case type in Pega, follow these basic steps:

1. **Navigate to App Studio**: Start by accessing App Studio, which provides a user-friendly interface for creating and managing case types.
2. **Define the Case Type**: Click on "Case types" and create a new case type, providing a name and description.
3. **Add Stages**: Outline the primary stages that the case will go through. Use drag-and-drop tools to organize the stages in the desired order.
4. **Insert Steps**: Within each stage, add the required steps, such as assignments, subprocesses, or automated tasks.
5. **Configure Transitions**: Set up conditions for moving between steps and stages, ensuring that the case progresses smoothly.
6. **Test and Iterate**: Use the built-in testing tools to simulate case progression and make necessary adjustments to optimize the workflow.

7. Best Practices for Effective Case Management

To maximize the effectiveness of case management in Pega, consider these best practices:

- **Design for Flexibility**: Anticipate potential exceptions and build alternate paths to handle them without disrupting the primary process.
- **Utilize SLAs**: Set realistic SLAs to keep processes on track and manage performance expectations.
- **Leverage Subcases**: Break down complex cases into subcases to simplify management and enhance visibility.
- **Monitor and Optimize**: Regularly review case performance data to identify areas for improvement and make adjustments as needed.

Mastering the basics of case management sets the stage for creating more complex and dynamic applications in Pega.

Section 3:
Designing and Building Applications

Creating Your First Pega Application

Creating your first Pega application marks a significant step in harnessing the platform's powerful capabilities for process automation. This chapter will guide you through the essential steps of building a basic Pega application, from initial setup to launching a functional prototype. By following these steps, you will gain a hands-on understanding of the foundational aspects of Pega application development.

1. Setting Up Your Project

Before you start building, it is essential to set up your project correctly to ensure a smooth development process.

- **Accessing App Studio**: Log in to the Pega platform and navigate to **App Studio**, which is tailored for low-code development and ideal for creating initial application prototypes.
- **Creating a New Application**:
    1. Click on **"New Application"** in the App Studio dashboard.
    2. Choose a template or framework that aligns with your business needs (e.g., Customer Service or generic case management).
    3. Provide a name for your application and select the organizational context (e.g., division, unit) in which it will be built.
- **Application Structure**: Pega will generate a basic application structure, including preconfigured case types, data types, and a starting workflow.

2. Defining Your Case Types

Case types are the primary building blocks of any Pega application, representing business processes that need to be managed from initiation to resolution.

- **Creating a Case Type**:
    - In **App Studio**, click on **"Case types"** and select **"Add case type"**.
    - Name the case type according to the process it represents (e.g., "Customer Onboarding").
- **Configuring the Case Life Cycle**:
    - Add **stages** to outline the major phases of the case.
    - Insert **steps** within each stage to detail tasks that need to be completed. These can include user assignments, automated processes, or data collection activities.

3. Building Your Workflow

Designing the workflow is a critical aspect of creating a case type, as it dictates how the process flows from one stage to the next.

- **Adding Steps and Assignments**:
    - Drag and drop assignments and tasks into the stages to define the workflow.
    - Configure assignment details, such as the user or team responsible for completing the task, and set any necessary instructions.
- **Configuring Transitions**:

    - Define the conditions that trigger movement between stages, such as completing a task or meeting specific criteria.
    - Use **decision rules** to create dynamic paths within the workflow, allowing cases to adapt based on data and user input.

4. Designing User Interfaces

A well-designed user interface (UI) is essential for enhancing the user experience and ensuring that interactions with the case are intuitive.

- **UI Creation in App Studio**:
    - Open the **"Views"** tab within a case step to design the user interface for that particular task.
    - Use drag-and-drop tools to add fields, labels, and interactive elements to the form.
- **Customizing Layouts**:
    - Choose from Pega's pre-built templates or create custom layouts to organize UI elements.
    - Add validation rules to ensure data is entered correctly before progressing to the next step.

5. Integrating Data Types

Data types help manage the information associated with your cases, ensuring data is stored and accessed efficiently.

- **Creating a Data Type**:
    - Navigate to **"Data types"** in App Studio and select **"Add data type"**.
    - Name the data type and define its properties (e.g., text fields, numeric values).
- **Connecting to External Data Sources**:
    - Integrate external databases or systems by configuring **data pages** and connectors.
    - Ensure the data integration is secure and efficient by testing data retrieval during the development phase.

6. Testing Your Application

Testing is a crucial step to verify that your application functions as expected and meets business requirements.

- **Previewing Your Case**:
    - Use the **"Preview"** button in App Studio to test the case life cycle and view the application from a user's perspective.
- **Debugging Tools**:
    - Utilize Pega's built-in **tracer tool** and **clipboard viewer** in Dev Studio for in-depth testing and debugging.
- **Simulating Case Progression**:
    - Run test cases to simulate the completion of assignments and the progression through stages, ensuring all transitions and rules work correctly.

7. Deploying Your Application

Once your application has been tested and refined, it is ready for deployment.

- **Deployment Steps**:
    - Verify that all configurations, security settings, and integrations are complete.
    - Promote the application from the development environment to the testing or production environment using Pega's **deployment manager** or other DevOps tools.
- **User Training and Documentation**:
    - Provide training sessions or documentation to end-users, ensuring they understand how to interact with the new application and perform their roles effectively.

8. Best Practices for Building Pega Applications

To create a robust and maintainable Pega application, follow these best practices:

- **Start Simple**: Build a minimal viable product (MVP) and iterate based on feedback and testing.
- **Modular Design**: Use reusable components and rules to simplify maintenance and improve scalability.
- **Regular Reviews**: Collaborate with stakeholders regularly to validate that the application meets business goals and adjust as necessary.
- **Performance Optimization**: Monitor application performance and refine processes to ensure smooth and efficient operation.

Creating your first Pega application is an empowering step toward mastering the platform's capabilities. By following these guidelines, you can build an effective and user-friendly application that automates processes and meets business needs.

Case Lifecycle Design

Designing an effective case lifecycle is fundamental to creating robust Pega applications that align with business processes. The case lifecycle represents the flow of work and helps guide cases through various stages, ensuring that each step is completed efficiently and in the correct sequence. This chapter will provide an in-depth overview of case lifecycle design, covering essential principles, best practices, and advanced techniques to optimize your workflow.

1. Understanding the Case Lifecycle Concept

The **case lifecycle** in Pega is a visual representation of how a case progresses from initiation to resolution. It breaks down the workflow into stages and steps, allowing developers to map out processes clearly and manage complex workflows.

Key Components:

- **Stages**: High-level phases that organize the work of a case, each representing a significant portion of the case's journey.
- **Steps**: Actions within a stage that must be completed to move to the next stage. These can be user assignments, data collection points, automated system actions, or subprocesses.
- **Alternate Stages**: Special stages that handle exceptions, errors, or alternate paths outside the primary flow.

2. Defining Stages in the Case Lifecycle

Stages are the building blocks of a case lifecycle. Designing clear and effective stages helps structure the process logically and ensures that cases progress smoothly.

Designing Primary Stages:

- **Outline Major Phases**: Identify the key phases of the process that will form the primary stages. For example, in a customer onboarding case, primary stages might include "Application Review," "Verification," and "Approval."
- **Logical Progression**: Arrange stages in the order that reflects the natural flow of the process. Ensure that each stage transitions logically to the next.

Alternate Stages for Exceptions:

- **Exception Handling**: Create alternate stages to manage special scenarios such as rejections or additional information requests.
- **Re-entry Points**: Design alternate stages to allow cases to return to the primary stages when necessary, maintaining continuity and adaptability.

3. Designing Steps and Workflows

Steps are the specific tasks that users or the system must complete within each stage. They define the detailed actions required to progress a case through its lifecycle.

Types of Steps:

- **User Assignments**: Tasks that require input or action from a user. These steps often involve forms or data entry.
- **Automated Actions**: Processes completed by the system without user interaction, such as sending notifications or updating records.
- **Subprocesses**: Embedded workflows that can run independently within a stage, useful for complex tasks that require multiple steps.

Configuring Steps:

- **Add and Arrange Steps**: In Pega's App Studio, use the drag-and-drop interface to add steps to stages and arrange them in the required order.
- **Set Step Properties**: Configure each step's properties, such as instructions for the user, deadlines, and dependencies.
- **Conditional Logic**: Implement decision rules to guide cases through different paths based on data or user input, creating a more dynamic and responsive workflow.

4. Transitions and Conditional Navigation

Transitions dictate how a case moves from one stage or step to another. Properly configured transitions help maintain the flow and adapt to different outcomes.

Stage Transitions:

- **Automatic Progression**: Configure stages to move forward automatically when the last step is completed.
- **Manual Progression**: Allow users to advance the case manually, providing flexibility when needed.
- **Condition-Based Transitions**: Use when rules and conditions to trigger stage transitions based on case data, ensuring cases take appropriate paths.

Step Transitions:

- **Next Step Logic**: Define which step follows the completion of the current one. Utilize conditional paths to create workflows that change based on the data or user actions.

5. Implementing Advanced Case Design Features

For more sophisticated case lifecycle designs, Pega provides features to handle complex scenarios and improve user experience:

Parallel Processing:

- **Multiple Paths Simultaneously**: Enable steps or stages to run in parallel, allowing for concurrent tasks that improve efficiency.
- **Synchronization**: Use wait shapes or join conditions to ensure that parallel paths complete before progressing.

Dynamic Stages and Steps:

- **Adaptive Workflows**: Implement rules that add, remove, or reorder stages and steps dynamically based on case conditions or user interactions.
- **Real-Time Adjustments**: Allow changes to the case lifecycle during execution, making processes more flexible and responsive to unexpected needs.

Service-Level Agreements (SLAs):

- **Defining Timeframes**: Attach SLAs to steps or stages to set time goals for completion. Configure escalation actions if SLAs are breached, ensuring that important tasks receive attention.
- **Monitoring and Alerts**: Use SLAs to trigger alerts and notifications to users or supervisors when deadlines approach or pass.

6. Best Practices for Case Lifecycle Design

To design effective and maintainable case lifecycles, adhere to these best practices:

- **Keep It Simple**: Design clear and straightforward stages and steps. Avoid overly complex workflows that could confuse users or become difficult to manage.
- **Reuse Components**: Use reusable case templates and subprocesses to streamline development and ensure consistency across applications.
- **Validate with Stakeholders**: Collaborate with business users and stakeholders during the design phase to ensure the case lifecycle meets real-world needs and expectations.
- **Test Thoroughly**: Simulate different scenarios to test the case lifecycle's behavior, identifying potential issues or inefficiencies before deployment.
- **Document the Workflow**: Maintain detailed documentation of the case lifecycle to support ongoing maintenance and onboarding of new team members.

By understanding and implementing case lifecycle design principles, you can build applications that handle complex business processes effectively.

Implementing Workflows in Pega

Workflows form the backbone of any process automation solution, ensuring that tasks flow logically and efficiently from initiation to completion. Pega provides robust tools for implementing workflows that can adapt to business needs, improve productivity, and enhance user experience. This chapter will guide you through the essential elements of workflow implementation in Pega, offering practical insights and best practices to help you create effective and responsive workflows.

1. Understanding Workflows in Pega

A **workflow** in Pega represents the sequence of tasks or processes that a case follows from start to finish. It defines how work moves between users, systems, and stages, ensuring tasks are completed in the correct order and according to set rules.

Key Components of Workflows:

- **Flow Rules**: Visual representations of the workflow logic that outline the path a case follows.
- **Assignments**: Tasks assigned to users or groups to be completed within the workflow.
- **Decision Points**: Rules or conditions that guide the case's progression based on specific criteria or data.
- **Subprocesses**: Nested workflows that can be executed as part of a larger workflow for modular design.

2. Creating Flow Rules

Flow rules are the primary tools for building workflows in Pega. They are diagrammatic representations that map out the path of a case and define the sequence of actions.

Steps to Create Flow Rules:

1. **Access Dev Studio**: Navigate to **Dev Studio** to create or modify flow rules.
2. **Create a New Flow**: Go to the "Records" explorer, select **Process > Flow**, and create a new flow rule.
3. **Design the Flow**: Use drag-and-drop shapes such as **Start**, **Assignment**, **Subprocess**, **Decision**, and **End** to build the workflow.
4. **Configure Properties**: Customize each shape's properties, such as assignment instructions, routing options, and transitions.

Common Flow Shapes:

- **Start**: Indicates the beginning of the workflow.
- **Assignment**: Represents tasks assigned to users.
- **Subprocess**: Embeds another flow within the main workflow.
- **Decision**: Evaluates conditions to determine the path a case takes.
- **End**: Marks the conclusion of the workflow.

3. Assignments and Routing

Assignments are critical elements that dictate which user or team is responsible for completing a task. Pega's workflow engine supports various routing options to ensure that tasks are assigned efficiently.

Configuring Assignments:

- **Add Assignment Shapes**: Place **Assignment** shapes within the flow rule to indicate user tasks.
- **Set Routing Options**: Configure assignments to route to specific users, roles, or dynamically determined recipients using **when** rules or expressions.

- **Configure Instructions**: Add clear instructions to guide users on what needs to be done for each assignment.

Routing Strategies:

- **Worklist Routing**: Assigns tasks to a specific user's worklist.
- **Workbasket Routing**: Assigns tasks to a shared workbasket for team-based task completion.
- **Skill-Based Routing**: Routes assignments based on user skills or availability to optimize task completion.

4. Incorporating Decision Points

Decision points add conditional logic to workflows, enabling cases to follow different paths based on set criteria.

Types of Decision Points:

- **Decision Shapes**: Used in flow rules to evaluate conditions and direct the case to different paths.
- **When Rules**: Boolean expressions that return true or false, guiding the flow based on specific conditions.
- **Decision Tables and Trees**: Allow for more complex decision logic, evaluating multiple conditions and outputs.

Implementing Decision Logic:

1. **Add a Decision Shape**: Place the **Decision** shape in the flow rule.
2. **Link to a When Rule or Table**: Connect the decision shape to an existing when rule, decision table, or decision tree.
3. **Configure Paths**: Define which path the case will follow based on the decision outcome.

5. Integrating Subprocesses for Modular Design

Subprocesses enhance workflow design by enabling the reuse of smaller, self-contained workflows within larger ones. This modular approach improves maintainability and scalability.

Creating a Subprocess:

- **Add a Subprocess Shape**: Insert a **Subprocess** shape within your main flow.
- **Select or Create a Flow**: Link the subprocess shape to an existing flow rule or create a new one.
- **Configure Entry and Exit Conditions**: Set the conditions under which the subprocess starts and how it returns control to the main workflow.

Use Cases for Subprocesses:

- Handling specific tasks like approvals, escalations, or notifications.
- Reusing common processes across different case types, such as data validation or user verification.

6. Automating Workflow Tasks

Pega supports automation within workflows, allowing certain tasks to be completed without user intervention.

Automated Steps:

- **Utility Shapes**: Perform backend operations such as sending emails, updating records, or calling external systems.

- **Integrations**: Use connectors (e.g., **Connect-REST**, **Connect-SOAP**) within workflows to interact with external systems and automate data exchange.
- **Data Transforms**: Automatically modify or map data between steps to streamline case progression.

7. Best Practices for Workflow Implementation

To design effective workflows, follow these best practices:

- **Keep It Simple**: Design workflows that are straightforward and easy to understand. Complex flows can be harder to maintain and troubleshoot.
- **Use Modular Design**: Implement subprocesses to create reusable components that simplify the workflow and enhance scalability.
- **Ensure Clarity in Assignments**: Provide clear and concise instructions for each assignment to reduce confusion and improve user productivity.
- **Test Thoroughly**: Simulate different scenarios to test the workflow's behavior and identify potential issues or inefficiencies.
- **Incorporate SLAs**: Apply service-level agreements (SLAs) to key steps to ensure tasks are completed within a reasonable timeframe and escalations are triggered when necessary.

By mastering the implementation of workflows in Pega, you can build efficient, dynamic, and adaptable processes that align with business goals.

Building Data Models in Pega

Data models play an essential role in building efficient, scalable, and maintainable applications in Pega. A well-structured data model allows seamless data handling and integration, enabling applications to process information smoothly across various stages and user interactions. This chapter will explore how to design, build, and optimize data models in Pega, equipping you with the knowledge to manage data effectively.

1. Understanding Data Modeling in Pega

Data modeling in Pega involves creating and structuring data types that represent the information your application needs to function. This data can come from user input, external systems, or be generated as part of business logic.

Key Components of Data Models:

- **Data Types**: Entities that define a set of properties used in applications (e.g., Customer, Order, Product).
- **Properties**: Fields that store specific pieces of data within a data type (e.g., Name, ID, Date of Birth).
- **Data Pages**: Containers that retrieve, hold, and manage data from various sources for use in your application.
- **Integration with Data Sources**: The ability to connect with external databases, services, and systems to access or store data.

2. Creating Data Types

Data types are the building blocks of data models, representing logical groupings of related data.

Steps to Create a Data Type:

1. **Navigate to App Studio**: Access the **App Studio** environment.
2. **Add a Data Type**:
    - Go to **"Data types"** in the navigation panel and select **"Add data type"**.
    - Provide a name and description for the data type (e.g., "Customer").
3. **Define Properties**:
    - Create properties by specifying their data types (e.g., Text, Integer, Date).
    - Assign relevant validation rules or constraints, such as format restrictions for phone numbers or email addresses.

Common Property Types:

- **Single Value (Text, Number, Date)**: Represents individual data points.
- **Page**: Represents a group of related properties (nested structure).
- **Page List**: Represents a list of pages, used for repeating groups of data like a list of orders or products.

3. Working with Data Pages

Data Pages are essential for handling and retrieving data within your Pega application. They serve as the mechanism to bring data into the application when needed and are key to optimizing performance by avoiding redundant database calls.

Types of Data Pages:

- **Thread-Level**: Data pages that are unique to a specific case or requestor thread.

- **Requestor-Level**: Shared data pages for a particular user session, accessible across multiple cases.
- **Node-Level**: Shared data pages across the entire system, useful for data that doesn't change frequently.

Configuring Data Pages:

1. **Create a Data Page**:
   - Navigate to **"Records"** in Dev Studio and select **"Data Page"** under **Data Model**.
   - Define the data source (e.g., database, web service).
2. **Set Refresh Conditions**:
   - Configure the conditions that determine when the data page should reload or refresh.
3. **Specify Parameters**:
   - If needed, use parameters to make the data page flexible and reusable for different inputs.

4. Connecting to External Data Sources

Integrating with external systems allows Pega applications to pull or push data from/to various sources. Pega provides built-in connectors and integration wizards for seamless connectivity.

Integrating External Data:

- **Use Connectors**: Utilize **Connect REST**, **Connect SOAP**, or **Connect SQL** to fetch data from external systems.
- **Map Data**: Use **Data Transforms** to map incoming data into your application's data structure.
- **Error Handling**: Implement error-handling mechanisms to manage issues such as network disruptions or invalid data.

Example Integration Workflow:

1. Configure a **Connect REST** rule to link to an external REST API.
2. Create a data page to call the connector and fetch data.
3. Map the retrieved data to properties within your data model using data transforms.

5. Best Practices for Data Modeling

Implementing best practices ensures your data models remain efficient, easy to maintain, and scalable.

Best Practices:

- **Normalize Data Structures**: Avoid data redundancy by structuring data types and properties logically.
- **Use Reusable Data Types**: Create generic data types that can be reused across different applications or cases.
- **Leverage Data Pages for Data Retrieval**: Minimize direct database calls by using data pages to fetch and cache data.
- **Apply Appropriate Security**: Implement data security to protect sensitive information through role-based access control and field-level encryption.
- **Test Thoroughly**: Validate your data model and integrations using Pega's **Unit Testing** tools to ensure data integrity and performance.

6. Common Challenges and Solutions

Challenge: Integrating data from multiple external sources can lead to performance issues. **Solution**: Optimize data retrieval by using node-level data pages for frequently accessed data and employing **caching strategies** to reduce load.

Challenge: Managing data consistency in complex workflows. **Solution**: Implement data transforms and business logic to synchronize and validate data as it moves through different stages of a workflow.

A well-designed data model is critical for creating efficient and effective Pega applications. By following these guidelines and leveraging Pega's data modeling tools, you can ensure that your application handles data seamlessly and supports business processes with agility.

Configuring User Interfaces

User interfaces (UIs) are a critical aspect of any application, directly impacting user experience and productivity. In Pega, configuring effective and intuitive UIs can significantly enhance the efficiency of case handling and user interactions. This chapter will guide you through the principles of UI configuration in Pega, covering design tools, best practices, and advanced customization techniques to create user-friendly and dynamic interfaces.

1. Introduction to User Interface Configuration in Pega

Pega's UI tools allow developers to create interactive, responsive, and aesthetically appealing user interfaces with minimal coding. By leveraging Pega's design capabilities, you can build applications that cater to user needs while maintaining consistency and adherence to best practices.

Key Components of Pega UI:

- **Sections**: Reusable UI elements that contain fields, labels, buttons, and other components.
- **Layouts**: Structures that organize sections and fields within an interface.
- **Dynamic UI Behaviors**: Rules and scripts that enable UI interactions, such as showing or hiding fields based on user input.

2. Using App Studio for UI Design

App Studio provides a low-code environment ideal for designing UIs quickly and efficiently.

Steps to Configure UIs in App Studio:

1. **Access App Studio**: Log in to Pega and navigate to **App Studio**.
2. **Open the Case Type**: Choose the case type you are working on and go to the **"Views"** tab.
3. **Add or Edit Sections**:
   - Use the drag-and-drop editor to add components like text input fields, dropdowns, buttons, and date pickers.
   - Configure properties for each component, such as labels, default values, and validation rules.
4. **Customize Layouts**:
   - Select from pre-defined layout types (e.g., column, grid, tab) or create custom layouts for more control.
   - Arrange sections within layouts to achieve the desired structure and flow.

Common UI Components:

- **Text Input**: Captures text-based user input.
- **Dropdown**: Provides a list of selectable options.
- **Button**: Triggers specific actions when clicked.
- **Date Picker**: Allows users to select a date from a calendar view.

3. Leveraging Dev Studio for Advanced Customization

For more complex UI requirements, Dev Studio offers advanced capabilities for developers who want greater control over the design and behavior of the interface.

Advanced UI Configurations:

- **Using Dynamic Layouts**: Create responsive UIs that adjust based on screen size and user interactions.

- **Adding Custom Styles**: Apply CSS classes and use the **Skin rule** to define custom styling that aligns with branding guidelines.
- **Incorporating JavaScript**: Add custom scripts for specific client-side interactions not natively supported by Pega.

Creating a Custom Section:

1. Go to **Records** > **User Interface** > **Section**.
2. Create a new section and design the layout by dragging and dropping UI components.
3. Configure properties and rules for dynamic visibility, editable conditions, and event handling.

4. Enhancing User Experience with Dynamic Behaviors

Dynamic behaviors make the UI more interactive and user-friendly. Pega supports various ways to implement dynamic actions without the need for extensive coding.

Configuring Visibility and Actions:

- **Show/Hide Conditions**: Set conditions for displaying or hiding fields based on user input or other criteria.
- **Refresh When**: Automatically update sections when certain conditions change (e.g., after a user selects an option).
- **Event Handlers**: Add actions to buttons and other elements that trigger data refreshes, navigate to other sections, or submit forms.

Examples of Dynamic UI Configurations:

- **Conditional Visibility**: Display additional form fields when a user selects a specific option (e.g., showing a "Reason for Leave" field only when "Leave Type" is set to "Other").
- **Interactive Buttons**: Configure buttons to save data, perform calculations, or trigger automation scripts.

5. Best Practices for UI Configuration

Designing a UI that is both effective and user-friendly requires adherence to certain best practices:

UI Design Best Practices:

- **Keep it Simple**: Avoid clutter by using only the necessary components and keeping the layout clean.
- **Maintain Consistency**: Ensure consistent styles, fonts, and component placements throughout the application for a seamless experience.
- **Use Reusable Sections**: Create sections that can be reused across multiple forms and case types to improve development efficiency.
- **Optimize for Responsiveness**: Test the UI across different devices and screen sizes to ensure accessibility and usability.
- **Provide Clear Labels and Instructions**: Make sure each UI element is clearly labeled, and provide brief instructions when needed to guide users through the process.

Accessibility Considerations:

- Ensure that UI components are accessible to users with disabilities by following **WCAG** (Web Content Accessibility Guidelines) standards.
- Implement keyboard navigation and screen reader compatibility for enhanced usability.

6. Testing and Reviewing Your UI

Testing your user interface is crucial to identify any issues and ensure that it meets user expectations.

Steps for Effective UI Testing:

1. **Preview the Interface**: Use the built-in preview functionality in App Studio to see how the interface looks and behaves.
2. **Simulate User Actions**: Test various user interactions, such as filling out forms, clicking buttons, and selecting dropdown options.
3. **Gather Feedback**: Engage with stakeholders and potential users to review the UI and suggest improvements.
4. **Refine Based on Feedback**: Implement changes based on test results and feedback to enhance the user experience.

Configuring user interfaces in Pega can greatly impact the overall efficiency and satisfaction of end-users interacting with your applications. By mastering UI design principles and leveraging both App Studio and Dev Studio, you can build applications that are not only functional but also intuitive and engaging.

Designing Business Rules and Logic

Effective business rules and logic are essential for creating responsive and intelligent Pega applications. These rules drive decision-making within workflows, allowing applications to respond dynamically to various scenarios. This chapter will guide you through the process of designing and implementing business rules and logic, focusing on best practices and tools available in Pega to create efficient, rule-driven applications.

1. Understanding Business Rules in Pega

Business rules in Pega are conditions or guidelines that determine the flow of processes and actions in an application. They help automate decision-making, enforce policies, and enhance overall application logic.

Key Types of Business Rules:

- **Decision Tables**: Simplify complex decision logic by mapping conditions and corresponding outcomes in a table format.
- **Decision Trees**: Provide a visual, hierarchical approach to decision-making, evaluating conditions sequentially.
- **When Rules**: Simple, reusable expressions that evaluate to `true` or `false` and are used to guide case behavior.
- **Declare Expressions**: Automatically compute property values based on changes in other properties, ensuring data consistency.

2. Creating and Configuring Decision Tables

Decision tables are a straightforward way to represent business logic involving multiple conditions and outcomes.

Steps to Create a Decision Table:

1. **Navigate to Dev Studio**: Go to **Records** > **Decision** > **Decision Table**.
2. **Create a New Decision Table**: Define input properties and specify conditions and results in the table.
3. **Configure Table Structure**:
   - **Conditions**: Define columns that represent the criteria for evaluation (e.g., "Order Amount" or "Customer Type").
   - **Results**: Map each row's condition to an outcome (e.g., "Discount Percentage").
4. **Test the Rule**: Use the built-in testing tool to simulate inputs and verify that the table returns the expected results.

Example Use Case: A decision table for determining loan eligibility might have input properties like "Credit Score" and "Income Level," with outputs defining "Loan Approval" or "Rejection."

3. Implementing Decision Trees for Hierarchical Logic

Decision trees are ideal for modeling complex, branched decision-making processes.

Steps to Create a Decision Tree:

1. **Go to Records** > **Decision** > **Decision Tree**.
2. **Build the Tree Structure**:
   - Add **branches** to define sequential decisions based on conditions.
   - Configure **conditions** at each node to guide the flow.
3. **Configure Outcomes**: Set specific actions or values to return when a path's conditions are met.

4. **Optimize Performance**: Limit the depth of decision trees to maintain performance and simplicity.

Use Case for Decision Trees: An insurance claim process might use a decision tree to check multiple criteria such as policy coverage, claim amount, and claimant history, routing the case accordingly.

4. Creating and Using When Rules

When rules are simple, reusable expressions that evaluate conditions and are used throughout Pega applications to direct behavior.

Creating a When Rule:

1. **Navigate to Records** > **Decision** > **When**.
2. **Define Conditions**:
   - Create logical expressions (e.g., `.OrderAmount > 500`).
   - Use logical operators (`AND`, `OR`) to combine multiple conditions.
3. **Test and Validate**: Ensure the rule behaves as expected by testing with sample data.

Application of When Rules: Use when rules in user interfaces, workflows, or data transforms to dynamically enable, disable, or guide actions based on specific conditions.

5. Automating Business Logic with Declare Expressions

Declare expressions are used to automatically calculate and maintain property values, enhancing data consistency.

Setting Up Declare Expressions:

1. **Navigate to Records** > **Decision** > **Declare Expression**.
2. **Select Target Property**: Choose the property whose value will be computed.
3. **Define the Calculation Logic**:
   - Use mathematical operations or reference other properties.
   - Set the expression to run **conditionally** or **unconditionally**.
4. **Monitor Dependencies**: Pega tracks changes in properties to ensure that dependent expressions recalculate as needed.

Use Case Example: A declare expression can be used to calculate the total price of an order based on item prices and quantities, updating automatically if any item changes.

6. Best Practices for Designing Business Rules and Logic

Adhering to best practices ensures that business rules remain efficient, maintainable, and scalable.

Best Practices:

- **Modularize Logic**: Break down complex rules into smaller, reusable rules to enhance readability and reusability.
- **Document Thoroughly**: Maintain clear documentation and annotations for business rules, making it easier for teams to understand their purpose.
- **Test Extensively**: Use Pega's testing tools to validate rules against different scenarios and data sets.
- **Leverage Version Control**: Keep track of rule versions and changes, facilitating rollback and comparison if needed.
- **Avoid Redundancy**: Reuse existing rules whenever possible to reduce duplication and streamline maintenance.

Performance Considerations:

- **Optimize When Rules**: Combine conditions logically to minimize processing.
- **Simplify Decision Tables**: Limit the number of conditions and avoid overly complex tables.
- **Use Declare Expressions Judiciously**: Avoid excessive use of declare expressions that recalculate frequently, as this may impact performance.

By mastering the design and implementation of business rules and logic in Pega, you can create intelligent, adaptive applications that streamline decision-making and process flow.

Integrating Business Policies into Applications

Business policies are the guiding principles and rules that define how an organization operates. Integrating these policies effectively within Pega applications ensures compliance, consistency, and alignment with strategic goals. This chapter explores how to embed business policies seamlessly into your Pega solutions, detailing best practices, tools, and examples to streamline their implementation.

1. Importance of Business Policy Integration

Integrating business policies directly into applications provides the following benefits:

- **Consistency**: Ensures that all users and processes follow standardized procedures.
- **Compliance**: Helps maintain regulatory and organizational compliance automatically.
- **Efficiency**: Reduces the need for manual oversight and adjustments.

Examples of Business Policies:

- Approval workflows that require manager sign-off for transactions over a certain amount.
- Customer service response times aligned with service level agreements (SLAs).
- Data handling protocols that comply with data protection regulations.

2. Identifying Business Policies for Integration

Before embedding policies into your Pega application, it is essential to identify and document which business policies need automation. Key steps include:

- **Collaboration with Stakeholders**: Work with business analysts, policy makers, and end-users to understand critical policies.
- **Documenting Requirements**: Clearly outline each policy's objectives, conditions, and actions.
- **Assessing Impact**: Determine how the integration of each policy will affect the current workflow and user interactions.

3. Tools and Features for Policy Integration in Pega

Pega offers a variety of tools and features that can be leveraged to integrate business policies effectively.

Key Pega Features for Policy Implementation:

- **Business Rules Engine**: Use decision tables, decision trees, and when rules to implement business logic.
- **Case Management**: Design case workflows that incorporate business policies directly into their stages and steps.
- **SLA Rules**: Set SLAs to automate the timing of specific actions, such as escalation policies.
- **Role-Based Access Control (RBAC)**: Ensure that business policies involving user access and permissions are embedded into the application logic.

Example Use Case: A financial services company needs to automate the policy that any transaction exceeding $10,000 must be reviewed by a senior manager. This policy can be implemented using a decision table within the case workflow to trigger an approval step when the transaction amount exceeds the set limit.

4. Steps for Embedding Business Policies into Applications

Step-by-step approach:

1. **Design the Workflow**:

- Map out the case lifecycle and identify where policies need to be integrated.
- Ensure policies are logically placed to avoid bottlenecks and optimize process flow.

2. **Create Business Rules**:
   - Use **decision tables** or **decision trees** to capture the conditions and outcomes of the policy.
   - Configure when rules for conditional logic that guides user actions and system behaviors.
3. **Configure SLAs and Escalation Points**:
   - Define SLA rules to monitor and enforce timelines related to policies, ensuring that cases adhere to critical deadlines.
4. **Test and Validate**:
   - Implement thorough testing to ensure that the policies work as intended without causing disruptions.
   - Use Pega's testing tools to simulate different scenarios and validate the correct application of the policies.

5. Advanced Techniques for Policy Integration

For more complex policy requirements, Pega offers advanced features that provide additional control and customization.

Using Data Transforms:

- Data transforms can be used to modify or transfer data as part of policy implementation, ensuring that conditions are met before an action is triggered.

Leveraging Declarative Rules:

- **Declare OnChange** and **Declare Expressions** can be utilized to monitor and respond to changes in property values, automatically enforcing policies without explicit user intervention.

Integration with External Systems:

- For policies that require data or input from external systems (e.g., regulatory databases), use **Connect REST** or **Connect SOAP** to integrate and retrieve relevant information dynamically.

6. Best Practices for Integrating Business Policies

Best Practices:

- **Modularize Rules**: Keep business policies modular to make future updates easier.
- **Maintain Clarity**: Use descriptive names and annotations for rules, ensuring that the purpose and function are clear.
- **Optimize for Performance**: Evaluate the impact of complex rules on application performance and optimize as needed.
- **Regular Audits**: Periodically review integrated policies to ensure they align with any changes in organizational strategy or regulations.

Example of Best Practices in Action: A retail company integrates its return policy within its Pega application. The policy specifies that returns within 30 days are approved automatically, while returns after 30 days require manual review. This is implemented using decision tables and SLA rules to monitor the timeline of the return requests.

7. Troubleshooting Common Challenges

Challenge: Business rules conflict with one another, leading to unintended outcomes. **Solution**: Regularly review and test business rules as a cohesive unit to identify overlaps or conflicts. Use rule-based debugging tools provided in Pega to trace and resolve issues.

Challenge: Changes in regulations require updates to embedded policies. **Solution**: Structure business rules to be modular and easily editable so that modifications can be made quickly without overhauling the entire application.

Integrating business policies into Pega applications ensures that processes run smoothly, align with organizational goals, and adhere to regulations. By following the strategies outlined in this chapter, you can create flexible, policy-driven applications that support dynamic business environments.

Leveraging Pega's Visual Modeling Tools

Visual modeling tools are a cornerstone of Pega's development environment, empowering users to design, build, and maintain robust applications without extensive coding. By using these tools effectively, application development becomes more intuitive, collaborative, and efficient. This chapter will guide you through leveraging Pega's visual modeling capabilities to create powerful applications that align with business goals and processes.

1. The Importance of Visual Modeling in Pega

Visual modeling helps streamline development by:

- **Enhancing Clarity**: Simplifies complex business processes and decision-making paths.
- **Facilitating Collaboration**: Allows non-technical stakeholders to contribute to the design process.
- **Accelerating Development**: Reduces the need for manual coding, enabling rapid prototyping and implementation.
- **Ensuring Consistency**: Standardizes the design approach across teams and projects.

2. Overview of Pega's Visual Modeling Tools

Pega offers an array of visual modeling tools that cater to different stages of application development:

- **Case Designer**: A tool to visually define case structures and lifecycle stages.
- **Process Modeler**: Used for mapping process flows and defining stages, steps, and transitions.
- **Decision Management**: Visual tools like decision tables and decision trees to design and implement business logic.
- **UI Designer**: A drag-and-drop interface for building user interfaces and forms.
- **Data Modeler**: Simplifies the creation and management of data objects and their relationships.

3. Designing Case Lifecycles with Case Designer

The **Case Designer** allows you to create and manage cases using a visual representation. It helps define:

- **Stages and Steps**: Outline the flow from initiation to resolution.
- **Paths and Conditions**: Specify alternative paths for different business scenarios.
- **SLAs and Escalations**: Integrate service level agreements and automated escalation triggers.

Example: For an insurance claim application, use the Case Designer to define stages such as "Submission," "Review," "Approval," and "Payout," each containing specific steps and conditions.

4. Mapping Workflows with the Process Modeler

The **Process Modeler** is a powerful tool for detailing the flow of work:

- **Drag-and-Drop Interface**: Easily add and arrange stages, tasks, and transitions.
- **Event-Based Controls**: Integrate timers, wait conditions, and event triggers to enhance workflow automation.
- **Parallel Processing**: Design processes that allow tasks to run concurrently for increased efficiency.

Best Practice: Keep processes modular and use sub-processes for complex workflows to improve maintainability.

5. Crafting Business Logic Visually with Decision Management

Decision logic is crucial for applications that need dynamic behavior. Pega's visual tools for decision management include:

- **Decision Tables**: Represent complex logic with multiple conditions and outcomes in a grid format.
- **Decision Trees**: Provide a hierarchical approach to decision-making with branching logic.
- **Map Value Rules**: Allow for mapping values based on various input conditions, which are visually represented for easy adjustments.

Use Case: Implement a decision table to handle customer discount eligibility based on variables like order size and customer loyalty tier.

6. Designing User Interfaces with UI Designer

The **UI Designer** facilitates the creation of user-friendly interfaces:

- **Drag-and-Drop Components**: Add fields, buttons, grids, and panels with ease.
- **Live Preview**: View changes in real-time as you build forms and pages.
- **Reusable Sections**: Create UI sections that can be reused across various parts of the application to maintain consistency.

Tip: Ensure that the user interface aligns with best practices for usability and accessibility to enhance the user experience.

7. Building Data Structures with Data Modeler

The **Data Modeler** simplifies the creation and management of data objects:

- **Visual Data Relationship Mapping**: Establish relationships between data types using a visual diagram.
- **Automatic Data Type Creation**: Create properties and structures without manual coding.
- **Integration**: Link data types to external data sources using connectors and integration rules.

Example: Design a customer profile data model that includes personal details, order history, and preferences, linking it to external CRM systems through connectors.

8. Best Practices for Using Pega's Visual Modeling Tools

Best Practices:

- **Maintain Simplicity**: Avoid overcomplicating models with excessive details; keep diagrams clean and comprehensible.
- **Leverage Templates**: Use pre-defined templates and out-of-the-box components to speed up development.
- **Document as You Go**: Annotate visual models to provide context and facilitate future updates by team members.
- **Iterative Refinement**: Start with a high-level design and iteratively refine it as the project evolves.

Performance Considerations:

- **Optimize Performance**: Ensure that complex decision trees and workflows do not hinder performance; review and streamline models regularly.
- **Test Thoroughly**: Use Pega's built-in testing tools to validate that visual models function as intended under different conditions.

9. Challenges and Troubleshooting Tips

Challenge: Complex decision logic becomes hard to manage visually. **Solution**: Break down the logic into smaller, modular decision components and integrate them using sub-decision rules.

Challenge: Visual models become cluttered as the application grows. **Solution**: Regularly refactor and organize the models, and use collapsible stages and sub-processes to manage complexity.

Leveraging Pega's visual modeling tools can significantly enhance the efficiency, clarity, and effectiveness of application development. These tools empower both technical and non-technical team members to contribute to building robust, policy-compliant applications that meet business needs.

Section 4:
Advanced Application Development Techniques

Incorporating Complex Case Types

Complex case types are essential for organizations that require multi-faceted workflows involving multiple participants, subprocesses, and conditional paths. Integrating these complex structures within Pega enables businesses to manage intricate processes seamlessly while maintaining transparency and efficiency. This chapter explores the key concepts, tools, and strategies for incorporating complex case types in your Pega applications.

1. Understanding Complex Case Types

Complex case types represent sophisticated workflows that often include:

- **Multiple Stages and Steps**: A case that progresses through numerous stages, each with unique steps and subcases.
- **Dynamic Paths**: Conditional routing and decision points that change the flow based on data inputs or user actions.
- **Parallel Processes**: Subprocesses or tasks that can run concurrently, enabling more efficient handling of related activities.

Example Use Case: Consider a loan processing application where a case type includes initial review, credit assessment, document verification, underwriting, and approval stages. Each stage can involve different teams and conditional paths based on customer criteria.

2. Designing Complex Case Structures in Pega

Steps to Create Complex Case Types:

1. **Define Case Stages**:
   - Use the **Case Designer** to outline high-level stages and identify key steps within each stage.
   - Define conditions under which cases move from one stage to another.
2. **Incorporate Subcases**:
   - Create subcases for tasks that can be handled independently but contribute to the main case outcome. For example, document verification as a subcase within a loan application.
3. **Set Up Parallel Processing**:
   - Use **parallel processing** to allow multiple stages or steps to run simultaneously. This is particularly useful in processes that do not require sequential task completion.
4. **Establish Dynamic Routing**:
   - Integrate decision rules and conditional logic to route cases dynamically. This ensures that cases follow different paths based on business rules, such as customer risk level or document completeness.

Tip: Modularize subcases for reusability across different case types and applications.

3. Utilizing Advanced Pega Tools for Complex Cases

Pega provides robust tools for managing complex cases effectively:

- **Stage Transitions**: Configure transitions between stages using entry and exit criteria to create flexible, condition-based stage movement.
- **Wait and Timer Events**: Implement wait steps or timer events to pause cases until certain conditions are met or until a set timeframe expires.
- **Dynamic Subprocesses**: Integrate subprocesses that can be invoked conditionally or looped based on runtime data, allowing adaptability in case handling.

Example Implementation: In a compliance review process, use dynamic subprocesses to trigger specialized checks only when certain risk factors are present. This ensures that resources are allocated efficiently without processing unnecessary steps for low-risk cases.

4. Best Practices for Implementing Complex Case Types

Best Practices:

- **Start with High-Level Design**: Map out the entire process flow before creating individual stages and subcases.
- **Use Clear Naming Conventions**: Ensure that stages, steps, and subprocesses are clearly named for ease of understanding and maintenance.
- **Monitor Performance**: Regularly review the performance of complex cases to identify potential bottlenecks or inefficiencies.
- **Test Thoroughly**: Validate complex cases with different scenarios to ensure that all paths and decision points function as intended.

Optimization Tips:

- **Limit Nested Subcases**: Avoid excessive nesting of subcases to reduce complexity and improve maintainability.
- **Leverage Reusable Components**: Use reusable rules and templates for common subcases and decision logic to streamline future development.

5. Troubleshooting Common Challenges

Challenge: Cases become too large or difficult to manage. **Solution**: Break down the case into smaller, manageable subcases and leverage Pega's process modeling capabilities to visualize and simplify the flow.

Challenge: Decision logic conflicts create unexpected behavior. **Solution**: Regularly audit decision rules and use Pega's rule validation tools to identify and resolve conflicts.

Challenge: Parallel processes create synchronization issues. **Solution**: Use wait steps and synchronization points to ensure that dependent tasks complete before advancing to the next stage.

6. Real-World Example of Complex Case Types

Case Study: A multinational insurance company implemented complex case types in Pega for processing claims. The application included:

- **Main Case**: Claim submission and evaluation.
- **Subcases**: Document verification, fraud assessment, and medical report review.
- **Dynamic Paths**: Claims under $5,000 followed a streamlined path, while higher-value claims triggered additional assessments and manual reviews.
- **Parallel Processing**: Document verification and medical report review ran concurrently to expedite the overall process.

This approach significantly reduced processing time and improved accuracy by ensuring that claims followed appropriate paths based on predefined criteria.

Incorporating complex case types in Pega applications allows organizations to build comprehensive, adaptive workflows that align with business goals and customer expectations. With a well-structured approach and adherence to best practices, complex cases can enhance process automation and operational efficiency.

Implementing Decision Rules

Decision rules in Pega play a critical role in creating dynamic, intelligent applications that respond to data inputs and business logic. They are essential for automating decision-making processes, enabling seamless and accurate outcomes across various workflows. This chapter delves into understanding and implementing decision rules to elevate your Pega applications.

1. The Importance of Decision Rules

Decision rules allow applications to make logical decisions based on defined criteria. These rules ensure that processes are adaptive and aligned with business objectives by automating actions based on inputs and conditions.

Use Cases of Decision Rules:

- **Loan Application Approval**: Automatically approve or decline applications based on pre-set criteria such as credit scores and income levels.
- **Customer Routing**: Direct customer inquiries to appropriate service representatives based on urgency or issue type.
- **Product Recommendations**: Display personalized product suggestions based on user behavior and past purchases.

2. Types of Decision Rules in Pega

Pega offers a variety of decision rules that cater to different scenarios:

- **Decision Tables**: Use tables to define rules with multiple conditions and outcomes, making complex decision logic more manageable.
- **Decision Trees**: Apply hierarchical logic to evaluate conditions sequentially and return specific outcomes.
- **Map Values**: Leverage this rule type for simple lookups based on one or more inputs.
- **When Rules**: Define conditions that evaluate to true or false, used for simple logical decisions.
- **Scorecards**: Calculate scores based on various weighted criteria, often used in risk assessments or customer profiling.

Choosing the Right Rule: The type of decision rule to implement depends on the complexity of the decision logic and the nature of the application. Decision tables are best for multi-condition scenarios, while decision trees are useful for cascading logic.

3. Implementing Decision Tables

Steps to Create a Decision Table:

1. **Navigate to the Decision Table Rule**: Access this through the Pega platform by creating a new rule under the “Decision Table” type.
2. **Define Inputs**: Specify the input properties or parameters that will be evaluated.
3. **Set Conditions and Results**: Populate the table with conditions in each column and corresponding results in the outcome cells.
4. **Test the Rule**: Use Pega’s test functionality to simulate inputs and validate the decision paths.

Example: In a customer support application, a decision table can be used to assign priority levels to support tickets based on criteria such as issue type, customer tier, and reported impact.

4. Creating Decision Trees for Complex Logic

Decision trees are suitable for more complex decision-making processes where conditions need to be evaluated in a sequence.

How to Create a Decision Tree:

1. **Open a New Decision Tree Rule**: Navigate to the "Decision Tree" option within Pega's rule types.
2. **Define the Conditions**: Create branches with different conditions that guide the decision path.
3. **Specify Outcomes**: Assign results or actions for each condition met.
4. **Optimize and Test**: Ensure the tree is optimized for performance by avoiding redundant checks and testing it with sample data.

Example: An insurance claim processing application can use a decision tree to route claims based on claim type, claim amount, and claimant's history.

5. Best Practices for Implementing Decision Rules

- **Modularize Logic**: Break down complex decision logic into smaller, reusable components for easier maintenance.
- **Document Rules Clearly**: Use descriptive labels and comments to make decision logic easier to understand and maintain.
- **Optimize for Performance**: Minimize the number of conditions checked within a single rule to maintain optimal system performance.
- **Test Extensively**: Use Pega's inbuilt rule testing capabilities to validate each rule under different scenarios to ensure accuracy and efficiency.

Tip: Utilize Pega's **Declarative Expressions** in conjunction with decision rules for more responsive, data-driven behavior across applications.

6. Integrating Decision Rules with Other Application Components

Decision rules can be integrated with:

- **Workflows**: To guide case flows dynamically based on rule outcomes.
- **Data Transforms**: For manipulating data based on decision results.
- **UI Components**: To show or hide user interface elements conditionally based on decision rule evaluations.

Example Implementation: In a financial services app, a decision rule can trigger an additional review step for high-value transactions that exceed a certain threshold, ensuring compliance and risk management.

7. Troubleshooting Common Challenges

Challenge: Decision logic is not producing expected results. **Solution**: Verify that all input data matches the conditions defined in the rule. Use Pega's **tracer tool** to debug and identify where the rule might be failing.

Challenge: Performance issues with decision rules. **Solution**: Optimize the decision logic by simplifying complex conditions and avoiding unnecessary nested evaluations. Leverage caching mechanisms where applicable.

8. Advanced Techniques for Decision Rule Management

- **Using Nested Decision Rules**: Embed smaller decision rules within larger ones for more granular control.

- **Rule Delegation**: Allow business users to manage specific decision rules without involving IT, enabling agility in business logic updates.
- **Version Control**: Implement versioning best practices for decision rules to track changes and revert to previous versions when needed.

Implementing decision rules in Pega enhances the automation, accuracy, and adaptability of business processes. By following best practices and leveraging the various decision rule types available, developers and business architects can create intelligent, responsive applications that align with business goals.

Designing Reusable Components

Designing reusable components in Pega is a strategic approach to enhancing efficiency and consistency across applications. By creating modular, reusable assets, developers can save time, reduce redundancy, and ensure adherence to best practices. This chapter covers the core principles and techniques for designing reusable components in Pega, enabling streamlined development and a scalable, maintainable system architecture.

1. Importance of Reusability in Application Design

Reusability is fundamental to creating flexible and scalable Pega applications. It minimizes code duplication, reduces maintenance efforts, and promotes a standardized approach to solving common business challenges.

Benefits of Reusable Components:

- **Reduced Development Time**: By leveraging pre-built components, developers can focus on more complex logic without reinventing basic functionalities.
- **Consistency Across Applications**: Reusable components help maintain uniformity in user experience and business logic across different parts of an application or multiple applications.
- **Simplified Maintenance**: Centralized, reusable components are easier to update and maintain, reducing the risk of inconsistent changes.

2. Identifying Opportunities for Reusable Components

Before designing reusable components, it's important to identify opportunities where reusability can be implemented.

Common Areas for Reusability:

- **User Interface Sections**: Common UI sections, such as headers, footers, or navigation panels, can be reused across various screens.
- **Data Transforms**: Standard data manipulation processes can be packaged for reuse in different workflows.
- **Validation Rules**: Frequently used validation logic, such as verifying customer data or product details, can be made reusable.
- **Flows and Subflows**: Common workflow patterns, like approval processes or notifications, can be standardized for reuse.

Identifying Reusable Logic:

- **Analyze Existing Processes**: Identify repetitive logic that appears in multiple places within your application.
- **Feedback from Teams**: Collaborate with business analysts and development teams to pinpoint processes that could benefit from reusability.
- **Best Practices Review**: Regularly review application design for areas where modularization could improve development efficiency.

3. Designing Reusable Components in Pega

When designing reusable components, consider the following principles to ensure their effectiveness:

Modular and Independent: Ensure that each component performs a single function and can operate independently without reliance on specific contexts or data structures.

Standardized Input and Output: Define standard input parameters and outputs for components to ensure seamless integration into different parts of the application.

Example: Creating a reusable data transform that formats customer addresses can take parameters like country and postal code format to return standardized output.

Documentation: Document the purpose, usage, and parameters of each reusable component for easy reference by developers and business users.

Version Control: Leverage Pega's version control to track changes to reusable components, ensuring that updates do not inadvertently affect existing processes.

4. Creating and Implementing Reusable Components

Step-by-Step Guide:

1. **Create the Component**:
   - Navigate to the rule type that you wish to make reusable (e.g., Data Transform, Section, Flow).
   - Design the component with generic logic that can apply to various use cases.
2. **Parameterize the Component**:
   - Use parameters to make the component adaptable to different inputs and outputs.
   - Ensure that input parameters are well-defined to minimize misconfiguration.
3. **Test the Component**:
   - Use Pega's test features to validate the component with different input scenarios.
   - Check for compatibility and consistency when integrated into different parts of the application.
4. **Deploy and Integrate**:
   - Deploy the component into a shared library or relevant rule set for easy access.
   - Train development teams on the proper usage of the component and its expected inputs and outputs.

Example Implementation: Creating a reusable **approval subflow** that can be integrated into any case type requiring an approval step:

- **Step 1**: Design the subflow with stages for request submission, review, and approval decision.
- **Step 2**: Parameterize the subflow to accept case data and approver details.
- **Step 3**: Test with various case types to ensure seamless integration.

5. Best Practices for Reusable Component Design

- **Keep It Simple**: Ensure that each component addresses a specific function without becoming overly complex.
- **Modularize Code**: Break down complex logic into smaller, manageable sub-components that can be assembled as needed.
- **Use Naming Conventions**: Adopt a clear and consistent naming convention to identify reusable components easily.
- **Encapsulation**: Protect the internal logic of components by using private access where appropriate, exposing only necessary parameters and outcomes.

Avoid Over-Engineering: Strive for balance between making components reusable and maintaining simplicity. Overly generalized components can be hard to use and maintain.

6. Managing Reusable Components

Effective management of reusable components ensures that they continue to add value over time. This involves:

Component Library: Maintain a centralized library or repository of reusable components accessible to the entire development team. This can be managed through Pega's rule management capabilities or external documentation.

Regular Audits: Conduct periodic audits of the application to identify components that may need updates or enhancements. This helps keep reusable components aligned with evolving business needs.

Feedback Loop: Encourage feedback from developers and business users to improve existing components and identify new opportunities for reusability.

7. Integrating Reusable Components into Your Workflow

Integrate reusable components into new and existing workflows to achieve optimal results. Train team members on how to identify opportunities for reuse during the design phase and integrate these components effectively.

Example Integration: Integrating a reusable notification section into different case types:

- Add the pre-built section into case type workflows where notifications are needed.
- Configure it with parameters like notification type and message content to fit various use cases.

By designing reusable components with these best practices, developers can achieve greater efficiency, consistency, and maintainability in their Pega applications.

Introduction to Pega Expressions and Calculations

In Pega, expressions and calculations form the backbone of dynamic decision-making and data manipulation within applications. These features empower developers to implement complex logic and business rules efficiently. This chapter delves into the essential concepts, types of expressions, and practical applications of expressions and calculations in Pega, providing you with the tools to optimize workflows and enhance functionality.

1. Understanding Pega Expressions

Expressions in Pega are snippets of code or logic that calculate values based on predefined conditions, user input, or data transformations. They are versatile, used across various components such as decision rules, validation logic, and user interface elements.

Key Characteristics of Pega Expressions:

- **Declarative**: Automatically calculated based on changes in related data, ensuring that values remain current.
- **Reusable**: Can be integrated across multiple rules and processes for consistency.
- **Dynamic**: Support conditional logic and nested expressions, enabling complex operations.

Syntax Overview: Pega expressions use Java-based syntax but are simplified for easy integration. For example:

- `@Sum(.orderAmount)`
- `@IndexInList(.customerID, .customerList)`

2. Types of Pega Expressions

Pega offers several types of expressions, each suited to different needs within the platform:

Simple Expressions: Used for straightforward calculations and value assignments. Examples include:

- `10 + .discount`
- `@DateTime.addToDate(.orderDate, 0, 0, 7)`

Conditional Expressions: Enable developers to set conditional logic within rules. For instance:

- `@if(.age > 18, "Eligible", "Not Eligible")`

Declarative Expressions: Automatically triggered when input data changes, maintaining the up-to-date status of calculated values. Declarative expressions often use Pega's **Declare Expression rules.**

Complex Expressions: These involve nested logic, multiple functions, or iterative calculations. They are used for advanced data manipulation and decision-making processes.

3. Creating and Using Pega Expressions

Building Expressions: Expressions can be created within the Pega Rule Form under sections like Decision Tables, Decision Trees, and Map Values. The following steps outline how to create a basic expression:

1. **Navigate to the Rule Form**: Open the relevant rule (e.g., Decision Table).
2. **Enter the Expression**: Add your logic in the designated input field.
3. **Test and Validate**: Use the **Run Rule** feature to test the expression with various inputs.

Common Use Cases:

- **Data Validation**: Ensuring that user input meets certain criteria.
- **Dynamic Calculations**: Automatically updating totals or scores in forms.
- **Decision Rules**: Driving workflow actions based on calculated values.

Example: A simple declarative expression to calculate the total cost with tax:

```
.TotalCost = .BaseCost + (.BaseCost * .TaxRate)
```

4. Working with Calculations in Pega

Types of Calculations: Calculations in Pega are not limited to expressions; they extend to functions and pre-built libraries that simplify complex logic.

Built-In Functions: Pega provides a range of functions to handle tasks such as date manipulation, list processing, and string operations. Commonly used functions include:

- **@DateTime**: For handling date and time operations.
- **@Sum**: To aggregate values from lists or arrays.
- **@Contains**: To check for the presence of elements within a collection.

Using Custom Functions: Developers can create custom functions if built-in options don't meet their needs. Custom functions can be developed using **Java** and incorporated into Pega applications as part of rule sets.

5. Best Practices for Pega Expressions and Calculations

Keep It Simple:

- Start with simple expressions and expand as necessary.
- Avoid nesting too many conditions within a single expression to maintain readability.

Reuse and Refactor:

- Use reusable components such as **Declare Expressions** for logic that appears in multiple places.
- Regularly review expressions to refactor and consolidate repetitive logic.

Test Rigorously:

- Test expressions in various scenarios to ensure expected behavior.
- Utilize Pega's **Tracer Tool** and **Live UI** for debugging.

Document Expressions:

- Include comments or notes explaining complex expressions for easier maintenance and collaboration.

6. Troubleshooting Common Issues

Performance Concerns:

- Overly complex expressions may impact performance. Simplify logic or break down calculations into smaller, manageable parts.
- Monitor the use of looping constructs within expressions to avoid excessive processing time.

Debugging Techniques:

- Use **Pega's Tracer Tool** to step through expressions and identify points of failure or unexpected behavior.
- Leverage **Unit Testing** to validate expressions as standalone rules.

Error Handling:

- Ensure expressions handle null or unexpected values gracefully to prevent application errors.
- Use built-in functions like `@coalesce` to provide default values and avoid null pointer exceptions.

7. Real-World Application Examples

Case Study: Automating Discounts: An online retailer uses a Pega application to apply dynamic discounts based on customer loyalty. An expression calculates the discount:

```
.DiscountAmount = @if(.LoyaltyLevel = "Gold", .BasePrice * 0.15, .BasePrice * 0.05)
```

Advanced Example: Loan Eligibility: A financial institution uses a nested conditional expression to determine loan eligibility:

```
@If(.creditScore > 700 && .income > 50000, "Approved", @If(.creditScore > 650,
"Review", "Denied"))
```

Mastering expressions and calculations in Pega is essential for creating sophisticated, data-driven applications. By leveraging these capabilities, you can implement flexible, dynamic logic that meets complex business requirements.

Managing Data Transforms

Data transforms in Pega play a pivotal role in controlling and mapping data within an application. They offer a method for efficiently moving and modifying data between various properties, systems, and processes. Mastering data transforms is essential for developers looking to optimize data management and enhance the functionality of their Pega applications.

1. What Are Data Transforms?

Data transforms in Pega are rule types that allow developers to define a series of instructions for data transformation. They are used to map, set, and manipulate data between source and target properties or structures. The process of using data transforms ensures that data handling is efficient, consistent, and easy to maintain within Pega applications.

Key Features of Data Transforms:

- **Declarative**: They can automatically apply data changes when rules are triggered.
- **Versatile**: Suitable for various use cases such as initialization, data copying, and validation.
- **Reusable**: Can be shared across different processes, promoting consistency and reducing redundancy.

2. Creating and Configuring Data Transforms

Steps to Create a Data Transform:

1. **Navigate to the Data Transform Rule Form**: Go to `App Studio` or `Dev Studio`, locate the relevant class, and create a new data transform rule.
2. **Define the Purpose and Name**: Provide a meaningful name that reflects its use, such as `CopyOrderDetails` or `InitializeCaseProperties`.
3. **Configure Steps**: Add steps to define specific actions, such as copying data, mapping fields, or performing calculations.
4. **Set Conditions**: Use conditional logic to execute specific steps based on predefined criteria.
5. **Test and Validate**: Run and debug the data transform to ensure it functions as expected under different scenarios.

Basic Structure of a Data Transform: A data transform is comprised of a series of steps, each specifying:

- **Action Type**: What the step will do (e.g., `Set`, `Append and Map`, `When`).
- **Target**: The property or object to be manipulated.
- **Source**: The value or property being assigned.

Example: A data transform to initialize customer order data might include:

```
1. Set .orderDate = @DateTime.CurrentDate()
2. Set .customerID = .inputCustomerID
3. When .orderAmount > 1000
   - Set .priority = "High"
4. Otherwise
   - Set .priority = "Standard"
```

3. Common Use Cases for Data Transforms

Data Mapping: When integrating with external systems or APIs, data transforms help map incoming data to the properties used within Pega. For instance, mapping a JSON response from an API to a Pega data structure.

Data Initialization: During case creation or process initiation, data transforms can set default values for properties, ensuring that necessary data points are pre-populated.

Conditional Logic: Data transforms support `When` and `Otherwise` conditions, allowing for conditional data modifications based on specific criteria.

Data Copying and Aggregation: They are often used to copy data from one structure to another or aggregate data for reporting and analysis.

Example: Mapping data from an external system to Pega properties might look like:

```
1. Set .customerName = .externalResponse.name
2. Set .customerAddress.city = .externalResponse.address.city
3. Append and Map to .orderList
   - Source: .externalResponse.orders
   - Target: .orderList
```

4. Advanced Techniques in Data Transforms

Using Functions: Pega provides various built-in functions that can be incorporated into data transforms for enhanced functionality. For example, `@String.concat()` can concatenate strings, and `@Math.round()` can round numbers to a specific precision.

Nested Data Transforms: Data transforms can call other data transforms within them, promoting modular and maintainable code. This technique is useful when complex transformations need to be broken down into smaller, reusable parts.

Append and Map to: This step is used to map data from one list or page group to another, making it ideal for processing collections of data such as lists of orders or customer accounts.

Using Iterative Loops: Data transforms support iterative operations through loops that apply transformations to each item in a collection. This is useful for processing lists and repeating data transformations.

Example of Advanced Use: A data transform for updating customer loyalty points based on recent purchases:

```
1. Append and Map to .purchaseHistory
   - Source: .recentPurchases
   - Target: .purchaseHistory
2. For Each Page in .purchaseHistory
   - When .purchaseAmount > 500
     - Set .loyaltyPoints = .loyaltyPoints + 50
   - Otherwise
     - Set .loyaltyPoints = .loyaltyPoints + 10
```

5. Best Practices for Using Data Transforms

Maintain Simplicity: Avoid over-complicating data transforms with excessive logic. For complex operations, consider breaking them into smaller, manageable data transforms.

Ensure Reusability: Design data transforms that can be reused across different cases or applications, enhancing maintainability and reducing duplication.

Leverage Naming Conventions: Use clear and consistent naming conventions for data transforms to indicate their purpose, such as `InitOrderData` or `CopyCustomerDetails`.

Testing and Debugging: Regularly test data transforms with the **Clipboard Tool** and **Tracer Tool** to verify data changes and identify issues.

Document Complex Logic: Include comments or documentation within complex data transforms to help team members understand the purpose and functionality of each step.

6. Troubleshooting Common Issues

Incorrect Data Mapping: Ensure that source and target properties are correctly referenced. Misaligned mappings can result in errors or data not being populated as expected.

Performance Considerations: Optimize data transforms that handle large datasets or are invoked frequently to avoid performance bottlenecks.

Conditional Logic Errors: Verify that `When` conditions are correctly evaluated and that there are no missing branches or logic paths.

Debugging Techniques:

- Use **Tracer** to trace data transform execution and pinpoint issues.
- Review the **Clipboard** to inspect the current state of data and validate changes.

7. Practical Example: Customer Onboarding Process

Scenario: A financial services company uses a data transform to streamline customer onboarding. The process includes verifying customer details, setting default values, and mapping external data to internal structures.

Key Steps:

1. **Set Initial Values**: Set default account type and verification status.
2. **Map Data**: Map data from an external KYC (Know Your Customer) API response.
3. **Conditional Logic**: Assign risk levels based on the verification result.
4. **Append Data**: Add verified customer documents to a document list.

Data Transform Steps:

```
1. Set .accountType = "Standard"
2. Set .verificationStatus = "Pending"
3. Map to .customerDetails from .kycResponse.customerInfo
4. When .verificationScore > 80
   - Set .riskLevel = "Low"
5. Otherwise
   - Set .riskLevel = "High"
6. Append and Map to .documentList
   - Source: .kycResponse.documents
   - Target: .documentList
```

Mastering data transforms in Pega equips developers with the tools to handle complex data manipulation efficiently. This enhances application performance, streamlines processes, and ensures that business logic is both maintainable and scalable.

Implementing SLA and Escalation Policies

Service Level Agreements (SLAs) and escalation policies are essential components of modern process automation that help organizations maintain efficiency, prioritize tasks, and meet critical deadlines. In Pega, SLAs are used to define time-based goals for completing assignments, stages, or cases. This chapter will guide you through the key concepts, implementation strategies, and best practices for effectively using SLAs and escalation policies within your Pega applications.

1. Understanding SLAs in Pega

SLAs in Pega serve as time-bound commitments that specify the target duration within which a task should be completed. These SLAs help ensure timely processing of cases and improve adherence to organizational standards.

Key Elements of an SLA:

- **Goal**: The time by which the assignment or case should be completed under normal conditions.
- **Deadline**: The maximum time allowed for the completion of the assignment or case.
- **Passed Deadline**: Actions that occur when the task exceeds the defined deadline.
- **Urgency**: A numerical measure that prioritizes the task relative to others.

Example: An SLA might specify that a customer service ticket should be resolved within 24 hours (goal), with a maximum resolution time of 48 hours (deadline). If the deadline is surpassed, an escalation action might trigger a notification to the supervisor.

2. Configuring SLAs in Pega

Steps to Create an SLA:

1. **Navigate to SLA Rule Creation**: Open the `Dev Studio` and create a new SLA rule by navigating to `Records > Process > Service Level`.
2. **Define the SLA Properties**:
    - **Name**: Assign a meaningful name (e.g., `ResolveCustomerQuerySLA`).
    - **Time Intervals**: Set the values for the goal, deadline, and passed deadline.
    - **Urgency**: Adjust the urgency value to determine the priority of the task as the time progresses.
3. **Configure Escalation Actions**:
    - **At the Goal**: Specify actions such as sending notifications or updating urgency.
    - **At the Deadline**: Set actions like routing the task to a different user or team.
    - **Passed Deadline**: Implement automatic task escalation or further notifications.

Example Configuration:

```
Goal: 24 hours, urgency increment of 10 points
Deadline: 48 hours, urgency increment of 20 points
Passed Deadline: Every 12 hours post-deadline, send a notification and increase
urgency by 5 points
```

3. Implementing Escalation Policies

What Are Escalation Policies? Escalation policies in Pega are triggered when an assignment or case surpasses its defined deadline or goal. They can include notifications, reassignment of tasks, or automated reminders to ensure that the task receives attention.

Types of Escalation Actions:

- **Email Notifications**: Notify team members or supervisors about the delayed task.
- **Reassign Tasks**: Move the assignment to a different user or team for expedited handling.
- **Modify Urgency**: Increase the urgency level to bring the task to the forefront of the work queue.
- **Automatic Processing**: Trigger specific actions, such as transferring data or closing a case under predefined conditions.

Configuring Escalation Policies:

1. Within the SLA rule form, navigate to the **Escalation Actions** section.
2. Add escalation activities for the goal, deadline, and passed deadline.
3. Specify actions such as `Notify Manager`, `Reassign to Supervisor`, or `Increase Urgency`.

Example of Escalation Action: An assignment's passed deadline may trigger an automatic email alert to the operations manager, followed by reassignment to a senior team member for priority handling.

4. Applying SLAs to Assignments and Cases

Assignments: SLAs can be applied directly to assignments in the workflow to ensure timely task completion. For example, an assignment to review a client document may have a goal of 2 hours and a deadline of 4 hours, ensuring swift processing.

Case-Level SLAs: Applying SLAs at the case level ensures that the entire case process adheres to defined timelines. This is particularly useful for long-running cases where time management is critical.

Steps to Apply SLAs to Assignments:

1. Open the `Flow` rule where the assignment resides.
2. Select the assignment shape and set the SLA property.
3. Choose the appropriate SLA rule to attach to the assignment.

Steps to Apply SLAs to Cases:

1. Navigate to the `Case Type` rule.
2. Access the `Settings` tab and choose the `Service Level` section.
3. Attach an SLA rule that governs the entire case lifecycle.

5. Best Practices for Implementing SLAs and Escalations

Set Realistic Timeframes: Ensure that the goal and deadline times reflect realistic processing capabilities. Overly stringent timelines can lead to unnecessary escalations and increased workload.

Use Notifications Judiciously: Too many notifications can desensitize users. Only use notifications for critical milestones or when immediate action is required.

Monitor and Adjust: Regularly review SLA performance metrics and adjust the goal, deadline, or escalation policies as needed to align with changing business requirements.

Combine SLAs with Work Prioritization: Integrate SLAs with Pega's work prioritization capabilities to ensure that the most urgent and overdue tasks are addressed first.

Document and Train: Ensure that team members understand the SLA rules and escalation policies implemented within their processes. Proper documentation and training can prevent confusion and improve task management.

6. Troubleshooting SLA and Escalation Issues

Common Issues and Solutions:

- **SLA Not Triggering**: Ensure that the SLA rule is correctly associated with the assignment or case.
- **Incorrect Urgency Levels**: Review urgency calculations and increments within the SLA rule to ensure they reflect the intended logic.
- **Escalation Actions Not Executing**: Check the associated activities or actions and ensure that permissions and access rights are properly configured.

Debugging Tools:

- **Tracer Tool**: Use the Tracer tool to monitor SLA events and actions during process execution.
- **Clipboard**: Verify the urgency and SLA properties on the clipboard to ensure they are being set and updated correctly.

Example Debugging Scenario: An escalation action that should notify a supervisor at the deadline fails to execute. Use the **Tracer tool** to trace the SLA rule and identify where the process deviates from expectations. Check that the **notification activity** is configured properly and that email services are enabled.

Conclusion

Implementing SLAs and escalation policies in Pega can significantly enhance the management of tasks and case timelines, ensuring that business processes run smoothly and efficiently. By following the best practices outlined in this chapter, you can leverage Pega's SLA features to optimize workflows, maintain high performance standards, and meet service commitments consistently.

Enhancing User Experience with Dynamic Interfaces

User experience (UX) is pivotal in creating applications that are intuitive, efficient, and engaging. Pega provides robust tools and capabilities for designing dynamic interfaces that adapt in real-time to user interactions, enhancing overall usability and ensuring that business processes run smoothly. In this chapter, we will explore how to build dynamic user interfaces in Pega to improve user satisfaction and productivity.

1. Importance of Dynamic Interfaces

Dynamic interfaces allow applications to respond to user inputs and changing data, providing a seamless experience that guides users through complex processes. Implementing these interfaces helps:

- **Increase User Engagement**: Interactive and responsive screens keep users focused and involved.
- **Simplify Processes**: By adapting to user actions, interfaces can reduce clutter and present only relevant information.
- **Enhance Usability**: Dynamic UI elements streamline navigation and reduce cognitive load.

2. Core Concepts in Dynamic Interface Design

To design effective dynamic interfaces in Pega, it's essential to understand the following core concepts:

- **Visibility Conditions**: Rules that show or hide sections, fields, or controls based on specific criteria.
- **Declarative Expressions**: Used to automatically refresh or calculate field values when underlying data changes.
- **Refresh Strategies**: Methods to update sections or data without refreshing the entire page.
- **UI Templates and Layouts**: Predefined structures in Pega that form the foundation for building responsive designs.

3. Implementing Visibility Conditions

Visibility conditions control the appearance of UI elements based on certain parameters. For instance, you can set conditions to display additional form fields when a user selects a particular option.

Steps to Implement Visibility Conditions:

1. **Navigate to the Section Rule**: Open the section where you want to apply visibility conditions.
2. **Select the Element**: Click on the element (e.g., a field or container).
3. **Set Visibility Condition**: In the properties panel, select `Visibility > Condition (expression)` and input the logic (e.g., `.UserRole == "Manager"`).
4. **Test the Configuration**: Preview the section to ensure that the element behaves as expected.

Example: If a customer selects "Yes" to a question about needing additional support, a set of fields asking for more details can appear automatically.

4. Using Declarative Expressions for Real-Time Data Updates

Declarative expressions allow specific fields to automatically update when underlying data changes. This capability is particularly useful in forms where calculations or data dependencies are required.

Creating a Declarative Expression:

1. **Access Data Transform or Property Rule**: Open the relevant data transform or property.
2. **Configure Expression**: Add an expression that defines how the field value is calculated (e.g., `.TotalAmount = .Quantity * .UnitPrice`).
3. **Apply Context**: Ensure the expression is applied in the appropriate context (e.g., on change of `.Quantity` or `.UnitPrice`).

Example: In an order form, updating the `Quantity` field instantly recalculates the `Total Amount` without requiring the user to refresh the page.

5. Implementing Refresh Strategies

Refresh strategies are essential for keeping data current without requiring full page reloads. Pega offers a few different ways to refresh sections and data sources.

Types of Refresh Strategies:

- **Auto-Refresh on Data Change**: Set a section to refresh when a specific property changes.
- **Refresh When Condition Is True**: Refresh a section based on the outcome of a logical condition.
- **Manual Trigger**: Users click a button to refresh a section or data source.

Implementing Auto-Refresh:

1. **Open the Section Rule**.
2. **Configure the Refresh Condition**: Select the section properties and set `Refresh When` logic.
3. **Set Properties for Refresh**: Define which properties trigger the refresh.

Example: A form that displays dynamic pricing based on selected options can refresh the price field whenever the user changes a dropdown selection.

6. Leveraging UI Templates and Layouts

Pega offers a variety of templates and layouts that provide a consistent and responsive design for user interfaces. Using these predefined structures can significantly reduce development time and ensure consistency across the application.

Commonly Used Layouts:

- **Dynamic Layouts**: Adapt to the content and screen size, providing a flexible and user-friendly display.
- **Column Layouts**: Split content into columns for better organization.
- **Tab Layouts**: Organize content into tabs to save space and improve navigation.

Steps to Use a UI Template:

1. **Select the Appropriate Template**: In `App Studio` or `Dev Studio`, choose a dynamic or column layout that fits the user interface needs.
2. **Add Content**: Drag and drop UI components into the layout.
3. **Customize Appearance**: Adjust style, colors, and formatting as needed to align with branding requirements.

7. Best Practices for Enhancing User Experience

- **Keep It Simple**: Design interfaces that are straightforward and minimize user confusion.
- **Prioritize Important Information**: Ensure critical information is prominent and easily accessible.
- **Test Responsiveness**: Check how the interface adapts to different devices and screen sizes.

- **Use Feedback Mechanisms**: Provide users with visual or text-based feedback when an action is completed or data is processed.

8. Example Use Case: Dynamic Loan Application Form

Consider a loan application form that needs to adjust based on user inputs. If an applicant indicates they are applying for a home loan, additional fields related to property details and mortgage information appear.

Implementation Steps:

1. **Configure Conditional Visibility**: Set visibility conditions on sections related to home loan details.
2. **Use Declarative Expressions**: Calculate loan eligibility automatically when users fill out income and loan amount fields.
3. **Implement Auto-Refresh**: Refresh the section displaying the estimated approval timeline whenever data changes.

Conclusion

Enhancing user experience with dynamic interfaces in Pega ensures that your application not only looks professional but also functions in a way that improves productivity and user satisfaction. By leveraging visibility conditions, declarative expressions, refresh strategies, and robust UI templates, you can build an adaptable and intuitive interface that aligns with business goals and user expectations.

Developing Mobile-Compatible Pega Applications

In the digital age, businesses and their customers increasingly rely on mobile solutions for greater flexibility and improved user engagement. Pega's platform is designed to support the development of mobile-compatible applications that are responsive, functional, and capable of handling complex business processes on-the-go. This chapter will guide you through the essentials of building mobile-compatible Pega applications that meet the demands of modern users.

1. Importance of Mobile-First Development

Mobile-first development emphasizes designing applications with the mobile user experience in mind, ensuring that applications function seamlessly on smaller screens before scaling up to desktop versions. This approach provides:

- **Wider Accessibility**: Enables users to access the application from anywhere at any time.
- **Enhanced User Engagement**: Mobile-friendly designs promote higher user satisfaction and usability.
- **Improved Productivity**: Mobile solutions allow employees and clients to interact with systems outside traditional office settings.

2. Key Considerations for Mobile Development in Pega

When developing mobile-compatible applications in Pega, consider the following aspects:

- **Responsive Design**: Ensure that UI components adapt fluidly to different screen sizes and orientations.
- **Touch Optimization**: Design interfaces that are easy to navigate and interact with using touch controls.
- **Performance Optimization**: Optimize applications for speed and efficiency to prevent lag on mobile devices.
- **Offline Capabilities**: Integrate offline functionality for users who may not always have internet access.

3. Setting Up Mobile Compatibility in Pega

Pega offers tools and configurations to make applications mobile-friendly. The Mobile Client and Pega App Studio are particularly useful for these purposes.

Steps for Initial Mobile Configuration:

1. **Access Pega App Studio**: Open the application in Pega App Studio to access mobile development features.
2. **Enable Mobile View**: Use the preview function to see how the application appears on different devices and make necessary adjustments.
3. **Select a Mobile Template**: Choose from pre-defined templates optimized for mobile use or customize your template as needed.
4. **Configure Responsive Layouts**: Ensure that dynamic and column layouts adjust properly based on screen size.

4. Designing Mobile-Friendly Interfaces

Designing user interfaces that are optimized for mobile involves creating intuitive and simplified layouts. Best practices include:

- **Minimalist Design**: Keep the layout clean and avoid excessive information on a single screen.

- **Larger Interactive Elements**: Ensure buttons and interactive elements are big enough to be tapped comfortably.
- **Use of Icons and Visual Cues**: Utilize icons to reduce text-heavy layouts and guide users through processes.

Example: A mobile-friendly customer service application should have large, easy-to-tap buttons for submitting requests, navigation tabs for different service categories, and a responsive search bar that adjusts in size depending on the screen orientation.

5. Incorporating Mobile-Specific Features

Pega applications can leverage the unique capabilities of mobile devices such as cameras, GPS, and notifications.

Common Mobile Features to Integrate:

- **Camera Access**: For document scanning or image uploads directly from the mobile device.
- **Location Services**: For applications that need to capture or use the user's geographical location.
- **Push Notifications**: For alerting users about important updates or actions needed in the app.

Implementation Steps:

1. **Add Mobile Components**: Use Pega's mobile design options to incorporate components that interact with device hardware.
2. **Configure Data Capture**: Set up fields to accept inputs from the camera or location services.
3. **Test Notification Functionality**: Ensure push notifications are set up properly and can be sent based on user interactions or system events.

6. Offline Support for Mobile Applications

Offline functionality is essential for mobile users who may face connectivity challenges. Pega allows for limited offline access, enabling users to interact with certain application features even without an active internet connection.

Setting Up Offline Mode:

1. **Determine Features for Offline Use**: Identify which parts of the application should be available offline.
2. **Configure Data Synchronization**: Set up data sync rules to upload changes made offline once the device reconnects.
3. **Test Offline Behavior**: Simulate offline scenarios to ensure that the application performs as expected when not connected to the internet.

Example: A field service application that allows employees to record maintenance tasks or inspections should include offline capabilities for use in remote areas. Data entered offline should be queued for automatic submission when connectivity is restored.

7. Testing and Optimizing Mobile Performance

Mobile applications must be tested rigorously to ensure they perform well under different conditions. Key aspects of performance testing include:

- **Load Times**: Ensure that the app loads quickly and efficiently on mobile networks.
- **Interaction Response**: Verify that all touch inputs respond without delays.
- **Cross-Device Functionality**: Test the application across various mobile devices and operating systems for consistency.

Optimization Tips:

- **Minimize Data Load**: Only load necessary data when the user interacts with a component to reduce the initial load time.
- **Use Caching Wisely**: Implement caching strategies to speed up the retrieval of frequently accessed data.
- **Compress Images and Files**: Optimize multimedia elements for faster loading without compromising quality.

8. Best Practices for Mobile App Development in Pega

- **Use Adaptive Layouts**: Implement adaptive layouts that automatically adjust based on device size.
- **Regular Updates**: Update the mobile app regularly to keep it compatible with the latest operating systems and devices.
- **User Feedback Integration**: Gather feedback from mobile users to continuously improve the app's design and functionality.

Conclusion

Developing mobile-compatible Pega applications ensures that businesses can provide flexible and efficient solutions to their users. By prioritizing responsive design, leveraging mobile-specific features, and incorporating offline capabilities, developers can create applications that meet the dynamic needs of modern enterprises.

Section 5:
Automation and Integrations

Integrating Pega with External Systems

In today's interconnected business environment, integrating Pega with external systems is vital for ensuring smooth communication, data flow, and functionality across platforms. Pega's robust capabilities allow organizations to create seamless integrations that enhance operational efficiency and promote comprehensive automation across various business functions. This chapter delves into the essentials of integrating Pega with external systems and the tools and techniques required to do so effectively.

1. Importance of Integrating Pega with External Systems

Integration helps organizations maintain an interconnected ecosystem where Pega applications can interact seamlessly with other software and databases. This capability:

- **Enhances Workflow Efficiency**: Reduces manual data entry and duplication of efforts by synchronizing data automatically.
- **Improves Decision-Making**: Access to data from different systems provides a comprehensive view for better decision-making.
- **Supports Real-Time Processes**: Ensures up-to-date information across applications, enabling real-time monitoring and updates.

2. Key Integration Scenarios

Pega's integration capabilities can be employed in numerous scenarios, such as:

- **Connecting with ERP Systems**: Synchronizing with systems like SAP or Oracle to streamline data processing and workflows.
- **Linking CRM Platforms**: Integrating with Salesforce or other CRM tools for improved customer service and data management.
- **Interfacing with Legacy Systems**: Connecting with older platforms to leverage existing data and operations without complete system overhauls.
- **Web Services Integration**: Using REST or SOAP APIs for communication between Pega and other web-based services.

3. Integration Tools and Features in Pega

Pega offers a comprehensive suite of built-in tools and connectors for integration:

- **Integration Designer**: This tool provides a visual representation of integrations, making it easier to manage and configure connections between Pega and external systems.
- **Connectors and Services**: Pega supports REST, SOAP, SQL connectors, and services, allowing applications to communicate with external databases, web services, and other software.
- **Data Pages (D-Page)**: These pages are used for fetching data from external sources and making it available for use within Pega applications.
- **Pega API**: A built-in API that allows external systems to interact with Pega applications, facilitating bi-directional communication.

4. Setting Up Integrations with External Systems

To set up an integration in Pega, follow these steps:

1. **Identify Integration Requirements**: Determine the type of data to be exchanged, the format, and the external system involved.
2. **Configure the Connector**:
    - **REST/SOAP Connector**: Use Pega's REST or SOAP connector wizard to configure the connection. Provide the endpoint URL, authentication details, and request/response data mappings.
    - **Database Connector**: Configure the connection to external databases by defining the database connection string and SQL queries.
3. **Create Data Pages**: Set up data pages to fetch and cache data from the external source. Specify the connector as the source for the data page.
4. **Map Data**: Use Pega's Data Transform feature to map the incoming data structure to the Pega application's data model.
5. **Test the Integration**: Run test cases to ensure the integration works as expected and data is correctly received and processed.

Example: For integrating with a CRM system like Salesforce, a REST connector can be configured using the Salesforce API endpoint. The data fetched from Salesforce can be displayed in a Pega case type to provide users with real-time customer information.

5. Best Practices for Pega Integrations

Implementing integrations effectively requires adhering to best practices:

- **Use Asynchronous Processing**: For long-running processes, consider using asynchronous integration to prevent bottlenecks in Pega applications.
- **Secure Connections**: Ensure data exchanged between Pega and external systems is encrypted using secure protocols like HTTPS and OAuth for authentication.
- **Error Handling**: Implement error handling mechanisms to manage connection failures, data mismatches, and other issues that may arise during integration.
- **Data Transformation**: Standardize data transformation processes using Data Transforms and Parse rules to handle incoming data formats efficiently.

6. Troubleshooting Common Integration Issues

Integrating Pega with external systems can sometimes result in challenges. Common issues and their solutions include:

- **Connection Failures**: Ensure that the endpoint URLs and network configurations are correct and accessible from Pega's environment.
- **Data Format Mismatches**: Use Pega's data mapping and transformation tools to align data structures between Pega and the external system.
- **Authentication Issues**: Verify that API keys, tokens, or other authentication credentials are valid and correctly configured.
- **Performance Bottlenecks**: For high data loads, consider batching data retrieval and optimizing connector performance through configuration tweaks and caching strategies.

7. Case Study: Integration with a Payment Gateway

Consider a scenario where a Pega application is integrated with an external payment gateway to facilitate online transactions. The integration can be set up as follows:

- **Connector Configuration**: A REST connector is configured to send payment requests and receive responses from the payment gateway.

- **Data Mapping**: The transaction data structure is mapped to Pega's internal model, ensuring smooth data flow between the systems.
- **Security Measures**: The integration is secured with token-based authentication and encrypted data transmission.
- **Error Handling**: Custom error messages are configured to inform users in case of transaction failures or connectivity issues.

Outcome: The integration results in seamless payment processing, providing users with a reliable and efficient transaction experience within the Pega application.

Conclusion

Integrating Pega with external systems is a critical aspect of creating a cohesive and efficient business process environment. By utilizing Pega's robust integration tools and adhering to best practices, organizations can enhance their workflows, optimize data exchange, and provide superior functionality to users. Understanding and implementing these integrations effectively enables businesses to leverage the full potential of Pega as part of a larger enterprise ecosystem.

API Management and Web Services in Pega

The effective use of Application Programming Interfaces (APIs) and web services is essential for creating an interconnected ecosystem where Pega can communicate with other applications and services. In this chapter, we will explore how Pega facilitates API management and how it leverages web services to extend its capabilities, streamline operations, and integrate seamlessly with external systems.

1. Overview of API Management in Pega

Pega provides built-in capabilities for developing and managing APIs that allow external systems to interact with Pega applications. This feature helps organizations expose Pega functionalities, making them accessible for integrations, mobile apps, and third-party services.

Key aspects of Pega's API management include:

- **RESTful and SOAP Services**: Pega supports the development and management of both RESTful and SOAP web services, enabling flexible integration with a variety of systems.
- **Secure Access**: Pega APIs are designed with security in mind, supporting authentication mechanisms such as OAuth 2.0 and basic authentication to protect data and control access.
- **Endpoint Management**: Pega allows developers to configure, test, and manage endpoints efficiently for smoother integrations.

2. Creating and Configuring APIs in Pega

To create and manage APIs in Pega, developers can follow these key steps:

a. Configuring REST and SOAP Services:

- **REST Services**:
  - Use the **REST Integration wizard** in Pega to set up RESTful services quickly.
  - Define the resource path and HTTP methods (GET, POST, PUT, DELETE) for data retrieval and submission.
  - Map input and output parameters using **JSON** or **XML** formats.
- **SOAP Services**:
  - Utilize the **SOAP Integration wizard** to create SOAP services.
  - Configure the WSDL (Web Services Description Language) for the service and map data as required.

b. Establishing Connectors:

- Pega provides connectors for consuming third-party services.
- **Connect REST and Connect SOAP rules** enable Pega to call external RESTful and SOAP web services.
- Specify details such as endpoint URLs, authentication credentials, and data mappings in the rule configuration.

Example: To set up a REST connector in Pega:

1. Navigate to **Records > Integration-Connectors > Connect REST**.
2. Configure the connector with the endpoint URL.
3. Define request and response data transforms to map data appropriately.
4. Test the connection to ensure smooth interaction.

3. Securing APIs and Web Services

Security is a paramount concern when exposing APIs or integrating web services. Pega incorporates several mechanisms to ensure that APIs are secured:

- **Authentication Protocols**: Implement OAuth 2.0 for secure token-based access. Basic authentication and custom authentication schemes can also be configured.
- **Access Groups and Roles**: Assign specific access groups and roles to control who can use or modify APIs and web services.
- **Data Encryption**: Use HTTPS for encrypted data transmission to prevent unauthorized data access or interception during transfer.

Best Practices:

- Regularly review and update API keys and tokens.
- Implement rate limiting to prevent excessive usage or potential denial-of-service attacks.
- Monitor API usage with Pega's monitoring tools to detect anomalies and secure endpoints.

4. Utilizing Pega's Out-of-the-Box APIs

Pega comes with prebuilt APIs, such as the **Pega API**, which facilitates interaction with cases, assignments, and data objects in Pega. These APIs provide endpoints that can be used to:

- **Create and manage cases**: Start new cases or update existing ones.
- **Retrieve assignments**: Access tasks assigned to users or work queues.
- **Fetch data**: Use the API to pull data for reports and dashboards.

Example Use Case: A company wants to integrate its customer support system with Pega. By using Pega's REST API, the support system can create new cases in Pega whenever a customer submits a request, ensuring that support staff have immediate visibility and can take appropriate action.

5. Testing and Debugging Integrations

To ensure that integrations are set up correctly, Pega provides various tools for testing and debugging:

- **Tracer Tool**: Use the Tracer tool to monitor the processing of service and connector rules and identify issues in real-time.
- **Postman/SoapUI**: Test external API calls using tools like Postman or SoapUI to verify that Pega services are responding as expected.
- **Log Analysis**: Review Pega logs for any errors or issues related to service calls and integrations.

6. Advanced Topics: API Management and Scalability

For enterprises that require extensive API usage, managing and scaling APIs is crucial:

- **Version Control**: Pega allows versioning of APIs to manage changes without affecting existing integrations.
- **Load Management**: Integrate with Pega's system performance tools to monitor API load and ensure optimal performance under high traffic.
- **Caching**: Use data page caching for frequently accessed data to reduce response times and API load.

7. Real-World Application Example

A global e-commerce company integrates Pega with its warehouse management system via RESTful APIs. This integration allows real-time updates on order status and inventory levels:

- **Inbound Integration**: The warehouse management system notifies Pega when inventory levels change.

- **Outbound Integration**: Pega sends case updates and shipment requests to the warehouse system.

This seamless integration helps maintain synchronized operations between order management and warehouse logistics, reducing errors and improving customer satisfaction.

Conclusion

API management and web services in Pega play a vital role in creating a connected digital ecosystem. By leveraging Pega's capabilities for developing, managing, and securing APIs, businesses can enhance their process automation, improve communication between systems, and provide comprehensive service offerings. Understanding and implementing these integrations effectively ensures that organizations remain agile and efficient in an increasingly interconnected world.

Automating Processes Using Robotics

Robotic Process Automation (RPA) has revolutionized the way businesses operate, offering a way to automate repetitive tasks and workflows that traditionally required human intervention. Pega Systems, with its comprehensive suite of automation tools, integrates robotics seamlessly to enhance operational efficiency, reduce costs, and improve accuracy. This chapter will guide you through understanding how Pega facilitates process automation using robotics and how to effectively leverage these capabilities in business operations.

1. Introduction to Robotic Process Automation (RPA)

Robotic Process Automation (RPA) involves using software robots or 'bots' to automate routine tasks that do not require human decision-making. These tasks can include data entry, data extraction, form processing, and simple decision-making processes. Pega's RPA capabilities enable businesses to automate processes across various applications and systems without the need for complex integrations.

Key Benefits of RPA in Pega:

- **Enhanced productivity**: Automates high-volume, repetitive tasks.
- **Improved accuracy**: Reduces human error, ensuring consistency in task execution.
- **Cost reduction**: Saves costs associated with manual labor.
- **Scalability**: Easily scales to meet business demands.

2. Understanding Pega's Robotics Architecture

Pega's RPA is designed as part of the Pega Robotics suite, which includes Pega Robot Manager and Pega Robotics Studio. These tools provide the infrastructure for building, deploying, and managing bots in business processes.

Components of Pega's Robotics Architecture:

- **Pega Robotics Studio**: The development environment where bots are designed and configured.
- **Pega Robot Manager**: The tool that monitors and manages bots, their workload, and performance.
- **Pega Workforce Intelligence**: An analytics tool that identifies automation opportunities and enhances workforce efficiency.

3. Designing Robotic Automation with Pega Robotics Studio

Pega Robotics Studio is the starting point for creating automation scripts and bots. The process involves using a visual, drag-and-drop interface to design automation workflows.

Steps to Create an RPA Workflow:

1. **Define the Process**: Identify the business task you wish to automate, such as data entry or report generation.
2. **Build the Workflow**: Use Pega Robotics Studio to configure the automation logic by dragging and dropping components, defining actions, and mapping data flows.
3. **Set Automation Rules**: Configure conditions under which the bot operates, including decision trees and exception handling.
4. **Test the Bot**: Run the bot in a controlled environment to validate its performance and ensure it behaves as expected.
5. **Deploy the Bot**: Use Pega Robot Manager to deploy the bot to production and monitor its activity.

Example: Automating invoice processing by creating a bot that extracts invoice data from emails and inputs it into an ERP system.

4. Integrating Bots into Pega Workflows

Pega makes it easy to integrate bots into business processes and workflows. Bots can work alongside human operators, taking on repetitive tasks while users handle more complex activities.

Methods of Integration:

- **Attended RPA**: Bots that work alongside employees, triggering actions based on human input.
- **Unattended RPA**: Bots that operate independently, executing processes based on predefined triggers or schedules.
- **Hybrid Automation**: Combines attended and unattended RPA, enabling seamless collaboration between bots and human workers.

5. Managing and Monitoring RPA with Pega Robot Manager

Pega Robot Manager is the centralized platform for managing RPA deployments. It allows administrators to:

- **Allocate and distribute workloads**: Ensure that bots are utilized effectively to handle incoming tasks.
- **Monitor bot performance**: View dashboards and reports that provide insights into bot activity and success rates.
- **Manage exceptions**: Identify and resolve issues where bots encounter unexpected scenarios.

Example Use Case: A financial services firm uses Pega Robot Manager to monitor bots that automate loan application processing, ensuring that all required data points are entered into the system without delays.

6. Advanced RPA Features and Best Practices

To make the most of Pega's RPA capabilities, consider the following best practices and advanced features:

- **Exception Handling**: Implement robust exception handling to ensure bots can recover from errors gracefully.
- **Bot Scalability**: Design bots that can scale to meet changing business needs without significant reconfiguration.
- **Security Measures**: Use encryption and secure authentication to protect data processed by bots.
- **Continuous Improvement**: Regularly analyze bot performance and make adjustments to improve efficiency.

Best Practices:

- **Document Processes**: Maintain detailed documentation of automation scripts and processes for future reference and training.
- **Optimize Task Segmentation**: Break down complex processes into smaller, automatable tasks to enhance bot performance.
- **Regular Updates**: Keep Pega Robotics Studio and Robot Manager updated to access the latest features and security patches.

7. Real-World Application of Pega RPA

Companies across various industries have successfully implemented Pega RPA to streamline processes:

Case Study: A global logistics company used Pega RPA to automate the processing of shipment tracking updates. The bots retrieved shipment data from various carrier websites and updated the company's internal systems. This automation reduced manual workload by 40% and improved tracking accuracy.

8. Challenges and Solutions in Implementing RPA

While RPA provides significant advantages, it's essential to address potential challenges:

- **Bot Maintenance**: Bots may need regular updates if the integrated systems or interfaces change.
- **Process Selection**: Choose processes with a high volume and low complexity for the best automation results.
- **Change Management**: Prepare the workforce for RPA implementation by offering training and support to adapt to new workflows.

Solutions:

- Implement comprehensive training programs.
- Conduct pilot tests before full-scale deployment.
- Involve IT and business teams in collaborative planning and execution.

Conclusion

Automating processes using robotics in Pega empowers organizations to transform operations by minimizing manual effort, improving task accuracy, and optimizing resources. By leveraging Pega's RPA capabilities, businesses can achieve substantial operational efficiencies and maintain a competitive edge in the digital landscape.

Utilizing Pega's Robotic Process Automation (RPA)

Robotic Process Automation (RPA) has become a cornerstone for businesses seeking to automate high-volume, repetitive tasks that do not require human judgment. Pega's RPA capabilities extend beyond basic automation, providing comprehensive solutions that integrate with existing workflows to optimize operations and reduce operational costs. In this chapter, we will explore how to utilize Pega's RPA effectively to enhance your business processes.

1. Overview of Pega's RPA Capabilities

Pega's RPA is designed to mimic human actions in executing digital tasks within various software systems. Unlike traditional automation, Pega's RPA integrates seamlessly with the Pega Platform to enable cohesive workflow automation.

Key Features of Pega's RPA:

- **Seamless Integration with BPM**: Pega's RPA can be combined with Business Process Management (BPM) to create end-to-end automated workflows.
- **Low-Code Development**: Utilize Pega Robotics Studio to design bots with minimal coding.
- **Attended and Unattended Automation**: Supports both attended (human-assisted) and unattended (independent) bots for diverse use cases.

2. Building RPA Solutions in Pega Robotics Studio

Pega Robotics Studio serves as the core development environment for creating RPA solutions. This low-code platform allows developers to build automation workflows by dragging and dropping components.

Steps to Create RPA Bots:

1. **Define the Process**: Identify repetitive tasks within your business operations that can be automated.
2. **Design the Workflow**: Use the visual interface in Pega Robotics Studio to construct the bot's logic and actions.
3. **Configure Automation Logic**: Map out the decision-making logic and sequence of actions for the bot.
4. **Integrate with Pega Platform**: Link the bot with existing Pega workflows for cohesive process execution.
5. **Test and Deploy**: Validate the bot's functionality in a test environment before deploying it to production.

Example: Automating customer onboarding by creating an RPA bot that extracts customer information from emails and updates the CRM system.

3. Attended vs. Unattended Bots

Pega offers both attended and unattended bots, each serving unique business needs.

- **Attended Bots**: Work alongside human operators to assist with tasks such as data validation or information retrieval. These bots are activated by user interactions and work in real-time.
- **Unattended Bots**: Operate independently to perform batch processing or complete tasks triggered by predefined events or schedules. Ideal for back-office operations that do not require human intervention.

Use Case: An insurance company uses unattended bots to process claims overnight, ensuring faster response times and workload management.

4. Implementing Pega RPA in Business Workflows

Integrating Pega RPA into your business workflows involves a strategic approach that ensures alignment with process goals and business outcomes.

Steps for Implementation:

- **Process Mapping**: Identify and document the tasks that will be automated.
- **Bot Development**: Develop the bot logic using Pega Robotics Studio, including data handling, navigation, and exception management.
- **Testing and Quality Assurance**: Conduct thorough testing to catch potential issues and refine the bot's performance.
- **Deployment and Monitoring**: Deploy the bots using Pega Robot Manager and monitor their activity to ensure optimal operation.

5. Managing and Monitoring RPA with Pega Robot Manager

Pega Robot Manager is the command center for managing and monitoring deployed bots. It provides an interface for tracking bot performance, managing workloads, and handling exceptions.

Features of Pega Robot Manager:

- **Real-Time Monitoring**: Keep track of bot activities and overall performance.
- **Workload Distribution**: Allocate tasks dynamically to optimize resource use.
- **Performance Analytics**: Gain insights into bot efficiency and success rates through reports and dashboards.

Example: A retail company uses Pega Robot Manager to oversee bots responsible for updating inventory records, ensuring data accuracy and process consistency.

6. Best Practices for Successful RPA Implementation

To maximize the benefits of Pega RPA, adhere to the following best practices:

- **Select High-Impact Processes**: Automate tasks that deliver significant efficiency gains and are high in volume but low in complexity.
- **Design for Scalability**: Ensure bots can be scaled up or down based on business needs.
- **Incorporate Robust Error Handling**: Plan for exceptions and create fallback mechanisms to handle unexpected scenarios.
- **Continuous Optimization**: Regularly review and optimize bot performance based on operational data and feedback.

7. Case Studies: Real-World Applications of Pega RPA

Case Study 1: A financial institution implemented Pega RPA to automate loan application processing. Bots extracted applicant data from multiple sources, validated it, and inputted it into the approval system. This reduced processing time by 50% and improved accuracy.

Case Study 2: A healthcare provider utilized Pega RPA for patient record management, automating the transfer of patient data between departments. This streamlined operations and allowed staff to focus on patient care rather than administrative tasks.

8. Addressing Common Challenges in Pega RPA Deployment

Despite its benefits, implementing RPA can come with challenges such as maintaining bots in dynamic environments where software interfaces change frequently.

Solutions:

- **Regular Maintenance**: Schedule routine updates and audits to ensure bots adapt to changes in the system environment.
- **Employee Training**: Provide training for staff to understand how to collaborate with RPA bots and report issues effectively.

Conclusion

Pega's RPA offers powerful tools for automating routine and time-consuming tasks, enabling businesses to optimize their processes and allocate human resources more effectively. By integrating Pega RPA into your business, you can achieve greater operational efficiency, reduce errors, and improve overall productivity.

Integrating AI and Machine Learning Capabilities

In today's fast-evolving technological landscape, the integration of Artificial Intelligence (AI) and Machine Learning (ML) capabilities is pivotal for organizations aiming to stay competitive and agile. Pega's AI and ML tools offer comprehensive solutions that enhance decision-making, automate complex processes, and deliver personalized customer experiences. This chapter explores how to effectively integrate AI and ML into your Pega applications to maximize business impact.

1. Overview of Pega's AI and ML Capabilities

Pega's AI and ML features are embedded within the platform, allowing businesses to leverage powerful analytics, predictive modeling, and real-time decisioning. These capabilities facilitate smarter workflows that adapt to changing circumstances and user needs.

Key Features of Pega's AI and ML:

- **Predictive Analytics**: Use historical data to forecast outcomes and trends.
- **Adaptive Models**: Continuously learn from new data to optimize decision strategies.
- **Natural Language Processing (NLP)**: Enhance user interactions through text analysis and automated responses.
- **AI-Powered Decisioning**: Real-time decision-making to guide next-best actions for improved outcomes.

2. Implementing AI-Powered Decisioning in Pega

Integrating AI into business processes allows for intelligent decision-making that goes beyond static, rule-based systems.

Steps to Implement AI-Powered Decisioning:

1. **Define Business Objectives**: Identify where AI decision-making can have the most impact, such as customer service, sales, or risk management.
2. **Create Decision Strategies**: Use Pega's Decision Strategy Manager to outline the flow of decisions, incorporating predictive and adaptive models.
3. **Leverage Data Sources**: Connect internal and external data sources to enrich decision models and improve the accuracy of outcomes.
4. **Configure Adaptive Models**: Set up adaptive learning models that update their predictions based on new data without manual intervention.
5. **Integrate with Processes**: Embed these decision strategies within workflows to enable automated, AI-driven responses.

Example Use Case: A telecommunications company using Pega's AI-powered decisioning to recommend tailored service plans to customers based on usage patterns and feedback.

3. Building Predictive Models

Predictive models analyze historical data to predict future trends, helping businesses make data-driven decisions.

Steps to Build Predictive Models:

1. **Data Preparation**: Collect and preprocess data for training models.
2. **Model Training**: Utilize Pega's machine learning tools to train the model using data sets.
3. **Validation**: Test the model with new data to ensure reliability and accuracy.
4. **Deployment**: Integrate the predictive model into workflows for real-time decision support.

Tips for Effective Predictive Modeling:

- Ensure data diversity to avoid biased predictions.
- Continuously update models to reflect changes in business conditions.
- Monitor model performance and retrain as needed for sustained accuracy.

4. Utilizing Adaptive Learning

Pega's adaptive learning models offer a significant advantage by learning from user interactions and outcomes to improve predictions and decisions.

Adaptive Learning Implementation:

- **Setup**: Integrate adaptive models into decision strategies for real-time learning.
- **Feedback Loops**: Ensure the system receives feedback on the outcomes to improve future decision accuracy.
- **Real-Time Adjustments**: Adaptive models adjust their behavior in response to new data, providing a flexible and responsive approach to automation.

Example: A financial institution that uses adaptive models for fraud detection, where the system learns from flagged transactions to better identify potential fraud in the future.

5. Enhancing Customer Interactions with NLP

Natural Language Processing (NLP) capabilities in Pega allow for better customer interactions through automated text understanding and responses.

Applications of NLP in Pega:

- **Chatbots and Virtual Assistants**: Implement chatbots that can understand and respond to customer queries using Pega's NLP features.
- **Text Analytics**: Analyze customer feedback, emails, and social media mentions to extract actionable insights.
- **Automated Case Management**: Use NLP to classify and route incoming requests based on content, ensuring efficient case handling.

Implementing NLP:

- **Configuration**: Set up NLP models to analyze text data and identify patterns or intents.
- **Training**: Train NLP models with relevant data to improve their accuracy in understanding customer queries.
- **Deployment**: Deploy NLP-powered solutions in customer service workflows to enhance user experience.

6. Best Practices for Integrating AI and ML in Pega

To effectively implement AI and ML in Pega, consider the following best practices:

- **Start Small, Scale Gradually**: Begin with specific processes or tasks and scale up as the models prove effective.
- **Ensure Data Quality**: High-quality data is essential for reliable AI and ML outputs.
- **Prioritize Transparency**: Maintain transparency in decision-making models to ensure they are understandable and auditable.
- **Monitor and Optimize**: Regularly review the performance of AI and ML models and make adjustments as needed to optimize outcomes.

7. Case Studies: Real-World Examples of AI Integration

Case Study 1: An e-commerce platform implemented Pega's predictive analytics to recommend products based on customer browsing history and previous purchases. This resulted in a 20% increase in customer engagement and sales.

Case Study 2: A healthcare provider used Pega's AI-powered decisioning to streamline patient appointment scheduling, improving efficiency and patient satisfaction by 30%.

Conclusion

Integrating AI and ML capabilities in Pega offers a robust way to automate decision-making and enhance process intelligence. By leveraging Pega's advanced tools, organizations can build smarter workflows, improve customer experiences, and drive operational efficiency.

Handling Data Integration Challenges

Data integration is a crucial aspect of process automation, ensuring seamless connectivity between different systems and data sources. In Pega, efficient data integration leads to more comprehensive workflows and a unified user experience. However, integrating diverse data sources can come with its set of challenges. This chapter explores these challenges and offers practical solutions within Pega to overcome them.

1. Understanding Common Data Integration Challenges

Before integrating data into Pega, it's important to identify potential issues that can hinder the process:

- **Data Silos**: Organizations often have data stored across disparate systems that do not communicate with each other. This lack of connectivity can limit the effectiveness of automated workflows.
- **Inconsistent Data Formats**: Different systems may use various formats and structures, making it difficult to synchronize data accurately.
- **Data Quality Issues**: Poor data quality, such as missing or inaccurate information, can lead to flawed processes and outputs.
- **Latency and Performance Bottlenecks**: Real-time integration is necessary for many business processes, and any latency can impact the overall performance and responsiveness of the system.
- **Security and Compliance**: Ensuring that data integration aligns with regulatory standards and internal security policies is crucial to maintain trust and avoid legal repercussions.

2. Pega's Tools for Data Integration

Pega provides a robust set of tools and features designed to handle data integration challenges effectively:

- **Integration Designer**: A visual tool that allows developers to map and connect external data sources with Pega applications seamlessly.
- **Connectors**: Pre-built connectors for various systems, such as REST, SOAP, JMS, and database integrations, facilitate communication with external data sources.
- **Data Pages**: Reusable components that act as a central point to pull and refresh data, ensuring consistency and reducing the need for multiple calls to external systems.
- **Integration Error Handling**: Built-in mechanisms to capture and respond to integration failures with customized error-handling workflows.
- **Data Transform Rules**: Enable data transformation from one format to another, ensuring compatibility between Pega applications and external data sources.

3. Strategies for Addressing Data Integration Challenges

To address the challenges associated with data integration in Pega, consider the following strategies:

A. Mitigating Data Silos

- **Unified Data Models**: Develop a comprehensive data model within Pega that aggregates data from various sources to create a unified view.
- **Centralized Integration Strategy**: Implement a centralized data integration approach to connect different data silos through Pega's data management tools.

B. Managing Inconsistent Data Formats

- **Use Data Transforms**: Employ data transforms within Pega to map and convert data from external sources into the required format.

- **Data Preprocessing**: Preprocess data at the source, if possible, to ensure consistency before it enters Pega's ecosystem.

C. Ensuring Data Quality

- **Validation Rules**: Establish robust validation rules to check data for completeness and accuracy before it is integrated into workflows.
- **Cleansing Mechanisms**: Implement data cleansing procedures using Pega's decisioning capabilities to identify and rectify errors in incoming data.

D. Addressing Latency and Performance Issues

- **Optimize Data Calls**: Reduce unnecessary calls to external systems by leveraging Pega's data pages and caching mechanisms.
- **Batch Processing**: Where real-time integration is not essential, use batch processing to handle data updates during off-peak hours to minimize system load.

E. Maintaining Security and Compliance

- **Encryption and Authentication**: Utilize Pega's built-in security features to encrypt data during transmission and ensure that only authorized users have access.
- **Audit Trails**: Enable audit trails for data integration activities to maintain transparency and comply with regulatory standards.
- **Compliance Checks**: Regularly review integration processes to ensure they align with current data privacy regulations, such as GDPR or HIPAA, depending on the business's needs.

4. Best Practices for Data Integration in Pega

- **Design for Scalability**: Build data integration processes that can scale as data sources and business needs evolve.
- **Regular Monitoring**: Implement monitoring tools to oversee data flows and address issues proactively.
- **Documentation**: Keep detailed documentation of data integration points, data sources, and mapping logic to facilitate future updates and troubleshooting.
- **Use Test Environments**: Test data integrations in a non-production environment to identify and resolve potential issues before deployment.
- **Collaborate Across Teams**: Ensure open communication between business, IT, and data management teams to align integration efforts with organizational objectives.

5. Case Study: Overcoming Data Integration Challenges

Scenario: A financial services company needed to integrate customer data from multiple legacy systems into its Pega-based customer service platform. The challenges included inconsistent data formats, latency, and data quality issues.

Solution:

- The team used Pega's Integration Designer and pre-built connectors to streamline connections to the legacy systems.
- Data transforms were employed to standardize the incoming data format.
- To enhance data quality, validation rules were set up to flag and correct incomplete or inaccurate data before processing.
- Caching strategies and batch processing were implemented to manage latency and improve performance.

Outcome: The company achieved seamless data integration, enabling a unified view of customer interactions and improved service response times by 40%.

Conclusion

Handling data integration challenges effectively requires leveraging Pega's suite of tools and adopting strategic best practices. By addressing common issues such as data silos, inconsistent formats, and latency, businesses can create robust and reliable integrations that support comprehensive, efficient processes. Through careful planning and the right implementation approach, Pega ensures that integrated data enhances decision-making and operational excellence.

Section 6:
Security and Compliance

Pega Security Framework Overview

As organizations increasingly rely on digital transformation and process automation, securing these systems and the data they handle becomes critical. Pega provides a comprehensive security framework designed to safeguard data, applications, and infrastructure while complying with industry standards and regulations. This chapter explores Pega's security features, architecture, and best practices to create a secure, compliant environment for automated business processes.

1. Key Principles of Security in Pega

Pega's security framework is based on several core principles, including:

- **Confidentiality**: Ensuring that only authorized users have access to sensitive information.
- **Integrity**: Protecting data from being altered or tampered with by unauthorized sources.
- **Availability**: Maintaining accessibility to authorized users whenever needed, even under adverse conditions.
- **Accountability**: Ensuring that actions are tracked and can be audited to uphold responsibility.

These principles guide Pega's design for access controls, data protection, encryption, and monitoring tools, providing a holistic approach to security.

2. Layers of Pega Security

Pega's security framework spans several layers to protect applications and data at various points of interaction:

- **Network Security**: Pega supports secure communication channels via HTTPS, SSL, and TLS protocols, ensuring data privacy during transmission across networks.
- **Application Security**: Pega's role-based access controls, authentication mechanisms, and encryption policies protect applications and their components.
- **Data Security**: Data security measures ensure that sensitive data is encrypted at rest and in transit. Pega also provides fine-grained access controls for data elements, preventing unauthorized access.
- **Operational Security**: Pega's infrastructure is designed to support secure deployment, configuration management, and auditing, enabling a secure operational environment.

3. Role-Based Access Control (RBAC)

RBAC is a fundamental aspect of Pega's security model, allowing administrators to define and control user permissions based on roles and responsibilities. This model ensures that users have only the necessary access levels required for their job functions, minimizing the risk of unauthorized access to sensitive functions or data.

- **Roles**: Each user is assigned a role that specifies permissions within the Pega environment.
- **Access Groups**: Access groups define a set of privileges and functionalities for users, specifying which applications or components they can access.

- **Privileges and Permissions**: Fine-grained controls allow administrators to set specific privileges within each role, ensuring that users only access the necessary areas within the system.

4. Authentication Mechanisms

Pega provides robust authentication options to validate users' identities before granting access to the platform. These include:

- **Single Sign-On (SSO)**: Pega integrates with SSO providers such as SAML and OAuth, enabling users to authenticate once and access multiple applications securely.
- **Multi-Factor Authentication (MFA)**: MFA adds an additional layer of security by requiring users to provide two or more verification factors, such as a password and a code sent to a mobile device.
- **Federated Authentication**: Pega supports federated authentication, allowing organizations to manage user credentials across multiple domains securely.

5. Data Encryption and Protection

Pega's security framework incorporates encryption to protect sensitive data from unauthorized access and tampering:

- **Encryption at Rest**: Sensitive data is encrypted while stored in databases and file systems, ensuring protection even if the data storage is compromised.
- **Encryption in Transit**: Data transmitted between users, systems, or services is encrypted using SSL/TLS protocols, protecting data integrity and confidentiality.
- **Field-Level Encryption**: Pega supports encryption at the field level, allowing organizations to secure specific data fields based on sensitivity requirements.

6. Auditing and Logging

Pega provides comprehensive auditing and logging features, enabling organizations to track user activity, system changes, and access attempts for security and compliance purposes. Key components include:

- **Audit Trails**: Track actions performed by users within the system, creating a record for accountability and traceability.
- **Security Event Logging**: Capture events such as failed login attempts, unauthorized access, and configuration changes for monitoring and investigation.
- **Compliance Reporting**: Pega's built-in reporting tools can generate compliance reports, assisting organizations in meeting regulatory requirements and demonstrating adherence to security standards.

7. Configuring Security Settings in Pega

Pega's configuration options allow administrators to tailor security settings to organizational requirements:

- **Security Policies**: Define password policies, session timeouts, and MFA requirements to align with internal security standards.
- **User Access Settings**: Set permissions, roles, and access groups based on job functions, ensuring that users only access what is necessary.
- **System and Application Security Settings**: Enable specific encryption, logging, and auditing settings at the application and system levels to meet compliance needs.

8. Best Practices for Pega Security

Implementing a secure Pega environment requires adhering to best practices that align with industry standards and regulatory requirements:

- **Regularly Review Access Controls**: Periodically audit and update access permissions to ensure that users have the correct level of access based on current roles and responsibilities.
- **Apply the Principle of Least Privilege**: Limit user access to the minimum necessary for them to perform their tasks.
- **Monitor Security Events**: Regularly monitor logs and audit trails to detect suspicious activity and respond to security incidents promptly.
- **Update Security Configurations**: Periodically review and update security settings in line with evolving security threats and compliance requirements.
- **Educate Users**: Conduct security awareness training to ensure that users understand security protocols and their role in maintaining a secure environment.

Conclusion

Pega's security framework is designed to provide a robust, layered approach to protect applications, data, and users. By leveraging features such as role-based access control, encryption, multi-factor authentication, and comprehensive auditing, Pega enables organizations to secure their process automation environments effectively. Implementing Pega's security framework in line with best practices ensures that organizations can protect their systems, meet regulatory requirements, and maintain trust with stakeholders.

Implementing User Authentication and Authorization

In the realm of process automation, securing user access is paramount to prevent unauthorized access and maintain data integrity. Pega's framework for authentication and authorization ensures that users accessing the system are properly validated and that their access levels align with their roles and responsibilities. This chapter explores the essential components and best practices for implementing robust user authentication and authorization protocols within Pega.

1. Understanding Authentication and Authorization in Pega

- **Authentication**: The process of verifying the identity of a user attempting to access the system. It ensures that only valid users gain access.
- **Authorization**: The process of determining what authenticated users are permitted to do. Authorization defines specific access rights based on user roles and privileges.

Together, authentication and authorization create a secure environment where access is both restricted and controlled, ensuring users can perform necessary tasks without risking data exposure or compromise.

2. Authentication Options in Pega

Pega supports multiple authentication methods to address various organizational requirements. These methods ensure flexibility in balancing security with user experience.

- **Username and Password**: The most common method where users provide credentials stored securely within Pega. Password policies (e.g., complexity requirements and expiration rules) can be configured for additional security.
- **Single Sign-On (SSO)**: Allows users to access Pega along with other applications without repeatedly entering credentials. Pega supports SSO through protocols like SAML and OAuth, which streamline user experience while enhancing security.
- **Multi-Factor Authentication (MFA)**: Adds an extra layer of security by requiring a second form of identification beyond a password, such as a mobile device code. MFA is especially valuable for high-privilege accounts.
- **LDAP and Active Directory Integration**: Pega can integrate with LDAP or Active Directory, allowing organizations to leverage existing user directories for authentication. This approach centralizes identity management and simplifies user administration.

3. Configuring Authentication in Pega

To configure authentication within Pega, administrators can utilize Pega's built-in tools to define and manage authentication policies:

1. **Create Authentication Profiles**: Authentication profiles in Pega define the specific method and configuration parameters for each authentication type.
2. **Implement MFA**: For critical accounts, enable MFA as an additional security layer. Pega provides options to configure MFA policies tailored to organizational needs.
3. **Enable Session Management Policies**: Session policies help limit unauthorized access by automatically logging users out after a period of inactivity. Configuring session timeouts enhances security for authenticated sessions.
4. **Define Password Policies**: Password policies enforce password strength and rotation requirements. Regularly updating these policies can significantly reduce security risks associated with compromised passwords.

4. Role-Based Access Control (RBAC) for Authorization

Pega's authorization is based on Role-Based Access Control (RBAC), which aligns user permissions with roles and responsibilities:

- **Roles**: A role defines a set of permissions applicable to users assigned to it. For instance, administrators, analysts, and general users each have distinct access privileges tailored to their functions.
- **Access Groups**: Access groups are collections of roles that define the overall access level and privileges for specific user categories. Access groups can include multiple roles, allowing flexible and granular control.
- **Privileges**: Privileges are specific permissions assigned to roles, enabling precise access control within applications. For example, a privilege might allow or restrict access to a particular function or data type.

Pega's RBAC allows organizations to implement the principle of least privilege, ensuring users have only the access they need to perform their tasks.

5. Configuring Authorization in Pega

To set up authorization using RBAC in Pega, follow these steps:

1. **Define Roles and Access Groups**: Begin by identifying roles based on job functions, and assign users to corresponding access groups. Customize these access groups to fit organizational structures and workflows.
2. **Set Privileges and Permissions**: Assign specific privileges to each role, determining the functionalities and data the user group can access. Permissions should be regularly reviewed to align with evolving job roles and responsibilities.
3. **Establish Access Controls on Data and UI Elements**: Ensure data and interface elements are appropriately restricted based on user roles. Sensitive data and critical UI components should be visible only to users with relevant permissions.
4. **Regular Auditing and Review of Access**: Schedule regular reviews of access groups and roles to ensure they remain accurate and up-to-date, especially as users change roles or responsibilities within the organization.

6. Best Practices for Authentication and Authorization in Pega

Implementing best practices ensures that user authentication and authorization in Pega remain both secure and functional:

- **Apply the Principle of Least Privilege**: Only grant access necessary for each user's role, reducing exposure to sensitive data and functionalities.
- **Enforce Strong Password and MFA Policies**: Require complex passwords and, where possible, multi-factor authentication for added protection.
- **Regularly Review and Update Access Controls**: Ensure that access groups and roles accurately reflect current job responsibilities. Update these controls as roles evolve.
- **Log and Monitor Access Events**: Pega's logging features can track access attempts and changes in permissions, enabling proactive monitoring and quick identification of unauthorized activities.
- **Implement Session Timeout Policies**: Enforce session timeouts to automatically log users out after a specified period of inactivity, reducing the risk of unauthorized access in shared or unsecured environments.

7. Auditing and Reporting for Access Control

Pega includes built-in tools for auditing and reporting, making it easier to maintain transparency and accountability:

- **Access Audits**: Track changes to access groups, roles, and privileges over time, creating an audit trail for accountability.
- **User Activity Monitoring**: Monitor user actions, login attempts, and system access to detect suspicious behavior.
- **Compliance Reporting**: Generate reports that demonstrate compliance with organizational and regulatory access control standards.

Regularly generating these reports supports internal reviews and regulatory audits, ensuring that user access practices meet security standards.

Conclusion

Implementing robust authentication and authorization mechanisms is essential for any Pega environment, particularly those handling sensitive data and critical business processes. By leveraging Pega's authentication options, RBAC model, and best practices, organizations can ensure that only authorized users access necessary functions and data. Regular auditing, monitoring, and updating of these controls provide an ongoing defense against unauthorized access, creating a secure environment that aligns with industry standards.

Role-Based Access Control (RBAC) in Pega

Role-Based Access Control (RBAC) is a critical component in securing Pega applications, ensuring users access only the data and functions relevant to their roles. Implementing RBAC effectively enhances data protection, prevents unauthorized access, and aligns with regulatory compliance requirements. This chapter will cover the core concepts of RBAC, how it is structured within Pega, and practical steps to configure and manage access control for users.

1. Introduction to RBAC in Pega

RBAC is a security model that restricts system access based on user roles, rather than individual permissions. In Pega, roles are mapped to access groups, privileges, and permissions, defining what a user can see and do in the application. By assigning users to specific roles, administrators can enforce security policies while maintaining efficient workflows.

The RBAC model in Pega offers:

- **Granular control** over application resources
- **Simplified administration** by grouping permissions into roles
- **Alignment with compliance standards** through controlled access to sensitive data and actions

2. Components of RBAC in Pega

RBAC in Pega is built on three main components:

- **Roles**: These are collections of permissions that represent specific job functions. Roles define the capabilities assigned to users and are linked to access groups.
- **Access Groups**: Access groups in Pega are collections of roles that define the application areas a user can access and the specific rules or privileges applicable to them.
- **Privileges and Permissions**: Privileges are granular permissions within a role, providing further control over what actions users can perform within the application.

3. Setting Up Roles and Access Groups in Pega

1. **Defining Roles Based on Job Functions**: Start by identifying the different job functions and responsibilities within your organization. Typical roles may include Admin, Developer, Business User, or Read-Only User.
2. **Creating Access Groups**: Each access group corresponds to a set of roles and permissions required for a particular job function. For example:
    - **Admin Group**: Full access to manage the application, configuration, and user roles.
    - **Developer Group**: Access to design tools, but restricted from sensitive data functions.
    - **End-User Group**: Access to interface elements needed for daily operations with limited system settings.
3. **Assigning Privileges to Roles**: Privileges define specific actions users can perform within a role. Pega allows fine-tuning access by setting privileges for viewing, editing, deleting, or running certain operations. Each privilege aligns with a particular job function's requirements, such as the ability to modify workflows or manage customer records.

4. Configuring and Managing Access Levels

Pega provides several options for configuring RBAC and managing user access:

- **Portal and UI Access**: Define which interfaces or portals each role can access. For instance, admins might have access to configuration portals, while end users only see customer-facing interfaces.

- **Data Security**: Control which data types users can view or edit. In Pega, you can set data security policies for each role, limiting access to sensitive information based on role requirements.
- **Case and Process Access**: Roles can be configured to control which cases or processes a user can initiate, view, or update.

5. Implementing Security Controls for Each Role

Pega's RBAC model allows administrators to implement targeted security controls for different application areas:

- **Field-Level Security**: Limit visibility of specific data fields within cases or reports based on the user's role.
- **Workflow Permissions**: Control access to workflows, ensuring that only users with the right permissions can modify or approve specific processes.
- **Activity-Level Restrictions**: Set permissions to prevent unauthorized users from executing certain actions within the system, such as running reports or initiating tasks.

These controls provide additional granularity in enforcing security policies within Pega applications.

6. Auditing and Monitoring Role-Based Access

To maintain a secure environment, Pega includes auditing and monitoring features that help track access and ensure compliance:

- **Access Control Audits**: Pega logs access events, making it easy to trace which roles accessed specific data or performed certain actions. This is vital for identifying and addressing unauthorized access attempts.
- **User Activity Reports**: Regularly review activity reports to monitor user behavior and ensure compliance with internal policies.
- **Periodic Access Reviews**: Conduct periodic reviews of roles and privileges to verify that current permissions align with user roles and responsibilities.

7. Best Practices for Role-Based Access Control in Pega

Implementing RBAC effectively requires adherence to best practices to optimize security and maintain compliance. Key best practices include:

- **Principle of Least Privilege**: Only grant users the minimum access needed to perform their job functions. This reduces the risk of unauthorized access and exposure of sensitive data.
- **Regular Role Reviews and Updates**: Business needs evolve, and so should RBAC policies. Regularly review and update roles, access groups, and privileges to reflect changing job functions and compliance requirements.
- **Segregation of Duties (SoD)**: Separate critical duties across multiple roles to prevent conflicts of interest. For instance, the user who approves financial transactions should not be the same user who initiates them.
- **Implement Access Expiry Policies**: Set up temporary access for certain roles, expiring permissions after a specific period or upon project completion.

8. Configuring Custom Roles and Access Groups

Pega allows customization of roles and access groups to meet unique business requirements. Here's how to configure custom roles effectively:

1. **Define Custom Roles Based on Business Needs**: Work with business units to identify unique access needs and create custom roles that meet these requirements.

2. **Assign Specific Privileges and Permissions**: Customize privileges to control what actions users in custom roles can perform.
3. **Test Access Settings**: Before implementing custom roles, conduct testing to confirm that permissions work as intended, preventing unauthorized access while allowing necessary actions.
4. **Document Role and Access Policies**: Ensure that documentation is up-to-date for each custom role and access group, outlining the purpose, permissions, and intended users for future reference.

9. Leveraging Access Groups for Efficient User Management

Access groups are critical in RBAC as they consolidate roles and simplify user management. By grouping related roles, you can:

- **Streamline User Assignments**: Assign users to access groups instead of individual roles, reducing administrative overhead.
- **Facilitate Role Changes**: If a user's role changes, they can simply be moved to a different access group without the need to reconfigure individual permissions.
- **Implement Department-Specific Policies**: For large organizations, access groups can be tailored to specific departments, aligning permissions with team needs and job functions.

Conclusion

Pega's Role-Based Access Control (RBAC) model provides a comprehensive framework for managing user permissions, ensuring that users have appropriate access to perform their duties without exposing sensitive data. By establishing well-defined roles, access groups, and privileges, administrators can build a secure and compliant environment that meets organizational and regulatory standards.

Ensuring Data Privacy and Regulatory Compliance

Data privacy and regulatory compliance are crucial aspects of managing any enterprise application, and Pega's robust framework supports organizations in meeting these standards. By ensuring that sensitive data is protected and that Pega applications comply with relevant regulations, organizations can safeguard user information and maintain trust. This chapter explores Pega's tools and practices for implementing data privacy and adhering to regulatory standards within your BPM workflows.

1. Understanding Data Privacy and Compliance in Pega

Data privacy refers to safeguarding personal and sensitive information within your application, ensuring that unauthorized users cannot access, alter, or misuse this data. Compliance involves meeting industry-specific regulations, such as GDPR, HIPAA, and CCPA, which set standards for how organizations handle personal information.

The need for data privacy and compliance in Pega applications stems from:

- **Growing regulatory requirements**: Regulations impose strict guidelines on managing data and penalize non-compliance.
- **User trust and reputation**: Protecting data enhances trust and reputation, reducing the risk of customer attrition.
- **Internal security policies**: Many organizations have data governance policies requiring compliance to reduce the risk of breaches and unauthorized access.

2. Regulatory Standards and Pega Compliance

Pega's framework supports compliance with various regulations through built-in features that help organizations align with data protection requirements, including:

- **GDPR (General Data Protection Regulation)**: Requires that European Union residents' data be processed securely and gives users the right to access, correct, and erase personal data.
- **HIPAA (Health Insurance Portability and Accountability Act)**: Requires protection for healthcare information, ensuring confidentiality and integrity in how patient data is managed.
- **CCPA (California Consumer Privacy Act)**: Grants California residents rights over their data, including the ability to request information about data collection, sharing, and deletion.

By leveraging Pega's built-in privacy features, your application can address these requirements and ensure compliance with each regulation's specifics.

3. Configuring Data Privacy Controls in Pega

Pega provides various tools and settings to help organizations maintain data privacy and comply with regulations:

1. **Data Encryption**: Pega allows encryption for data at rest and in transit. By encrypting sensitive information such as user profiles, financial data, and healthcare records, you can prevent unauthorized access to critical data.
2. **Data Masking**: This feature hides sensitive data from users who don't require access. For instance, masking can be applied to Social Security numbers, credit card details, and other private information, ensuring that only authorized users view this data.
3. **Access Control Policies**: Implement role-based access controls (RBAC) to restrict data visibility based on job function. Role-based restrictions ensure that only users with a legitimate need can view or modify certain data fields.

4. **Audit Trails**: Pega provides detailed logs of user activity, making it possible to track access to sensitive data. These logs are essential for demonstrating compliance and identifying potential data access violations.

4. Implementing Compliance-Driven Workflows

Pega's framework allows the creation of workflows tailored to compliance requirements. Key elements include:

- **Consent Management**: Ensure workflows respect user consent. For instance, before processing personal data, a user's consent is requested and recorded. Consent management workflows in Pega ensure compliance with GDPR and CCPA regulations.
- **Data Deletion Requests**: Support users' right to data deletion by setting up workflows that respond to and confirm deletion requests. This feature is vital for GDPR compliance and helps users exercise control over their data.
- **Data Access and Rectification**: Pega enables users to access and update their data upon request. This workflow can automatically verify user identity, retrieve the necessary records, and allow users to update or rectify personal information as required by law.

5. Leveraging Pega's Data Privacy and Security Features

1. **Data Obfuscation and Masking Rules**: In Pega, you can configure rules to obfuscate specific data fields based on the user's role or access level. This feature is critical for protecting sensitive data and ensures that only authorized users can view complete data.
2. **Secure Data Transmission**: Pega uses HTTPS and SSL/TLS protocols to secure data transmission between users and the application. These protocols ensure that data remains private and unaltered during transit.
3. **Access Control to Data Objects**: Pega provides flexibility in defining access policies for data objects. With granular access control, administrators can create policies specific to certain fields or objects, adding an additional layer of security to sensitive data.
4. **Audit Logging for Compliance**: Pega's audit logging feature records actions taken within the application. Logs can be reviewed for compliance purposes to ensure data access policies are followed and that unauthorized access attempts are identified promptly.

6. Meeting Key Compliance Requirements with Pega

Pega can support your organization in meeting key compliance requirements, including:

- **Data Minimization**: Collect only the data necessary for specific processes. Data collection and storage fields can be customized in Pega to align with this principle, reducing exposure risk.
- **Right to Access**: Users must be able to view their data upon request. Pega's workflows can be configured to retrieve and display data in compliance with GDPR's "Right of Access" provision.
- **Right to Erasure (Right to be Forgotten)**: Users can request data deletion in compliance with GDPR and CCPA. Pega workflows can process these requests and confirm completion, ensuring legal compliance.
- **Data Integrity and Confidentiality**: Pega's encryption and access controls help maintain data integrity by preventing unauthorized modifications, ensuring data remains accurate and confidential.

7. Compliance Monitoring and Reporting

To maintain compliance, organizations must continuously monitor data access and report on their adherence to privacy standards. Pega provides:

- **Compliance Dashboards**: Pega's dashboards give a visual overview of compliance metrics, such as data access, audit logs, and consent records.
- **Automated Alerts**: Configure alerts to notify administrators of suspicious activity or policy violations, allowing for immediate corrective action.
- **Audit Reports**: Generate reports detailing data access, usage, and any policy breaches. These reports can be used as evidence during compliance audits and provide insight into privacy practices.

8. Best Practices for Data Privacy and Compliance in Pega

Adhering to best practices for data privacy in Pega strengthens your organization's compliance posture and reduces the risk of data breaches:

- **Data Minimization**: Collect only the data necessary for your processes to limit exposure.
- **Regular Data Audits**: Perform periodic reviews of data policies, access logs, and security configurations to ensure ongoing compliance.
- **User Training**: Educate users on data privacy policies and practices to reinforce a culture of compliance within your organization.
- **Use Pega's Compliance Tools**: Leverage the tools and settings available in Pega, such as encryption, masking, and audit logs, to maintain a secure environment.

9. Preparing for Future Privacy Regulations

As new privacy regulations emerge, your organization needs to be agile and ready to adapt. Pega's flexible framework enables quick adjustments to meet new compliance standards. Monitor industry trends, stay informed about regulatory changes, and review Pega's compliance capabilities regularly to stay ahead of emerging requirements.

Conclusion

Ensuring data privacy and regulatory compliance in Pega requires a comprehensive approach that combines technology, policies, and best practices. By implementing Pega's privacy features, creating compliance-focused workflows, and adhering to industry standards, organizations can build secure and compliant applications. These efforts not only safeguard sensitive information but also enhance customer trust and support regulatory adherence, strengthening the overall integrity and reputation of the organization.

Monitoring Security Events and Threats

Monitoring security events and identifying potential threats are essential components of maintaining a secure Pega environment. Given the sensitive nature of data processed in business operations, detecting, analyzing, and responding to security incidents is critical for safeguarding organizational assets. In this chapter, we explore best practices and tools available within Pega to establish a robust security monitoring framework, ensuring continuous protection against evolving cyber threats.

1. Importance of Security Event Monitoring in Pega

Security monitoring provides insights into the security posture of Pega applications by identifying unusual or unauthorized activities. The primary objectives of monitoring security events and threats in Pega include:

- **Identifying Suspicious Behavior**: Detecting unauthorized access, unusual data access patterns, or abnormal user behavior.
- **Ensuring Compliance**: Monitoring activities to comply with regulations and standards that require logging and reviewing of security-related events.
- **Preventing Data Breaches**: Early detection of security threats can help prevent data breaches and minimize impact.
- **Supporting Incident Response**: Monitoring provides necessary data for investigation, allowing teams to respond swiftly to security incidents.

2. Key Components of Security Monitoring in Pega

Pega offers several features and integration capabilities that facilitate effective security monitoring:

- **Audit Logs**: These logs capture critical user and system activities, providing a detailed view of actions taken within the system.
- **Alerting Mechanisms**: Alerts can be configured for high-risk events, such as failed login attempts, unauthorized access attempts, and unusual data retrieval patterns.
- **Role-Based Access Monitoring**: Ensuring that only authorized users access certain resources and monitoring any role changes that could indicate a threat.
- **Data Encryption Monitoring**: Verifying that data encryption policies are enforced, ensuring data is protected at all times.

3. Setting Up and Configuring Pega Audit Logs

Audit logs in Pega are instrumental in tracking and recording security-related events. To maximize their effectiveness:

1. **Enable Comprehensive Logging**: Activate logging for critical actions such as logins, logouts, password changes, data access, and modifications to user roles.
2. **Configure Log Retention Policies**: Retain logs for a suitable period to support long-term security analysis and compliance requirements.
3. **Audit Sensitive Data Access**: Focus on logging events that involve access to sensitive data, such as financial information, personal data, or confidential business details.

Audit logs serve as a vital tool in both proactive monitoring and post-incident investigation, helping administrators pinpoint the root causes of potential security incidents.

4. Real-Time Alerting and Notification Mechanisms

Real-time alerts are essential for immediate detection of security incidents. To set up effective alerting within Pega:

1. **Identify Key Security Events**: Define events that should trigger alerts, such as multiple failed login attempts, access by unauthorized users, and data access violations.
2. **Configure Thresholds and Sensitivity Levels**: Set thresholds to avoid alert fatigue. For example, alerts may trigger after a specific number of failed login attempts within a certain timeframe.
3. **Set Up Notifications**: Ensure alerts are routed to the appropriate personnel, such as security teams or administrators, for timely response.

Automated alerts allow for swift identification of potential threats, facilitating rapid response to mitigate risks before they escalate.

5. Integrating Pega with Security Information and Event Management (SIEM) Systems

Integrating Pega with an external SIEM system enhances security monitoring capabilities by aggregating, analyzing, and visualizing security events across the organization. Steps to consider:

1. **Select an SIEM Platform**: Choose a platform that integrates smoothly with Pega and supports real-time analysis of logs.
2. **Configure Data Feeds**: Set up data feeds to transfer Pega audit logs, alerts, and other relevant events to the SIEM system.
3. **Define Correlation Rules**: Create rules within the SIEM to correlate Pega events with other security data sources, identifying patterns that indicate potential threats.

By integrating Pega with SIEM, organizations gain a centralized view of security events, allowing for a comprehensive analysis of threats across all IT systems.

6. Monitoring User Activity and Access Patterns

Monitoring user activity, particularly around sensitive data access, is a key part of threat detection. Strategies for user activity monitoring include:

- **Track High-Privilege Users**: Closely monitor actions taken by users with elevated privileges, as these accounts can pose higher security risks.
- **Identify Unusual Access Patterns**: Look for signs of unusual behavior, such as data access at odd times or from atypical locations.
- **Monitor Role Changes**: Changes in user roles should be logged and reviewed to ensure they align with organizational policy and that no unauthorized access is granted.

User activity monitoring allows for early detection of insider threats and other forms of unauthorized access.

7. Leveraging Pega's Access Control Policies for Security Monitoring

Pega's access control policies can help prevent and detect unauthorized access by enforcing strict permissions. Steps to enhance security through access control include:

1. **Regular Review of Roles and Permissions**: Conduct periodic audits to ensure users have only the access necessary for their roles.
2. **Enforce Role-Based Access Control (RBAC)**: Ensure that access to sensitive data is restricted to authorized roles and that user access complies with organizational policies.
3. **Monitor Access Control Violations**: Set up alerts for access attempts that violate policy, such as unauthorized users attempting to access restricted areas.

Pega's access control policies help minimize security risks by limiting data exposure and restricting system access to authorized users only.

8. Utilizing Data Encryption and Protection Monitoring

Encryption is a critical component of data security, and Pega supports both encryption at rest and in transit. To ensure encryption policies are effective:

1. **Verify Encryption Configurations**: Ensure that data encryption is enabled and configured correctly within Pega's settings.
2. **Monitor for Encryption Failures**: Set up alerts for any instances where encryption protocols fail or are bypassed.
3. **Protect Encryption Keys**: Regularly review encryption key management practices to prevent unauthorized access to decryption keys.

Monitoring encryption compliance is vital to safeguarding sensitive data and ensuring that data privacy standards are upheld.

9. Incident Response and Security Reporting in Pega

Effective incident response involves having a well-defined process for investigating and addressing security incidents. Key steps include:

1. **Define Incident Response Procedures**: Establish a response plan for handling security alerts, including roles, responsibilities, and steps to contain and mitigate threats.
2. **Generate Security Reports**: Pega's reporting capabilities can be leveraged to create security-specific reports detailing recent incidents, user activity, and access violations.
3. **Conduct Post-Incident Analysis**: After an incident, analyze root causes and implement additional controls if necessary to prevent recurrence.

Security reports and post-incident analysis are crucial for continuous improvement of your security posture and for meeting compliance requirements.

10. Best Practices for Security Event Monitoring

To maximize the effectiveness of your security monitoring in Pega, consider the following best practices:

- **Automate Alerts for Critical Events**: Automate alerting for high-risk actions such as failed logins, unauthorized access attempts, and changes to critical configurations.
- **Regularly Audit Security Logs**: Conduct routine audits of security logs and access records to identify potential gaps and ensure compliance.
- **Educate Users on Security Policies**: Ensure that all users understand the importance of security policies and are trained to recognize potential threats.
- **Stay Updated on Threat Intelligence**: Regularly update your threat intelligence sources and adapt monitoring rules to address new and emerging threats.

Conclusion

Monitoring security events and threats in Pega is essential for protecting sensitive data, meeting compliance requirements, and proactively identifying potential risks. By leveraging Pega's security monitoring tools, integrating with SIEM systems, and establishing robust access controls, organizations can build a resilient security framework. Effective security event monitoring not only safeguards the application environment but also fosters trust among users and clients, supporting a secure and compliant operational framework.

Section 7:
Performance Optimization and Troubleshooting

Best Practices for Optimizing Application Performance

In the world of process automation, optimal application performance is essential for ensuring that business processes run smoothly and meet organizational goals. This chapter explores best practices and strategies to enhance the performance of Pega applications, focusing on system responsiveness, resource management, and efficient application design.

1. Understanding Performance Optimization in Pega

Performance optimization in Pega involves improving the system's response times, managing resources effectively, and minimizing potential bottlenecks. Achieving optimal performance requires a balanced approach, addressing both the technical and functional aspects of the application.

Objectives of performance optimization include:

- **Minimizing Response Times**: Ensuring fast responses to user actions and system requests.
- **Reducing System Resource Consumption**: Efficiently using system resources such as CPU, memory, and network bandwidth.
- **Enhancing User Experience**: Improving the overall usability and responsiveness of the application.

2. Application Design Best Practices

Effective design is the foundation of any high-performing Pega application. Here are some best practices for application design that contribute to performance optimization:

1. **Leverage Directly-Referenced Data**: Use data pages and reference data directly rather than relying on complex data joins. This minimizes database calls and reduces data retrieval time.
2. **Optimize Case and Process Design**: Streamline case and process designs by minimizing unnecessary steps or stages. Each additional component can add to processing time.
3. **Use Declarative Processing Sparingly**: Declarative rules like Declare Expressions and Declare OnChange are powerful but can lead to performance issues if overused. Reserve them for critical calculations or actions.
4. **Limit UI Components**: Excessive use of UI components, such as sections and layouts, can slow down rendering. Simplify user interfaces and avoid unnecessary elements where possible.

3. Database Optimization Techniques

The database is often a performance bottleneck, particularly when dealing with large datasets. Effective database optimization can greatly enhance Pega application performance:

1. **Optimize Database Queries**: Review and refine database queries to retrieve only the required data. Avoid using "SELECT *" and focus on selecting specific columns.

2. **Use Indexes Wisely**: Adding indexes to frequently queried columns can speed up retrieval times. However, too many indexes can increase database maintenance overhead, so apply indexes selectively.
3. **Implement Data Archiving**: Archive historical data periodically to reduce the database size, ensuring that current operations access only relevant data.
4. **Monitor Database Health**: Regularly check database health to ensure it meets performance requirements. Monitor parameters like cache size, read/write speeds, and transaction throughput.

4. Efficient Rule Management and Reuse

Effective rule management helps prevent redundancy and improves application performance. Best practices for rule management include:

1. **Reuse Rules Across Applications**: Reuse existing rules rather than creating new ones with similar functionality. Reusable rules reduce development time and maintenance effort.
2. **Optimize Rule Resolution**: Ensure that rules are appropriately scoped. For example, avoid using "any" scope if a narrower scope would suffice, as this reduces the system's rule resolution efforts.
3. **Version Control and Deprecation**: Maintain version control and deprecate outdated rules to prevent the system from evaluating unnecessary rule versions during execution.

5. Caching Strategies

Caching is an effective way to improve performance by storing frequently accessed data. Pega offers multiple caching options that can reduce processing load and enhance response times:

1. **Use Data Page Caching**: Configure data pages with caching enabled for frequently accessed, relatively static data. This minimizes repeated database calls for the same data.
2. **Leverage UI Caching**: Pega allows UI sections and elements to be cached, reducing the time required to render pages.
3. **Configure Declarative Rule Caching**: Declarative rules like Declare Expressions can be cached to avoid recalculating values unnecessarily.

When using caching, it's essential to establish a cache refresh policy to ensure data consistency, especially for data that changes frequently.

6. Memory and Resource Management

Efficient memory management is critical in a high-performance application. Consider the following best practices:

1. **Monitor JVM Performance**: Regularly monitor Java Virtual Machine (JVM) usage, including heap and non-heap memory. Ensure that memory allocation aligns with expected system loads.
2. **Optimize Data Pages**: Ensure data pages do not load excessive data into memory. Use parameterized data pages to retrieve only the necessary data for a particular use case.
3. **Garbage Collection**: Configure JVM garbage collection settings based on Pega and system requirements. Proper garbage collection settings can prevent memory leaks and improve application performance.

7. Asynchronous Processing and Queue Management

Pega supports asynchronous processing, allowing tasks to execute in parallel and freeing up resources for other operations. Best practices include:

1. **Use Background Processing for Long Tasks**: Shift long-running or resource-intensive tasks to background processing using agents, queues, and job schedulers.

2. **Monitor Queue Status**: Regularly monitor queue status and ensure that job queues do not become backlogged, which could indicate processing bottlenecks.
3. **Avoid Overusing Asynchronous Calls**: Excessive asynchronous processing can lead to resource contention, especially if too many tasks run simultaneously.

8. Leveraging Performance Analysis Tools in Pega

Pega provides built-in tools for analyzing and optimizing application performance. Key tools include:

1. **Performance Analyzer (PAL)**: PAL provides metrics on application performance, including rule processing times and system resource usage.
2. **Database Trace**: Database Trace captures database interactions, making it easier to identify inefficient queries and potential bottlenecks.
3. **Pega Predictive Diagnostic Cloud (PDC)**: PDC continuously monitors application health and provides alerts on performance issues. It can identify performance trends and offer insights for optimization.

Regularly using these tools can help maintain and improve application performance over time.

9. Monitoring Application Health and Performance

Continuous monitoring is essential for detecting and addressing performance issues promptly. Implement a monitoring strategy that includes:

1. **Real-Time Monitoring**: Use Pega's real-time monitoring capabilities to track key metrics, such as CPU utilization, memory usage, and response times.
2. **Historical Analysis**: Review historical performance data to identify trends and recurring issues. This can inform long-term optimization strategies.
3. **Set Performance Benchmarks**: Define acceptable performance benchmarks for response times, transaction speeds, and resource utilization. Use these benchmarks to measure application performance and make adjustments as needed.

10. Regular Load Testing and Capacity Planning

Load testing and capacity planning are essential to ensuring that applications perform well under expected workloads:

1. **Conduct Load Testing**: Simulate real-world usage scenarios to test application performance under load. Identify areas that require optimization based on the test results.
2. **Plan for Capacity Growth**: As applications grow, so do resource demands. Regularly review and adjust capacity to ensure the system can handle increased usage.
3. **Optimize Resource Allocation**: Allocate system resources, such as CPU and memory, based on the application's needs and workload demands.

11. Addressing Performance Issues in Production

Even with proactive optimization, issues may arise in production. Steps to address production performance issues include:

1. **Isolate and Identify**: Use Pega's diagnostic tools to identify specific rules, processes, or database interactions causing slowdowns.
2. **Prioritize Issues Based on Impact**: Address high-impact issues first to restore optimal performance as quickly as possible.
3. **Implement Temporary Fixes if Necessary**: In some cases, temporary fixes, like increasing memory or reconfiguring queues, may alleviate issues until a permanent solution is implemented.

Conclusion

Optimizing Pega application performance is a continuous process that requires a combination of best practices in design, resource management, caching, and monitoring. By implementing these best practices, you can ensure that your Pega application remains responsive, efficient, and capable of meeting user demands even as the application scales. With ongoing monitoring, performance analysis, and capacity planning, organizations can maintain a high level of performance, enhancing the user experience and supporting streamlined business operations.

Performance Tuning Tools in Pega

Optimizing the performance of Pega applications requires a thorough understanding of the platform's performance tuning tools. These tools help identify bottlenecks, monitor system health, and maintain optimal application performance. In this chapter, we'll explore key tools provided by Pega for performance tuning and how to effectively use them.

1. Performance Analyzer (PAL)

The Performance Analyzer, or PAL, is one of the most valuable tools in Pega for monitoring application performance. It collects statistics on various operations, helping to analyze resource consumption and identify potential bottlenecks.

Key Features of PAL:

- **Metrics Tracking**: PAL tracks a variety of performance metrics, such as rule execution times, database interactions, and resource utilization.
- **Time Intervals**: Users can measure performance over specific intervals, allowing for a focused analysis of certain transactions or processes.
- **Session Analysis**: PAL is useful for understanding individual user sessions and pinpointing where delays or inefficiencies occur.

Using PAL for Optimization:

- **Analyze Long Transactions**: Use PAL to find transactions that take longer than expected and determine if they are causing system-wide delays.
- **Track Resource Usage Trends**: PAL helps identify trends in resource usage that might lead to bottlenecks. For example, if database call times gradually increase, it may signal a need for optimization.

2. Database Trace

Database Trace is a tool specifically designed for monitoring database interactions. It captures all database calls made by Pega applications, helping identify inefficient queries and database-related performance issues.

Key Features of Database Trace:

- **SQL Query Logging**: Database Trace logs SQL queries executed by the application, allowing for a detailed examination of database interactions.
- **Elapsed Time Tracking**: It records the time taken for each query, helping identify slow or expensive database operations.
- **Filtering Capabilities**: Users can filter the types of queries to focus on specific interactions, such as SELECT, INSERT, or UPDATE statements.

Using Database Trace for Optimization:

- **Identify Expensive Queries**: Look for queries that consume significant resources and consider optimizing them with indexes or query refinement.
- **Optimize Query Execution Plans**: Database Trace provides insights into query execution plans, allowing you to make adjustments that improve efficiency, such as adding indexes or optimizing joins.

3. Log Analyzer (PLA)

The Pega Log Analyzer (PLA) is an offline tool that processes logs generated by the Pega platform, making it easier to analyze system behavior and troubleshoot issues. PLA provides a high-level overview of system performance based on log data.

Key Features of PLA:

- **Error Analysis**: PLA categorizes errors by type, source, and frequency, helping identify the root causes of recurring issues.
- **Performance Patterns**: It aggregates performance patterns over time, offering insights into periods of high usage or stress.
- **Historical Data**: PLA is valuable for identifying trends in historical data, making it easier to address long-term performance issues.

Using PLA for Optimization:

- **Detect Patterns in Error Logs**: PLA highlights common errors or warnings, which can indicate underlying performance issues.
- **Monitor Peak Times**: By analyzing usage patterns, you can identify peak times and ensure resources are allocated appropriately to handle high traffic.

4. Autonomic Event Services (AES)

Autonomic Event Services (AES) is a monitoring and alerting tool designed to continuously monitor the health and performance of Pega applications. AES detects issues in real time and can provide alerts, making it a valuable tool for proactive performance management.

Key Features of AES:

- **Real-Time Monitoring**: AES monitors the system in real time, providing alerts for potential issues such as CPU spikes, memory usage, or queue delays.
- **Threshold-Based Alerts**: AES allows administrators to set custom thresholds for metrics, enabling alerts when these thresholds are exceeded.
- **Performance Insights**: The tool provides a dashboard that gives a high-level view of application performance, making it easy to spot and resolve issues.

Using AES for Optimization:

- **Configure Alerts for Key Metrics**: Set up alerts for essential performance metrics, such as memory usage or CPU utilization, to ensure timely responses to potential problems.
- **Monitor Queues and Agents**: AES can track the performance of queues and agents, making it easier to identify backlogs or delays in background processing.

5. Tracer Tool

The Tracer tool in Pega captures detailed logs of rule execution, making it an essential tool for troubleshooting and fine-tuning application performance at the rule level.

Key Features of the Tracer Tool:

- **Step-by-Step Logging**: Tracer records each rule execution step, providing granular insights into rule processing and logic flow.
- **Conditional Filters**: Users can set filters to focus on specific rules, classes, or data transforms, making the output more manageable.
- **Error and Alert Tracking**: The Tracer highlights errors, warnings, and performance alerts, making it easy to identify problematic rules.

Using the Tracer Tool for Optimization:

- **Identify Inefficient Rules**: By tracing rule executions, users can identify rules that consume excessive time or resources.
- **Optimize Conditional Logic**: Tracer helps you fine-tune rule logic by showing the decision-making paths taken during processing, allowing for streamlined and optimized conditions.

6. Pega Predictive Diagnostic Cloud (PDC)

The Pega Predictive Diagnostic Cloud (PDC) is a cloud-based solution for monitoring and diagnosing Pega applications. It provides proactive insights and recommendations, helping administrators prevent issues before they impact performance.

Key Features of PDC:

- **Proactive Alerts and Recommendations**: PDC provides actionable insights based on predictive analytics, allowing teams to address issues before they escalate.
- **Real-Time and Historical Analysis**: PDC combines real-time monitoring with historical trend analysis, offering a complete view of application health.
- **User-Friendly Dashboard**: PDC's dashboard provides an overview of key performance metrics, enabling quick identification of performance bottlenecks.

Using PDC for Optimization:

- **Leverage Automated Recommendations**: PDC offers recommendations for addressing detected issues, making it easier to maintain optimal performance.
- **Use Predictive Insights**: PDC's predictive capabilities allow administrators to forecast potential issues based on usage patterns, enabling preemptive action.

7. Clipboard Tool

The Clipboard tool allows developers to view and modify the state of data objects in Pega. It provides insights into data values, structures, and interactions, making it useful for optimizing data handling.

Key Features of the Clipboard Tool:

- **Real-Time Data Access**: View data structures and values in real time, making it easy to analyze the state of data during rule execution.
- **Modify Data for Testing**: Test different scenarios by modifying data on the clipboard, enabling efficient troubleshooting and optimization.
- **Trace Data Flows**: The Clipboard tool helps track how data is manipulated and transferred within processes, identifying areas where data handling can be streamlined.

Using the Clipboard Tool for Optimization:

- **Analyze Data Load Patterns**: Use the Clipboard tool to identify large or unnecessary data loads, which can affect performance.
- **Optimize Data Pages**: Ensure data pages are configured efficiently, minimizing the data stored in memory and reducing processing overhead.

8. Application Profiler

The Application Profiler in Pega helps analyze and document the complexity of an application, providing insights into areas that may impact performance. It evaluates rule counts, dependencies, and overall application size.

Key Features of the Application Profiler:

- **Complexity Analysis**: Provides an overview of rule counts, dependencies, and application layers.

- **Resource Allocation Suggestions**: Offers insights into potential resource allocation adjustments based on application complexity.
- **Documentation Tool**: The profiler generates a summary of application structure, helping development teams focus on areas that could impact performance.

Using the Application Profiler for Optimization:

- **Identify Complex Components**: Focus on components with high complexity, as these are more likely to impact performance.
- **Plan for Resource Scaling**: Use profiler data to anticipate scaling needs, ensuring the application has adequate resources for expected usage.

Conclusion

Pega's performance tuning tools provide comprehensive support for identifying and addressing performance issues in applications. By using these tools regularly, developers and administrators can maintain optimal application performance, ensuring a smooth and responsive user experience. From identifying slow-running database queries with Database Trace to monitoring real-time health with PDC, Pega offers a range of solutions to meet performance optimization needs. Regular monitoring, proactive adjustments, and a solid understanding of these tools are essential to keeping applications running efficiently and meeting business demands.

Diagnosing Common Issues in Pega Applications

In any complex application environment, diagnosing and resolving issues quickly and efficiently is crucial to maintaining seamless performance. Pega applications, while robust, can encounter a range of issues that impact functionality, performance, and user experience. This chapter provides a structured approach to diagnosing common issues in Pega applications, including troubleshooting methods and best practices for identifying root causes.

1. Understanding the Types of Common Issues

Pega applications can encounter various types of issues, typically categorized as follows:

- **Performance Issues**: Slow response times, high CPU or memory consumption, and inefficient processing.
- **User Interface (UI) Issues**: Display problems, layout inconsistencies, and user experience flaws.
- **Data-Related Issues**: Data mismatch, data loss, or data integrity problems.
- **Rule Execution Issues**: Failures in rule execution, incorrect logic processing, and rule resolution conflicts.
- **Integration Issues**: Problems with external system communication, API failures, or data transfer delays.
- **Authentication and Authorization Issues**: Access control problems, permission errors, or security breaches.

Each category has unique diagnostics tools and methods to address underlying problems effectively.

2. Using Tracer for Root Cause Analysis

The **Tracer** tool in Pega is a powerful utility for capturing real-time execution logs, allowing developers to monitor and analyze rule execution at a granular level.

Using Tracer Effectively:

- **Focus on Specific Rules**: Configure Tracer to capture only relevant rules to avoid overwhelming output.
- **Filter by Rule Type or Event**: Apply filters to focus on certain types of events (e.g., activities, data transforms, and service interactions).
- **Identify Failures and Errors**: Look for execution failures, timeouts, or unexpected rule behaviors to pinpoint issues.
- **Capture External Data**: Tracer can also capture information from external sources, such as database calls or web service interactions, which is essential when diagnosing integration issues.

Best Practices:

- **Use in Lower Environments**: To avoid performance degradation, use Tracer in development or testing environments rather than in production.
- **Limit Trace Scope**: Run traces on specific transactions or interactions to minimize the amount of data and focus on potential problem areas.

3. Log Analysis with Pega Log Analyzer (PLA)

The **Pega Log Analyzer (PLA)** helps identify trends and common issues based on logs collected over time. PLA processes logs to reveal insights into performance, errors, and system health.

Common Logs to Analyze:

- **Alert Logs**: Highlight performance-related alerts, such as high response times or excessive resource utilization.
- **Error Logs**: Identify errors that occurred during rule execution, data handling, or API communication.
- **System Logs**: Provide insights into system events, background processing, and system-level interactions.

Interpreting Log Data:

- **Look for Patterns**: Consistent errors or alerts can indicate systemic issues or recurring bottlenecks.
- **Identify High-Frequency Errors**: Errors that occur frequently can significantly impact performance and user experience, warranting immediate attention.
- **Monitor Resource Usage**: Excessive CPU, memory, or I/O consumption identified in logs may indicate inefficient processing or memory leaks.

4. Diagnosing Database-Related Issues with Database Trace

Database issues are often a source of performance bottlenecks in Pega applications. **Database Trace** captures SQL queries executed by Pega, making it easier to analyze query performance and identify problematic interactions.

Steps for Using Database Trace:

1. **Enable Database Trace**: Activate tracing to capture SQL activity during specific transactions.
2. **Identify Slow Queries**: Look for queries with high execution times, indicating that optimization may be needed.
3. **Check Query Plans**: Analyze query execution plans to understand how the database processes queries and identify areas for optimization.
4. **Review Index Usage**: Ensure that queries are making use of indexes effectively; missing or inefficient indexes can lead to slow performance.

5. Utilizing Autonomic Event Services (AES) for Real-Time Monitoring

Pega's **Autonomic Event Services (AES)** monitors application performance in real-time, providing alerts and actionable insights.

Using AES for Diagnostics:

- **Set Threshold Alerts**: Configure alerts for essential metrics like CPU usage, memory consumption, and queue processing times.
- **Monitor Queue Health**: AES tracks queue processing, helping to diagnose issues with background jobs and agents.
- **Analyze System Health Trends**: Use AES insights to understand performance trends over time, which can reveal patterns and prevent future issues.

Common AES Alerts:

- **CPU or Memory Alerts**: High CPU or memory usage alerts indicate potential resource bottlenecks that could impact performance.
- **Queue Delays**: Alerts related to delayed queue processing can signal issues in batch processing or background tasks.
- **Database Connection Issues**: Alerts for database connectivity can indicate potential network or resource issues in the database infrastructure.

6. Diagnosing UI and User Experience Issues

User interface issues are often related to display problems, slow loading times, or inconsistent data presentation. Diagnosing UI issues requires a combination of tools and best practices.

Tools for Diagnosing UI Issues:

- **Clipboard Tool**: Use the Clipboard tool to verify data values and identify potential discrepancies in data presentation.
- **Browser Developer Tools**: Check for JavaScript errors, network requests, and console logs using browser developer tools.
- **Tracer for UI-Related Rules**: Run Tracer on UI-related rules like sections and data transforms to diagnose issues in rule execution.

Best Practices:

- **Test in Multiple Browsers**: Ensure compatibility and performance across different web browsers.
- **Optimize Data Pages**: Data pages that retrieve large data sets can slow down UI rendering. Optimize data pages to load only necessary information.

7. Handling Authentication and Authorization Issues

Authentication and authorization issues can prevent users from accessing necessary functionality or lead to security vulnerabilities.

Diagnosing Authentication Issues:

- **Check Authentication Logs**: Review authentication logs for login failures, incorrect passwords, or session timeout errors.
- **Test Authentication Policies**: Ensure authentication policies align with security requirements, and troubleshoot any policy misconfigurations.

Diagnosing Authorization Issues:

- **Validate Access Roles**: Confirm that users have the correct access roles and privileges to perform their tasks.
- **Review Security Policies**: Use Pega's role-based access control to fine-tune access permissions, ensuring that users have appropriate access without excessive privileges.

8. Common Integration Issues and Solutions

Integration issues in Pega can disrupt communication with external systems, affecting data flow and functionality. Diagnosing these issues often involves monitoring data transfers, API calls, and service responses.

Troubleshooting Integration Issues:

- **Use Tracer for Service Calls**: Capture and analyze service calls to diagnose data transfer issues or API errors.
- **Check Response Times**: High response times from external systems can indicate network delays or performance issues on the external system.
- **Analyze Connectivity Logs**: Review logs for errors related to service connections, such as authentication failures, timeouts, or data parsing issues.

Common Solutions:

- **Adjust Timeout Settings**: Increase timeout values for services interacting with slower systems to avoid unnecessary timeouts.

- **Implement Error Handling Logic**: Add error-handling logic in integrations to gracefully handle failed connections or data transfer issues.

9. Best Practices for Diagnosing and Resolving Issues

To effectively diagnose and resolve issues in Pega applications, it's essential to adopt a proactive approach. Here are some best practices to ensure efficient diagnostics and troubleshooting:

- **Regular Monitoring**: Use tools like AES and PDC for continuous monitoring, which enables early detection of issues before they impact users.
- **Document Issue Resolution**: Maintain a record of diagnosed issues and their resolutions to build a knowledge base that aids in future troubleshooting.
- **Collaborate Across Teams**: Engage cross-functional teams, including developers, database administrators, and network specialists, when diagnosing complex issues.
- **Optimize Configuration Settings**: Periodically review and adjust system configuration settings, such as cache sizes, query timeouts, and agent intervals, to ensure optimal performance.
- **Stay Updated on Best Practices**: Regularly update diagnostic processes and tools to align with Pega's latest best practices and platform updates.

Conclusion

Diagnosing common issues in Pega applications requires familiarity with the platform's diagnostics tools and a methodical approach to identifying and resolving problems. By utilizing tools like Tracer, Database Trace, and AES, and following best practices in issue resolution, Pega administrators and developers can maintain a high-performing, reliable application environment. Proactive monitoring, combined with a structured troubleshooting methodology, helps ensure that any issues are addressed efficiently, minimizing disruption to business operations and maintaining an optimal user experience.

Managing System Performance Metrics

Effective performance management is crucial in Pega applications to ensure seamless operation, optimal resource utilization, and consistent end-user experience. Monitoring and managing system performance metrics allow administrators to identify potential issues, optimize performance, and take proactive measures to prevent disruptions. In this chapter, we will explore essential performance metrics, tools to monitor them, and best practices to maintain an efficient Pega application environment.

1. Key System Performance Metrics in Pega

Understanding and tracking core performance metrics provides insights into how the application and infrastructure operate. The following are some of the most important metrics to monitor:

- **CPU Utilization**: Indicates the percentage of CPU resources in use, essential for detecting and resolving processing bottlenecks.
- **Memory Usage**: Reflects memory consumption and helps identify potential memory leaks or inefficient resource use.
- **Database Query Time**: Measures the response time of database queries, critical for diagnosing database-related performance issues.
- **Requestor Pools and Active Sessions**: Monitors active user sessions and concurrent requests, ensuring balanced load distribution.
- **Queue Processing Times**: Reflects the efficiency of background processing tasks, such as agent and queue-based jobs.
- **Application Response Time**: Tracks the end-to-end response time of user requests, which directly impacts user experience.
- **Error Rates**: Measures the frequency of errors within the application, indicating potential issues in processing, integrations, or configuration.

By focusing on these core metrics, administrators can maintain a high-performing application environment and prevent potential issues.

2. Tools for Monitoring Performance Metrics in Pega

Pega provides several tools and platforms for monitoring performance metrics and gaining insights into system health:

- **Pega Autonomic Event Services (AES)**: Pega AES is a real-time monitoring tool that provides alerts and insights on system performance, allowing administrators to take timely action.
- **Pega Predictive Diagnostic Cloud (PDC)**: PDC is a cloud-based tool that collects data on performance, errors, and potential issues, delivering proactive recommendations to maintain system health.
- **Performance Analyzer (PAL)**: PAL captures and analyzes individual requestor performance, helping diagnose performance problems at the transaction level.
- **System Management Application (SMA)**: SMA offers a comprehensive view of system metrics, queue processing, cache settings, and requestor sessions, providing administrators with detailed insights.
- **Database Trace**: Useful for tracking database interactions, identifying slow queries, and ensuring efficient data processing.

By leveraging these tools, administrators can monitor, diagnose, and optimize performance across various levels of the Pega environment.

3. Setting Up Effective Monitoring Dashboards

Dashboards provide a consolidated view of performance metrics, enabling quick analysis and identification of trends or abnormalities. Pega's dashboard capabilities allow administrators to customize views and prioritize metrics essential to their business requirements.

Configuring Dashboards:

- **Identify Key Metrics**: Select metrics that are most impactful for system performance, such as CPU, memory, queue processing, and response times.
- **Use Alerts for Critical Metrics**: Set alerts for thresholds on key metrics to receive immediate notifications for potential performance issues.
- **Leverage Real-Time and Historical Data**: Display both real-time metrics for immediate insights and historical data for trend analysis.

Dashboards provide an at-a-glance view of the system's health, helping administrators detect and resolve issues before they impact users.

4. Interpreting and Analyzing Key Metrics

Effectively managing performance metrics involves understanding what the numbers mean and how they impact the system's overall health. Below are strategies for interpreting core metrics:

- **CPU and Memory Usage**: High CPU usage may indicate processing bottlenecks, requiring load balancing or optimization of background processes. High memory usage, especially if persistent, could signal memory leaks.
- **Database Query Times**: Persistent high query times may indicate the need for database indexing, query optimization, or even hardware scaling.
- **Queue Processing and Agent Performance**: If queue processing times are high, investigate agent schedules, and consider optimizing agent configurations.
- **Error Rates**: A high error rate may indicate rule conflicts, misconfigurations, or integration issues, requiring immediate investigation to maintain system stability.

By understanding these metrics in context, administrators can apply targeted solutions to specific performance issues.

5. Best Practices for Optimizing Performance Metrics

Optimizing performance requires more than just tracking metrics; it involves proactive strategies to enhance system performance continually. Here are some best practices for managing Pega performance metrics:

- **Optimize Cache Settings**: Ensure cache settings are configured based on usage patterns to reduce redundant processing and enhance response times.
- **Regularly Review Agent Schedules**: Optimize agent schedules to reduce the load during peak times, improving overall system performance.
- **Conduct Routine Database Optimization**: Regularly analyze and optimize database queries, add necessary indexes, and consider partitioning large tables for better query performance.
- **Adjust Queue and Requestor Settings**: Configure queue and requestor settings to balance load and prevent over-utilization of system resources.
- **Implement Error Handling and Monitoring**: Set up robust error-handling processes to reduce error rates and improve system reliability.

Following these best practices ensures that the Pega system operates efficiently and is resilient to performance challenges.

6. Leveraging Predictive Analytics for Proactive Monitoring

Pega's Predictive Diagnostic Cloud (PDC) incorporates predictive analytics to help anticipate and resolve potential performance issues before they impact users. PDC analyzes historical and real-time data, providing actionable insights and recommendations.

Benefits of Predictive Analytics in Performance Management:

- **Early Detection of Anomalies**: Identify trends that may lead to performance issues, allowing proactive action.
- **Automated Recommendations**: Receive automated, data-driven recommendations to improve performance.
- **Enhanced Capacity Planning**: Plan for future demand and prevent capacity-related performance issues.

Predictive analytics can significantly enhance administrators' ability to maintain optimal performance by identifying and addressing potential issues early.

7. Troubleshooting Performance Metrics with Root Cause Analysis

When metrics indicate performance degradation, administrators can use root cause analysis techniques to identify underlying causes. This approach ensures that solutions address the root of the issue rather than just symptoms.

Root Cause Analysis Steps:

1. **Define the Problem**: Clearly identify the performance issue, such as high CPU usage or slow database queries.
2. **Analyze Relevant Metrics**: Gather and analyze relevant metrics to understand where the issue occurs and its impact.
3. **Identify Potential Causes**: Based on the data, determine possible causes, such as inefficient queries, heavy processing tasks, or integration delays.
4. **Validate with Diagnostics Tools**: Use tools like PAL, SMA, and Database Trace to confirm the cause of the issue.
5. **Implement and Test Solutions**: Apply the appropriate solution, such as optimizing rules or adjusting configurations, and test for improvement.

Root cause analysis ensures that performance improvements are sustainable and effective in the long term.

8. Continuous Improvement in Performance Management

Effective performance management is an ongoing process that requires regular monitoring, adjustments, and enhancements. Here are strategies for establishing a culture of continuous improvement:

- **Regular Performance Reviews**: Conduct periodic performance reviews to evaluate and adjust configurations, rules, and infrastructure based on current needs.
- **Performance Benchmarking**: Compare system performance against benchmarks or standards to identify areas for improvement.
- **Feedback Loops with Development Teams**: Foster a collaborative approach to performance management by sharing insights and feedback with development teams.
- **Stay Updated with Pega Best Practices**: Follow Pega's best practices and leverage the latest tools and updates for effective performance management.

Conclusion

Managing system performance metrics is critical to the success of any Pega application, impacting everything from user experience to operational efficiency. By understanding key metrics, leveraging

Pega's monitoring tools, and implementing proactive management strategies, administrators can maintain a high-performing, resilient application environment. Continuous monitoring, root cause analysis, and a culture of improvement ensure that Pega applications remain optimized and ready to handle evolving business demands.

Troubleshooting Workflows and Processes

Effective troubleshooting is essential in ensuring Pega workflows and processes perform smoothly, delivering seamless operations and user satisfaction. Workflow and process issues can stem from a range of sources, including rule configurations, database constraints, integrations, or system resource limitations. This chapter provides a comprehensive approach to diagnosing, isolating, and resolving workflow-related issues within Pega applications, enhancing both efficiency and reliability.

1. Understanding Common Workflow and Process Issues

To effectively troubleshoot workflows, it's essential to first understand common issues that may disrupt or degrade performance:

- **Process Flow Errors**: Errors that cause interruptions within specific steps of a process flow.
- **Stalled Cases**: Cases that fail to proceed past certain stages due to system misconfigurations or rule conflicts.
- **Data Constraints**: Problems arising from missing or mismatched data within forms, databases, or integrations.
- **Slow Processing Times**: Delays in workflows often resulting from resource bottlenecks, inefficient rule configurations, or long-running integrations.
- **Queue Management Issues**: Problems with processing tasks assigned to queues, causing delays in case progression.

By categorizing these common issues, administrators and developers can quickly narrow down troubleshooting approaches.

2. Tools and Techniques for Troubleshooting in Pega

Pega offers several diagnostic tools and features to help pinpoint issues within workflows and processes:

- **Tracer**: Tracer is essential for tracking rule execution and identifying where errors or unexpected behavior occurs within a process. By tracing specific requests or cases, developers can observe rule processing in real-time.
- **Clipboard Viewer**: The Clipboard Viewer provides insights into the data held in memory for each case. It's useful for examining property values, identifying missing or incorrect data, and validating data integrity.
- **System Management Application (SMA)**: SMA offers system-level insights, including JVM memory, requestor pools, and node performance. It can be used to identify resource constraints that may impact workflows.
- **Performance Analyzer (PAL)**: PAL captures performance statistics for specific requests, allowing you to analyze slow processes and identify where time is spent during execution.
- **Alerts and Logs**: Pega's logging framework captures errors, warnings, and performance alerts, which are invaluable for identifying recurring issues and their root causes.

Using these tools together provides a holistic view of the workflow, allowing for efficient troubleshooting and resolution.

3. Step-by-Step Workflow Troubleshooting Process

A structured troubleshooting process helps ensure that all potential causes are investigated and resolved systematically. Here's a step-by-step approach:

Step 1: Identify the Scope of the Issue

- Gather details on which workflows or processes are impacted, the frequency of the issue, and whether it affects specific users, cases, or actions.
- Check if the issue is isolated or system-wide, as this will influence where you start investigating.

Step 2: Reproduce the Issue

- Attempt to replicate the issue in a development or testing environment using the same conditions, data, and user permissions as the production environment.
- Reproducing the issue allows you to observe the behavior firsthand, facilitating targeted diagnostics.

Step 3: Trace the Execution Path

- Use the Tracer tool to monitor the execution path of rules and identify points where the process deviates or fails.
- Pay attention to any errors, warnings, or unexpected results in the Tracer output that could indicate misconfigurations or logic issues.

Step 4: Check Data Consistency with Clipboard Viewer

- Review the Clipboard data to validate that all necessary properties have the correct values.
- Ensure that required data is present at each step of the workflow and that data transformations are occurring as expected.

Step 5: Analyze Queue and Agent Performance

- If the workflow involves queues or background processing (such as agents), check SMA or Pega PDC for any processing delays, failures, or queue backlogs.
- Ensure that agents and queues are configured appropriately and are not overloaded.

Step 6: Review Logs and Alerts

- Review application logs for errors, warnings, or alerts associated with the workflow. Pay attention to alert types such as PEGA0001 (HTTP interaction time), PEGA0002 (Database response time), or PEGA0004 (Rule cache).
- Logs can reveal recurring patterns that may help identify persistent configuration issues or bottlenecks.

Step 7: Test and Validate Resolutions

- Apply potential fixes to address identified root causes, such as updating configurations, modifying rules, or optimizing integrations.
- Test the changes in a controlled environment to confirm that they resolve the issue without introducing new problems.

4. Troubleshooting Specific Workflow Scenarios

Different scenarios may require tailored troubleshooting approaches. Below are common workflow scenarios and how to address them:

Scenario: Stalled or Broken Case Flows

- **Issue**: Cases fail to advance beyond certain stages, often due to missing or incorrect rule configurations.
- **Solution**: Check process definitions and flow rules to ensure they are correctly configured. Validate entry conditions, connectors, and decision logic to ensure they route cases appropriately.

Scenario: Slow Workflow Processing Times

- **Issue**: Workflow steps experience significant delays, impacting user experience.
- **Solution**: Use PAL to identify time-intensive steps and review rule configurations, database queries, and integration calls. Address resource bottlenecks by optimizing queries, adjusting queue settings, or scaling system resources.

Scenario: Data-Related Errors

- **Issue**: Workflows generate errors due to missing or mismatched data.
- **Solution**: Use Clipboard Viewer to validate the data properties for each case. Ensure that all required fields are populated and that data is formatted correctly. If necessary, implement data validation rules to prevent incomplete cases from advancing.

Scenario: Integration Failures

- **Issue**: Integrations with external systems cause workflows to fail or stall.
- **Solution**: Use logs and Tracer to identify integration points. Check connection settings, API responses, and data mappings to ensure successful data exchange between systems.

5. Proactive Strategies to Prevent Workflow Issues

Implementing proactive measures can help reduce the frequency of workflow issues:

- **Robust Data Validation**: Enforce data validation at entry points to prevent incomplete or incorrect data from entering workflows.
- **Regular Process Audits**: Periodically review workflow configurations, rule structures, and decision logic to ensure they align with business requirements.
- **Optimize Resource Allocation**: Configure requestor pools, queues, and agents based on expected load and usage patterns to prevent bottlenecks.
- **Maintain Error Handling Rules**: Implement error-handling mechanisms to manage unexpected conditions gracefully, such as providing user-friendly error messages or allowing retries.
- **Monitor with PDC**: Use Pega Predictive Diagnostic Cloud (PDC) for continuous monitoring and proactive alerts on potential workflow performance issues.

By taking a proactive approach, administrators can mitigate common workflow issues, leading to smoother operations and enhanced user experience.

6. Case Study: Resolving a Workflow Bottleneck

Consider a case study of a Pega application with a workflow bottleneck during case assignment, where cases frequently stall due to agent processing delays.

Issue: Agents handling case assignments were experiencing backlogs, causing cases to be delayed.

Diagnosis:

- Using SMA and queue monitoring, administrators identified that the agent responsible for assignment processing had more tasks than it could handle, leading to significant delays.
- Tracer revealed that certain cases took longer to process due to complex decision logic and database interactions.

Solution:

1. **Optimize Agent Scheduling**: Adjusted agent scheduling to distribute workload more evenly throughout the day.
2. **Optimize Database Queries**: Refined database queries to improve processing time and reduce load on the agent.

3. **Add a Secondary Agent**: Configured a secondary agent to handle overflow tasks during peak times.

Outcome: By implementing these changes, the bottleneck was eliminated, and case processing returned to expected levels.

Conclusion

Troubleshooting workflows and processes in Pega is essential for maintaining a high-performing, reliable application environment. By using Pega's diagnostic tools, following a structured troubleshooting approach, and implementing proactive strategies, administrators can effectively identify and resolve workflow issues. Continuous monitoring, optimization, and regular audits will ensure that workflows run efficiently, meeting both business objectives and user expectations.

Section 8:
Monitoring and Reporting

Setting Up Monitoring Dashboards

Monitoring dashboards in Pega are essential tools for tracking application performance, identifying issues, and making data-driven decisions. Dashboards offer a visual interface that consolidates performance metrics, error logs, user activity, and more, allowing administrators and business users to gain insights at a glance. This chapter guides you through configuring monitoring dashboards in Pega, emphasizing best practices for layout, essential metrics, and tools to ensure effective monitoring.

1. Understanding the Importance of Monitoring Dashboards

Monitoring dashboards serve multiple roles in ensuring Pega applications function smoothly:

- **Proactive Issue Identification**: Dashboards help identify potential issues early, allowing administrators to address them before they affect users.
- **Performance Optimization**: Monitoring real-time and historical data helps to understand application usage patterns, optimize resource allocation, and manage workloads effectively.
- **Compliance and Audit**: Dashboards can display security and compliance metrics, ensuring that all actions and data access meet regulatory requirements.
- **User Experience Insights**: By monitoring user activity, Pega dashboards help you identify potential bottlenecks and adjust processes to enhance the user experience.

2. Key Components of Pega Monitoring Dashboards

Effective monitoring dashboards should be tailored to the needs of the organization, including the following key components:

- **Performance Metrics**: Track application response times, transaction processing times, and memory usage to ensure the application operates efficiently.
- **Error and Alert Tracking**: Monitor errors and alerts that provide insights into issues affecting specific modules or processes.
- **User Activity**: View user sessions, login patterns, and usage statistics to understand how users interact with the system.
- **Queue and Agent Monitoring**: Monitor processing queues and agent activities to ensure workflows and background tasks are processed without delays.
- **System Health**: Display key indicators of system health, such as CPU and memory utilization, database health, and requestor performance metrics.

By combining these components, a Pega dashboard provides a comprehensive view of application health and performance.

3. Steps to Configure Monitoring Dashboards in Pega

Creating an effective dashboard involves selecting relevant data sources, configuring widgets, and setting up alerts. Here's a step-by-step guide:

Step 1: Define the Monitoring Objectives

- Begin by defining the specific goals for your dashboard, such as monitoring performance, ensuring compliance, or tracking user behavior.
- Engage with stakeholders (such as business users, IT administrators, and security teams) to understand their requirements and tailor the dashboard to meet their needs.

Step 2: Select Data Sources and Metrics

- Choose relevant data sources for each objective. Common data sources include system logs, performance metrics from PAL (Performance Analyzer), and alerts.
- Define the metrics that align with your objectives, such as response times, error rates, and user session durations.

Step 3: Configure Dashboard Widgets

- Use Pega's dashboard widget options to create visual representations of the metrics, including graphs, tables, and counters.
- Common widgets include:
  - **Line Charts** for tracking performance trends over time.
  - **Bar Charts** for comparative data, such as agent processing volumes.
  - **Tables** for detailed logs of errors, alerts, or user sessions.
  - **Counters** for quick overviews of key indicators (e.g., total active sessions, average response time).

Step 4: Set Up Alerts and Thresholds

- Configure alerts for critical metrics to notify administrators of potential issues before they escalate. For example:
  - Set a threshold for high CPU usage to prompt investigation into potential resource bottlenecks.
  - Configure alerts for repeated errors within a module, signaling potential process issues.
- Use Pega's alert settings to define escalation paths, ensuring that notifications reach the appropriate personnel.

Step 5: Design Dashboard Layout

- Organize widgets and components based on priority, with critical metrics positioned prominently at the top.
- Group related widgets, such as performance metrics or error logs, to create a logical flow and make the dashboard intuitive to navigate.

Step 6: Test and Optimize the Dashboard

- Review the dashboard with stakeholders to ensure it meets all monitoring objectives and adjust as necessary.
- Conduct a test period to validate data accuracy, alert thresholds, and user-friendliness.
- Make iterative improvements based on feedback, refining widget layouts, data sources, and alert settings as needed.

4. Best Practices for Dashboard Design

To ensure the dashboard is effective and user-friendly, apply these best practices:

- **Clarity and Simplicity**: Use a clean design with a limited color palette to avoid visual clutter. Each widget should serve a specific purpose, and the dashboard should be intuitive to navigate.
- **Real-Time Data**: For high-priority metrics (such as performance and error tracking), use real-time or near-real-time data sources to provide up-to-date information.

- **Logical Organization**: Group widgets by functionality, such as performance, security, and user activity, making it easy for users to find relevant data.
- **Customizability**: Enable dashboard customization so that users can personalize views based on their specific needs, such as focusing on different metrics or adjusting time ranges.
- **Documentation and Training**: Provide documentation on dashboard functionality and conduct training for users to maximize the dashboard's effectiveness and ensure they understand how to interpret metrics.

5. Example Dashboard Use Cases

Below are two common scenarios where monitoring dashboards provide critical insights:

Use Case 1: Performance Monitoring

- **Objective**: Ensure that the Pega application maintains optimal performance under various conditions.
- **Metrics**: Track page load times, transaction processing durations, and memory utilization.
- **Widgets**: Line charts to show trends in response times, counters for current session counts, and tables for recent error logs.
- **Alerts**: Set up alerts for prolonged response times, high memory usage, or excessive error rates.

Use Case 2: Compliance Monitoring

- **Objective**: Ensure that the application meets regulatory standards for data security and access control.
- **Metrics**: Track login attempts, role-based access activity, and data export actions.
- **Widgets**: Tables listing recent user sessions, bar charts for failed login attempts by region, and counters for restricted data access attempts.
- **Alerts**: Configure alerts for multiple failed logins, data exports exceeding thresholds, or unauthorized access attempts.

6. Troubleshooting Dashboard Issues

Effective monitoring relies on dashboards functioning correctly. Here's how to troubleshoot common issues:

- **Missing Data**: If widgets display incomplete or missing data, check the data source connections and refresh intervals. Ensure that relevant logging is enabled.
- **Inaccurate Metrics**: Verify metric definitions and data sources to ensure that widgets reflect accurate and relevant information. Review configurations in the Performance Analyzer or SMA (System Management Application).
- **Excessive Alerts**: If alerts trigger too frequently, adjust thresholds to better align with realistic expectations and usage patterns, reducing noise and alert fatigue.

Conclusion

Setting up monitoring dashboards in Pega enhances visibility into system performance, security, and user activity. By following structured configuration steps, applying best practices, and tailoring the dashboard to meet specific objectives, administrators can maximize its value, proactively addressing issues, and supporting continuous optimization of the Pega application environment.

Using Pega's Reporting Capabilities

Pega's robust reporting capabilities enable users to gain valuable insights into business processes, monitor performance metrics, and make informed decisions based on data. By leveraging Pega's built-in tools, organizations can generate dynamic, interactive reports that help visualize trends, identify bottlenecks, and drive continuous improvement. This chapter explores how to harness Pega's reporting features, customize reports, and optimize data visualization to meet business needs.

1. Overview of Pega's Reporting Architecture

Pega's reporting system is integrated into the platform, allowing data from applications to be collected, analyzed, and presented in real-time. The key components include:

- **Report Definitions**: Templates used to define the data parameters, filters, and display options for reports.
- **Class-Based Reporting**: Reports are tied to specific classes, which means they pull data from defined structures within Pega's data model.
- **Report Browser**: A centralized interface where users can access, create, and manage reports.
- **Data Pages**: A tool to access data from both internal sources (Pega databases) and external sources for reporting purposes.

2. Creating Basic Reports

Creating a basic report in Pega involves selecting the data fields, defining filters, and choosing the desired format. Follow these steps to set up a report:

Step 1: Access the Report Browser

- Navigate to the Report Browser in Pega, which provides a user-friendly interface for creating and managing reports.

Step 2: Select the Report Class

- Choose the appropriate class, which will determine the data source. This ensures the report pulls the correct data set based on the business context.

Step 3: Define Data Fields and Filters

- Select the specific data fields to include in the report, such as customer name, case status, or resolution time.
- Set up filters to refine the data further. For instance, you can filter cases by status (open, resolved) or by date range.

Step 4: Choose the Report Format

- Decide on the format of the report. Pega offers options such as lists, summaries, or charts. Lists are ideal for detailed records, while summaries and charts are useful for analyzing trends and aggregated data.

Step 5: Save and Run the Report

- Save the report with a descriptive name and run it to view the output. You can access saved reports later in the Report Browser.

3. Advanced Report Configuration

To create more sophisticated reports, Pega provides advanced options for grouping, sorting, and calculations:

- **Grouping Data**: Organize report data by grouping related records. For example, group cases by priority to see the number of high, medium, and low-priority cases.
- **Sorting and Ordering**: Sort data fields to display records in ascending or descending order. Sorting by date or case resolution time helps identify recent trends.
- **Calculations and Aggregates**: Use functions like SUM, AVERAGE, and COUNT to generate aggregate data. For instance, calculating the average resolution time provides insights into process efficiency.

4. Visualizing Data with Charts and Graphs

Pega allows users to add visual elements to reports, making data more accessible and impactful:

- **Bar Charts**: Ideal for comparing data across different categories, such as case volumes by department.
- **Line Charts**: Useful for tracking changes over time, such as monthly case resolution rates.
- **Pie Charts**: Suitable for displaying proportions within a whole, such as case distribution by status.
- **Heatmaps**: Display density or intensity, making them useful for showing user activity or case distribution across regions.

Visual reports enhance understanding by providing a quick, graphical overview of key metrics.

5. Customizing Reports for Business Needs

Pega's reporting capabilities offer flexibility to tailor reports to unique business requirements:

- **Custom Columns**: Create calculated fields to display values derived from existing data fields, such as calculating total time in process stages.
- **Dynamic Filters**: Add filters that users can adjust when running the report, allowing them to view data based on real-time needs.
- **Parameterized Reports**: Set up parameters (e.g., date ranges or user roles) that users can define when generating a report. This allows a single report template to meet various needs.

6. Automating Report Generation and Scheduling

Pega enables users to automate report generation and distribution, helping keep stakeholders informed:

- **Scheduling Reports**: Set up a schedule to run reports automatically at regular intervals, such as daily, weekly, or monthly.
- **Email Delivery**: Configure automated email distribution to send reports to designated recipients, including executives or team leads.
- **Exporting Reports**: Export reports to formats like PDF, Excel, or CSV for offline analysis or sharing with external stakeholders.

7. Using Data Pages and External Data Sources

Data Pages in Pega allow reports to incorporate data from both internal and external sources:

- **Configuring Data Pages**: Set up Data Pages to pull data from sources like external databases or web services. This ensures reports include all necessary information.
- **Connecting to External Systems**: Integrate Pega reports with third-party applications, enabling reports to draw on data from CRM, ERP, or financial systems for comprehensive insights.

8. Best Practices for Effective Reporting

To maximize the value of reporting in Pega, consider the following best practices:

- **Focus on Key Metrics**: Identify and prioritize the most relevant metrics for each report to avoid overwhelming users with unnecessary details.
- **Use Visuals Wisely**: Choose visual elements thoughtfully to ensure they enhance understanding without cluttering the report.
- **Encourage Interactivity**: Enable dynamic filters and parameters where possible, allowing users to explore the data based on their specific needs.
- **Review and Refine**: Regularly review reports for accuracy and relevance, especially when business needs evolve.

9. Troubleshooting Common Reporting Issues

Effective reporting requires troubleshooting common issues to ensure data accuracy and relevance:

- **Incomplete Data**: Check data sources and filters if reports do not display complete records.
- **Inaccurate Aggregates**: Review calculations and grouping settings to ensure metrics like averages and sums are accurate.
- **Slow Performance**: If reports take too long to load, review report definitions and reduce the number of fields or filters to improve efficiency.

Conclusion

Pega's reporting capabilities are powerful tools for visualizing and analyzing business data, providing insights that drive better decision-making and operational efficiency. By following best practices, leveraging advanced configuration options, and optimizing reports for specific business needs, organizations can turn data into a strategic asset. Through well-designed reports, stakeholders gain a clearer view of processes, enabling continuous improvement and more agile responses to emerging challenges.

Designing Custom Reports and Metrics

Custom reports and metrics in Pega empower organizations to generate targeted insights that directly address specific business requirements. By designing custom reports, users can define unique metrics, configure data filters, and set up dynamic views that aid in making data-driven decisions. This chapter explores the steps for designing custom reports, selecting relevant metrics, and customizing the report layout to suit business needs.

1. Introduction to Custom Reporting in Pega

Custom reports in Pega provide a way to visualize and analyze specific business data, tailored to the needs of the organization or department. Through the Report Browser and Report Definition tools, users can:

- Create targeted views of data relevant to their operations.
- Define custom metrics that are most meaningful for their business processes.
- Apply custom filters, sorting, and grouping to organize data effectively.

2. Identifying Key Metrics for Custom Reports

Before creating custom reports, it's essential to identify the metrics that will provide meaningful insights. Common metrics for process automation and business process management (BPM) may include:

- **Case Resolution Time**: Tracks how long it takes to resolve a case from start to finish.
- **Process Efficiency**: Analyzes the number of tasks completed within a specified timeframe.
- **Customer Satisfaction Metrics**: Measures outcomes related to customer interactions and service quality.
- **Operational KPIs**: Custom KPIs that align with business goals, such as cost savings, productivity rates, or error reduction.

By defining these metrics upfront, you ensure that custom reports capture relevant and actionable data.

3. Creating a New Custom Report in Pega

Creating a custom report in Pega involves setting up the report definition, selecting data fields, and applying filters. Follow these steps to create a report tailored to your requirements:

Step 1: Access the Report Browser

- Open the Report Browser from the Pega Designer Studio. This provides access to available reports and the tools to create new ones.

Step 2: Define the Report Class

- Choose the class from which the report will pull data. This class determines the data structure and fields available for the report.

Step 3: Select Data Fields

- Select the specific data fields you want to include, such as "Case ID," "Customer Name," "Resolution Time," or "Agent Assigned." Choose only the fields that are directly relevant to avoid clutter.

Step 4: Set Up Filters and Sorting

- Apply filters to narrow down the data. For example, you can filter cases by date, status, or assigned user.
- Configure sorting options to arrange data by priority, date, or other relevant fields, ensuring that the report presents information in a logical order.

Step 5: Customize Report Layout

- Use Pega's layout options to design the visual structure of the report. Options include tables, lists, charts, and graphs, allowing you to create both detailed and summary views of the data.

4. Defining Custom Metrics for Reporting

Custom metrics help provide insights that are specific to your organization's needs. Define metrics by creating calculated fields or using formulas within the report definition:

- **Calculated Fields**: Use expressions to create custom calculations. For example, you might define "Average Case Resolution Time" by dividing the total resolution time by the number of cases.
- **Aggregations**: Set up aggregate functions like SUM, AVERAGE, MIN, and MAX to analyze data trends.
- **Percentages and Ratios**: Display metrics as percentages or ratios, such as "On-Time Completion Rate" or "Customer Satisfaction Score."

By defining these metrics within the report, you can ensure that critical performance indicators are easy to monitor and interpret.

5. Adding Visual Elements to Custom Reports

Visualizing data can make it easier to interpret, especially for high-level reports shared with stakeholders. Pega offers various options for adding visual elements:

- **Bar Charts**: Effective for comparing metrics across different categories, such as case types or user groups.
- **Line Charts**: Ideal for tracking changes over time, such as monthly trends in case resolution rates.
- **Pie Charts**: Useful for displaying proportions, such as the percentage of cases by status (e.g., open, in-progress, resolved).
- **Heatmaps**: Display data density or frequency, useful for visualizing customer demand or operational bottlenecks.

Choose visual elements that align with the report's purpose, as each chart type presents information differently.

6. Setting Up Interactive and Dynamic Reports

Pega allows you to add interactive features to custom reports, making it easy for users to adjust filters or view data in different ways:

- **Dynamic Filters**: Enable users to apply filters directly within the report, adjusting the data view based on criteria like date range, user role, or case status.
- **Parameterization**: Create reports that prompt users to enter parameters, such as selecting a specific department or process stage. This allows the same report to serve multiple needs.

Interactive reports improve the usability and flexibility of data analysis, allowing team members to explore data relevant to their current tasks.

7. Automating and Scheduling Custom Reports

To ensure consistent reporting and timely insights, Pega allows you to automate report generation and distribution:

- **Scheduling Reports**: Set up a schedule to generate reports at regular intervals (e.g., daily, weekly, monthly). This is useful for ongoing monitoring of key performance indicators.
- **Automated Email Delivery**: Configure the system to email reports to designated recipients, such as team leads or department heads.
- **Exporting Reports**: Export reports to formats like PDF, Excel, or CSV for easy sharing with external stakeholders or archiving.

Automating reports ensures that stakeholders receive updates consistently, without requiring manual report generation.

8. Best Practices for Designing Custom Reports and Metrics

To maximize the effectiveness of custom reports and metrics, follow these best practices:

- **Align Reports with Business Goals**: Design reports that directly support strategic objectives, ensuring that data insights contribute to decision-making.
- **Keep Reports Clear and Focused**: Avoid adding too many fields or metrics to a single report. Focus on key metrics that provide actionable insights.
- **Use Visuals Strategically**: Only add charts and graphs that enhance understanding. Avoid overusing visuals, as too many can make reports difficult to interpret.
- **Regularly Review and Update Reports**: Business needs evolve, so periodically review reports to ensure they remain relevant and valuable.

9. Troubleshooting Common Issues in Custom Reporting

Creating custom reports may occasionally lead to challenges. Here are solutions to some common issues:

- **Missing Data**: Verify that the correct class and fields are selected, and ensure filters are set up correctly to capture all relevant data.
- **Slow Loading Times**: Simplify the report by reducing the number of data fields or filters. Complex reports with large datasets may benefit from streamlined parameters.
- **Inaccurate Metrics**: Check calculations and custom expressions for accuracy. Errors in formula setup can lead to misleading results.

Conclusion

Designing custom reports and metrics in Pega provides organizations with tailored insights that align with their unique operational needs. By carefully selecting relevant metrics, customizing report layouts, and leveraging visual elements, users can create reports that drive informed decision-making. Additionally, with automated scheduling and distribution, custom reports can be consistently delivered to stakeholders, ensuring that insights are readily available for proactive management and continuous improvement.

Leveraging Real-Time Analytics for Decision Making

Real-time analytics in Pega enables organizations to monitor, analyze, and respond to business data as events occur. This proactive approach allows decision-makers to gain immediate insights into ongoing operations, make data-informed decisions swiftly, and address potential issues before they escalate. This chapter explores how to harness real-time analytics in Pega, the benefits it offers, and best practices for utilizing it in decision-making processes.

1. Understanding Real-Time Analytics in Pega

Real-time analytics in Pega involves the continuous analysis of data as it's generated, which helps organizations keep track of various performance indicators and respond to changes immediately. Unlike historical data analysis, which looks back on events after they've occurred, real-time analytics captures events as they happen, providing insights that reflect the current state of operations.

Key features of real-time analytics in Pega include:

- **Live Monitoring**: Observe key metrics and process indicators as they evolve.
- **Instant Alerts**: Get notified of specific conditions that require immediate action.
- **Automated Responses**: Configure rules to trigger automated actions when certain thresholds or events occur.

2. Setting Up Real-Time Data Feeds

To implement real-time analytics, you need to establish data feeds that supply live data from various sources, including Pega applications and third-party systems. This can be accomplished through:

- **Pega Data Pages**: Set up data pages that pull data from live systems, serving as real-time sources for reports and dashboards.
- **Integration with External Systems**: Connect Pega with external systems to feed real-time data, using APIs, web services, or direct database integration.
- **Event Streams**: Leverage Pega's support for event-driven architecture, where external events (e.g., user actions, system alerts) are streamed into Pega in real-time for instant analysis.

3. Configuring Real-Time Dashboards

A real-time dashboard provides a centralized view of critical metrics, allowing decision-makers to monitor and act on live data effectively. Steps for setting up a real-time dashboard in Pega include:

- **Defining Key Performance Indicators (KPIs)**: Identify the KPIs that are most relevant for your business. Examples include case resolution times, task completion rates, and customer satisfaction scores.
- **Designing Dynamic Charts and Visuals**: Configure charts and visuals that update automatically as data changes. Choose visualizations that offer a clear understanding of each metric.
- **Setting Up Filters and Views**: Allow users to filter data by different criteria, such as time frame, department, or case type, making it easier to explore specific aspects of the data.

By keeping the dashboard intuitive and accessible, teams can quickly understand and act on real-time insights without needing technical expertise.

4. Implementing Real-Time Alerts and Notifications

Real-time analytics becomes even more powerful when coupled with automated alerts. Pega can notify relevant stakeholders when predefined conditions are met, ensuring quick responses to important events. Steps to implement alerts include:

- **Defining Alert Criteria**: Set specific conditions that should trigger alerts, such as when a KPI crosses a threshold or an error rate rises.
- **Configuring Notification Channels**: Choose notification channels—such as email, SMS, or in-app messages—that suit the users receiving alerts.
- **Setting Priority Levels**: Classify alerts by priority to help users distinguish between urgent issues and informational updates.

These real-time alerts empower decision-makers to stay informed about critical developments and take action when needed, even when they're away from the dashboard.

5. Automating Decision-Making Processes with Real-Time Data

In some cases, real-time analytics can support not only monitoring but also automated decision-making. By establishing rules in Pega that respond to real-time data, organizations can automate certain actions, reducing the need for manual intervention. Examples include:

- **Dynamic Case Routing**: Automatically assign cases to the appropriate team or agent based on current workload, priority, or skillset.
- **Service-Level Agreements (SLAs)**: Trigger escalation procedures when SLAs are at risk of being breached.
- **Real-Time Customer Interactions**: Modify customer service responses based on real-time sentiment analysis, customer history, or other data.

These automated decisions increase responsiveness, reduce delays, and enhance overall efficiency by allowing the system to handle repetitive or predictable actions.

6. Using Predictive Analytics for Proactive Decision Making

In addition to real-time analysis, predictive analytics leverages historical data to anticipate future trends, enabling proactive rather than reactive decision-making. While not strictly "real-time," predictive models can be updated in near-real-time to adapt to changing data patterns. This includes:

- **Predicting Demand and Workload**: Forecast future demand or workload spikes, allowing the organization to allocate resources proactively.
- **Risk Assessment**: Estimate the likelihood of specific risks, such as system failures or compliance breaches, and take preventive measures.
- **Customer Behavior Insights**: Use predictive analytics to anticipate customer needs or behaviors, offering a more personalized experience.

7. Real-Time Analytics Best Practices for Decision Making

To ensure that real-time analytics in Pega drives valuable decisions, consider the following best practices:

- **Focus on Actionable Data**: Avoid information overload by focusing on metrics and alerts that lead to clear, actionable decisions.
- **Regularly Review and Update KPIs**: Ensure that KPIs remain aligned with evolving business goals by periodically reviewing and updating them.
- **Train Teams on Data Interpretation**: Equip users with the skills to interpret real-time data accurately, preventing misinterpretation and enabling more effective decision-making.
- **Optimize Alert Settings**: Strike a balance in alert configuration to avoid overwhelming users with too many notifications or missing critical updates.

8. Troubleshooting Common Issues with Real-Time Analytics

Implementing real-time analytics can come with challenges. Here are some common issues and their solutions:

- **Data Latency**: Real-time analytics requires minimal data delay. Work with your technical team to optimize data sources and reduce latency.
- **Alert Fatigue**: Over-notifying users can lead to alert fatigue, causing them to ignore important alerts. Review alert thresholds and adjust as necessary.
- **Data Accuracy**: Ensure that data sources are reliable and that data is verified before being used for critical decisions. Data inaccuracies can mislead users and lead to ineffective actions.

Conclusion

Real-time analytics in Pega enables organizations to make informed decisions at the moment, enhancing responsiveness and operational agility. By configuring real-time dashboards, implementing automated alerts, and integrating predictive models, businesses can monitor their most critical metrics, proactively address potential challenges, and continuously optimize their processes. Real-time analytics not only drives faster decisions but also empowers organizations to be more proactive, ultimately contributing to greater efficiency and a competitive edge.

Monitoring Key Performance Indicators (KPIs)

Monitoring Key Performance Indicators (KPIs) is essential for measuring the success of business processes and ensuring that goals are met. Within Pega, monitoring KPIs helps stakeholders understand how well processes perform, identify areas for improvement, and maintain alignment with strategic objectives. This chapter outlines how to define, configure, and monitor KPIs in Pega, with guidance on best practices for real-time insights and performance optimization.

1. The Importance of KPIs in Process Management

KPIs are quantifiable measures that gauge the success of a business process or project. In Pega, they serve as benchmarks for evaluating various aspects of system and process performance, such as efficiency, accuracy, customer satisfaction, and compliance. Effective KPI monitoring enables:

- **Real-Time Visibility**: Continuous tracking of KPIs helps teams identify issues early and respond quickly.
- **Objective Evaluation**: KPIs provide a concrete basis for measuring the impact of initiatives and making data-driven decisions.
- **Goal Alignment**: KPIs ensure that individual activities contribute to overall business goals, fostering a unified approach across teams.

2. Identifying Relevant KPIs for Pega Applications

Selecting the right KPIs is essential. The KPIs you choose should align with your organization's objectives and reflect critical process outcomes. Common KPIs monitored in Pega applications include:

- **Case Resolution Time**: Measures the average time taken to resolve cases, indicating efficiency.
- **Service-Level Agreement (SLA) Compliance**: Tracks adherence to SLAs, reflecting reliability and customer satisfaction.
- **Error Rate**: Monitors the frequency of errors or exceptions, revealing areas needing quality improvement.
- **Customer Satisfaction (CSAT) Score**: Evaluates customer feedback to gauge service quality.
- **Task Completion Rate**: Measures the proportion of completed tasks relative to initiated tasks, providing insights into productivity.

3. Setting Up KPIs in Pega

To monitor KPIs effectively, you need to configure them within Pega's reporting and analytics tools. This involves defining the metrics, setting targets, and configuring real-time tracking mechanisms. Steps to set up KPIs include:

1. **Define KPI Objectives**: Determine what each KPI aims to measure and why it's important.
2. **Set Target Values**: Establish specific, measurable targets for each KPI (e.g., "Resolve 95% of cases within 24 hours").
3. **Configure Reporting Tools**: Use Pega's reporting capabilities to capture data and track KPI performance over time.

KPIs can be displayed on real-time dashboards, allowing stakeholders to monitor them continuously.

4. Using Dashboards for KPI Monitoring

Dashboards provide a centralized view of critical KPIs, enabling users to track performance trends and make quick assessments. In Pega, dashboards can be customized to display the KPIs most relevant to each user or department. Key features of KPI dashboards include:

- **Real-Time Data Updates**: KPIs on dashboards reflect the latest data, ensuring that users always have current insights.
- **Visual Representations**: Charts, graphs, and other visuals make KPI data easy to interpret.
- **Drill-Down Capabilities**: Users can explore deeper insights by drilling down into specific KPI data points to understand underlying causes.

Well-designed dashboards support proactive decision-making by highlighting performance trends and deviations from targets.

5. Configuring Alerts for KPI Thresholds

Automated alerts for KPIs allow stakeholders to respond swiftly when performance deviates from acceptable thresholds. Pega can be configured to send alerts when KPIs cross predefined boundaries, helping teams address issues promptly. Steps to configure KPI alerts include:

1. **Set Thresholds**: Define acceptable ranges for each KPI and determine when alerts should be triggered.
2. **Choose Notification Channels**: Select the channels (e.g., email, SMS, or in-app) for alert delivery.
3. **Prioritize Alerts**: Classify alerts by priority to help users distinguish between critical and routine updates.

KPI alerts prevent delays in response by immediately notifying relevant teams about potential problems.

6. Best Practices for KPI Monitoring

For effective KPI monitoring, adhere to the following best practices:

- **Focus on Relevant KPIs**: Avoid overwhelming teams with too many metrics. Focus on the KPIs that align with strategic goals and directly impact business outcomes.
- **Set Realistic Targets**: Set achievable KPI targets based on historical data and industry benchmarks.
- **Regularly Review and Adjust KPIs**: Revisit KPIs periodically to ensure they remain aligned with evolving business needs.
- **Foster Data-Driven Culture**: Encourage teams to use KPI insights in their decision-making processes, embedding a data-driven approach across the organization.

7. Troubleshooting Common KPI Monitoring Challenges

Monitoring KPIs can present challenges, such as data accuracy issues, alert fatigue, or misaligned targets. Here's how to address these common challenges:

- **Data Accuracy**: Ensure data sources are reliable and that data entry errors are minimized to maintain accurate KPI tracking.
- **Alert Fatigue**: Configure thresholds carefully to avoid excessive alerts, which may lead users to ignore notifications.
- **Misaligned Targets**: Regularly evaluate KPI targets to ensure they match current business priorities and adjust them as necessary.

Conclusion

Monitoring KPIs in Pega is integral to tracking and enhancing business performance. By selecting meaningful KPIs, configuring real-time dashboards, and setting up alerts, organizations can gain visibility into critical metrics and ensure alignment with strategic goals. Adopting a disciplined approach to KPI monitoring supports continuous improvement, enhances responsiveness, and drives better decision-making across the organization.

Section 9:
Advanced Administration and Management

Managing Application Versions and Releases

In the dynamic world of software development, managing application versions and releases is essential for ensuring consistency, traceability, and efficient rollouts of new features or fixes. Pega's platform provides comprehensive tools and methodologies to streamline the version control and release management processes, enabling teams to maintain control over application updates and ensure alignment with business objectives. This chapter explores best practices, tools, and techniques for managing application versions and releases within Pega.

1. Importance of Version Control and Release Management

Efficient version control and release management are critical in complex enterprise applications, where multiple teams may be working concurrently. Effective management allows for:

- **Traceability**: Keeping track of changes across versions ensures that each update can be traced back to its origin, aiding in compliance and audit requirements.
- **Consistency**: Version control helps maintain consistency across development, testing, and production environments.
- **Efficient Rollouts**: A structured release management process enables seamless deployment of new features, enhancements, or bug fixes with minimal disruptions.
- **Risk Mitigation**: Proper release management minimizes the risk of introducing errors by controlling and testing changes before they reach production.

2. Understanding Versioning in Pega Applications

Versioning in Pega follows a hierarchical model, allowing for organized management of multiple versions and development streams. Key elements include:

- **Rulesets**: A collection of rules within a specific version. Each ruleset contains a version number (e.g., 01-01-01), which represents the major, minor, and patch levels.
- **Ruleset Versions**: Versions enable the encapsulation of specific ruleset changes, making it easier to promote only the desired updates during releases.
- **Branches**: Branches allow for isolated development streams. Each branch can have its own versioning, which is merged into the main application once development and testing are complete.

3. Planning a Release Cycle

A well-structured release cycle helps organize the process of application updates, ensuring timely delivery without compromising quality. Typical steps in a release cycle include:

1. **Define Objectives**: Identify the purpose of the release—whether it's a new feature rollout, a maintenance update, or a bug fix.
2. **Create a Timeline**: Establish deadlines for each phase, including development, testing, quality assurance, and deployment.
3. **Resource Allocation**: Assign resources based on the complexity and urgency of the release.
4. **Versioning and Documentation**: Update version numbers, document changes, and communicate to relevant stakeholders.

Effective release planning helps teams prepare for each stage of the cycle and reduces last-minute challenges during deployment.

4. Best Practices for Version Control in Pega

Managing versions effectively requires adhering to certain best practices. Key recommendations include:

- **Incremental Versioning**: Use incremental versioning to reflect major, minor, and patch-level changes. For instance, a change affecting core functionality might warrant a major version update.
- **Documentation**: Document each version, including features or fixes included, to provide a comprehensive history of changes.
- **Testing Environments**: Maintain multiple environments (e.g., development, testing, staging) to isolate versions and ensure they meet requirements before deploying to production.
- **Labeling and Tagging**: Use labels and tags for specific version releases to improve traceability, especially in cases of rollbacks.

5. Using Deployment Manager for Release Automation

Pega Deployment Manager is a powerful tool that simplifies the deployment process. It automates deployment pipelines, manages environments, and integrates with CI/CD processes. Key features include:

- **Automated Pipelines**: Configure deployment pipelines to automate the promotion of rulesets and data from one environment to another.
- **Environment Management**: Manage different environments, ensuring consistent configurations and dependencies across them.
- **Rollback Capabilities**: The Deployment Manager allows for rolling back to previous versions if issues are detected post-release.

Deployment Manager not only reduces manual efforts but also improves the reliability and speed of releases by automating routine tasks.

6. Change Management in Pega Releases

Change management is critical when deploying new versions to avoid disruptions. Best practices for managing changes include:

- **Stakeholder Communication**: Inform stakeholders about upcoming changes, expected benefits, and possible impacts on the workflow.
- **Approval Workflows**: Implement approval workflows to validate that changes meet business and technical standards before release.
- **Change Logs**: Maintain a detailed log of changes, which can help troubleshoot any issues and assist with future releases.
- **User Training**: Provide training or documentation for end-users affected by new features or changes to ensure smooth adoption.

By following structured change management practices, organizations can reduce the risk of unintended consequences and foster user confidence in updates.

7. Testing and Validation

Testing is a crucial component of release management, helping to ensure that each version meets quality standards. Testing phases should include:

- **Unit Testing**: Testing individual components to ensure they function as intended.
- **Integration Testing**: Verifying that the new version integrates seamlessly with other system components.

- **User Acceptance Testing (UAT)**: Allowing end-users to test the functionality to confirm it meets their needs and expectations.

Incorporate automated testing wherever possible to streamline these processes and improve accuracy.

8. Tracking Metrics for Release Success

After deploying a new version, track specific metrics to gauge the release's success. Important metrics include:

- **Deployment Time**: The time taken to deploy and stabilize the application after release.
- **Error Rate**: Monitoring errors or issues introduced with the release helps identify areas needing improvement.
- **User Feedback**: Collect feedback from users to assess satisfaction and identify any additional training needs or refinements.
- **Performance Metrics**: Monitor system performance post-release to ensure it meets expectations and that no regressions were introduced.

These metrics provide insights into the release process and help improve future version management practices.

Conclusion

Managing application versions and releases is vital for maintaining control over Pega applications as they evolve. By following structured release cycles, implementing best practices in version control, and leveraging tools like Pega Deployment Manager, organizations can enhance release efficiency and reliability. Additionally, maintaining robust change management, thorough testing, and performance tracking practices will ensure that each release contributes positively to business objectives and user satisfaction.

Configuring System Settings for Optimal Performance

Configuring system settings within Pega is essential to ensure applications operate efficiently and meet organizational performance standards. Proper configuration optimizes resource usage, minimizes latency, and supports smooth scaling as demand grows. This chapter provides guidelines for setting up Pega's system configurations to enhance performance, reduce downtime, and maintain stability.

1. Importance of Optimized System Configuration

A well-optimized configuration is critical for applications that handle high transaction volumes, complex business rules, or significant data processing. Key benefits of optimal settings include:

- **Enhanced System Stability**: Prevents unplanned downtime by maintaining efficient memory and resource usage.
- **Reduced Latency**: Minimizes processing delays, resulting in faster response times.
- **Improved User Experience**: Ensures seamless operation, especially during peak loads, enhancing user satisfaction.
- **Cost Efficiency**: Proper configuration avoids excessive resource consumption, reducing infrastructure costs.

2. Key System Settings in Pega

Pega provides several settings within its platform that impact performance. These settings can be managed through the System Management Application (SMA) or directly within Pega's administrative tools:

- **Memory Allocation**: Adjusting JVM (Java Virtual Machine) settings to allocate sufficient heap memory based on application demands.
- **Thread Pools**: Configuring the number of requestor pools and threads for optimal workload distribution.
- **Database Connections**: Setting limits on database connections to prevent overloading and bottlenecks.
- **Cache Management**: Configuring caches to optimize data retrieval times, particularly for frequently accessed information.

Each of these settings plays a crucial role in ensuring the efficient functioning of Pega applications, particularly under heavy loads.

3. Memory and JVM Configuration

Java Virtual Machine (JVM) settings directly impact Pega's performance. Key memory configurations include:

- **Heap Memory**: The main memory allocated to the application. It's important to configure both initial and maximum heap sizes based on expected load.
- **Garbage Collection (GC)**: JVM's garbage collection can affect performance if not optimized. Consider using GC algorithms like G1 or CMS for larger applications to manage memory reclamation effectively.

Best Practice:

- Regularly monitor memory usage to adjust heap sizes if necessary.
- Configure GC logs to detect any memory issues early.

4. Configuring Thread Pools for Concurrent Processing

Thread pools are essential for managing concurrent user requests and background processes. Configuration includes:

- **Number of Threads**: Set based on the expected user load and available CPU resources. More threads allow greater concurrency but can impact performance if CPU resources are limited.
- **Requestor Pools**: Configure requestor pools for different types of processing (e.g., web users, background processing) to ensure a balanced load.

Best Practice:

- Test thread pool settings under simulated loads to determine optimal values.

5. Database Connection Settings

Database settings directly affect data access and storage operations in Pega. Important configurations include:

- **Connection Pooling**: Enables efficient reuse of database connections, reducing the need to open new connections for each query.
- **Connection Timeout**: Defines how long the system waits for a database connection. Setting an appropriate timeout prevents delays if the database is busy.
- **Database Indexing**: Ensure proper indexing on frequently accessed tables to speed up query processing.

Best Practice:

- Monitor database performance and adjust connection pools as necessary based on peak load requirements.

6. Caching for Faster Data Retrieval

Pega's caching mechanisms can significantly improve performance by reducing the number of database calls:

- **Declarative Caches**: Store frequently accessed data such as reference tables and rule configurations.
- **Data Pages**: Use data pages with refresh intervals to cache data that's periodically updated, balancing freshness with performance.

Best Practice:

- Configure cache sizes based on data access patterns and review cache statistics to ensure effective usage.

7. Managing Background Processes

Pega applications often rely on background processes to handle scheduled tasks, data imports, and other asynchronous activities. Key configurations include:

- **Job Scheduler Settings**: Set job scheduler intervals based on the criticality and processing time of each task. Avoid overlapping jobs during peak hours to balance load.
- **Queue Processor Configuration**: Use queue processors for handling task queuing and processing. Configure the number of threads and queue sizes based on workload.

Best Practice:

- Regularly review job schedules to avoid conflicts and adjust thread counts for queue processors to handle peak loads efficiently.

8. Performance Monitoring and Adjustments

Ongoing monitoring is crucial for maintaining optimal performance, as system demands can change over time. Key monitoring tools include:

- **Pega Predictive Diagnostic Cloud (PDC)**: PDC provides real-time insights and analytics on application performance, allowing administrators to detect potential issues before they impact users.
- **System Logs**: Regularly review logs for warnings or errors related to performance, such as memory or database connection issues.
- **Alerts and Notifications**: Configure alerts for critical metrics like CPU utilization, memory usage, and database connection limits.

Best Practice:

- Establish a regular monitoring schedule and adjust settings based on performance trends.

9. Testing System Settings

Testing configurations before deployment is essential for verifying their effectiveness under real-world conditions. Recommended testing steps include:

- **Load Testing**: Simulate expected user loads to observe system behavior and identify potential bottlenecks.
- **Stress Testing**: Test system limits by gradually increasing load to find the maximum capacity.
- **Performance Benchmarks**: Establish benchmarks for response times, memory usage, and throughput to guide future configurations.

Best Practice:

- Conduct testing periodically, particularly when implementing new configurations or making significant updates.

Conclusion

Configuring system settings effectively is key to achieving optimal performance in Pega applications. By carefully managing memory allocation, thread pools, database connections, and caching, administrators can enhance stability and responsiveness, ensuring that Pega applications meet business needs efficiently. Regular monitoring, testing, and adjustments further support a high-performing environment, enabling organizations to maximize the value of their Pega investment.

Migrating Applications Across Environments

Migrating applications across different environments is a critical aspect of Pega Systems' deployment and maintenance strategy. Proper migration ensures that applications move seamlessly from development to testing, staging, and ultimately production, without loss of data, functionality, or performance. This chapter provides a comprehensive guide on Pega's best practices, tools, and processes for migrating applications across environments efficiently.

1. Understanding Pega's Environment Hierarchy

Pega applications typically move through several environments as they progress from development to production. Key environments include:

- **Development**: Where new features and updates are created and initial testing occurs.
- **Testing/QA**: The environment used for quality assurance, testing functionalities, and bug fixes.
- **Staging**: A pre-production environment that closely resembles the production setup, where final testing and user acceptance take place.
- **Production**: The live environment where the application is available to end users.

Migrating applications involves moving the application components, data structures, and configurations through these stages while maintaining integrity and performance.

2. Key Components of Migration

During migration, several core elements must be transferred across environments to ensure consistency:

- **Rules and Workflows**: These define the core business logic and processing flows within the application.
- **Data Instances**: Includes reference data, user roles, and permissions that the application depends on.
- **Configurations**: Settings specific to each environment, such as database connections, external integrations, and authentication details.
- **Custom Code and Integrations**: Any custom scripts, connectors, or API configurations necessary for application functionality.

Each of these components requires careful handling during migration to avoid issues like compatibility problems or incomplete functionality.

3. Tools and Techniques for Migration

Pega provides several tools and techniques to support smooth application migration across environments:

- **Product Rule**: The primary tool in Pega for packaging and migrating application components. The product rule allows you to create a package that includes specific rules, data instances, and configurations.
- **Deployment Manager**: An advanced tool that automates and manages the migration process, especially for DevOps setups with continuous integration and continuous delivery (CI/CD).
- **Application Import and Export**: Allows administrators to manually export applications from one environment and import them into another.

Best Practice:

- Use Deployment Manager for complex applications with frequent updates to maintain consistency and automate repetitive tasks.

4. Steps for Creating a Migration Package

The process of creating a migration package typically follows these steps:

1. **Define the Product Rule**: In the development environment, define a product rule that includes all necessary rules, data, and configurations.
2. **Select Components**: Carefully select the components to include, ensuring all dependencies are covered to avoid errors in the target environment.
3. **Specify Dependencies**: Add any required dependencies, including referenced rules, data classes, and custom code.
4. **Export the Package**: Once the package is defined, export it from the source environment, typically in a .ZIP format.

Best Practice:

- Test the package in a testing or staging environment before deploying to production to identify any potential issues.

5. Importing the Application in the Target Environment

After exporting the migration package, the next step is to import it into the target environment:

1. **Prepare the Target Environment**: Ensure that the target environment is configured correctly, including database connections, authentication, and necessary integrations.
2. **Import the Package**: Use the Application Import Wizard or Deployment Manager to upload and import the package into the target environment.
3. **Resolve Conflicts**: During import, Pega will detect conflicts or duplicate instances. Review and resolve these conflicts to ensure a smooth deployment.
4. **Run Validations**: Once imported, run validation tests to confirm that all components were transferred correctly and are functioning as expected.

Best Practice:

- Always maintain a backup of the target environment before importing a new application version to safeguard against potential issues.

6. Managing Environment-Specific Settings

Each environment often requires unique settings, such as database connections, API keys, and file storage configurations. To handle these variations, Pega allows for environment-specific configuration:

- **Dynamic System Settings**: Use dynamic system settings (DSS) to configure environment-specific variables, allowing these settings to be updated without modifying the application package.
- **JNDI Resource References**: Configure external resources, like databases, using Java Naming and Directory Interface (JNDI) references, which can be defined separately in each environment.

Best Practice:

- Use DSS for configurations that may change frequently across environments, providing flexibility without repackaging the application.

7. Testing the Migration Process

Testing is an essential part of the migration process to ensure that applications function as expected in the target environment. Recommended testing steps include:

- **Functional Testing**: Verify that all business rules, workflows, and integrations function as intended after migration.
- **Performance Testing**: Ensure the application performs efficiently in the target environment, especially if hardware resources differ between environments.
- **User Acceptance Testing (UAT)**: Involve end users in testing to validate that the application meets business requirements and performs reliably.

Best Practice:

- Perform testing incrementally, beginning with basic functionality and progressing to more complex scenarios, to isolate issues and address them effectively.

8. Managing Versions and Rollbacks

Pega supports version control within application migration to help track changes and manage rollbacks if necessary:

- **Versioning with Product Rules**: Track application versions by creating product rules with version numbers, making it easier to roll back to a previous version if issues arise.
- **Rollback Procedures**: Always maintain a backup of the current environment before deploying a new version. If issues arise, roll back to the previous stable version to ensure continuity.

Best Practice:

- Establish a rollback plan before deploying a migration package, especially for critical applications with high user impact.

9. Automating Migration with Pega Deployment Manager

Pega Deployment Manager simplifies and automates the migration process, making it especially useful for large applications with frequent updates. Key features of Deployment Manager include:

- **Automated Pipelines**: Set up automated pipelines for deployment, which streamline tasks like packaging, testing, and deploying applications.
- **Integrated Testing**: Integrate testing into the deployment pipeline to detect issues early.
- **Continuous Integration and Delivery (CI/CD)**: Supports CI/CD workflows, ensuring that updates move quickly and reliably through environments.

Best Practice:

- Use Deployment Manager in conjunction with version control to maintain a history of changes and ensure consistent application updates.

10. Monitoring and Troubleshooting Migration Issues

Even with careful planning, migration issues can arise. Common issues include dependency errors, missing components, and configuration conflicts. Effective troubleshooting involves:

- **Analyzing Logs**: Use Pega logs to identify errors during import or export, which may indicate missing components or conflicts.
- **Checking Dependency Warnings**: Review warnings related to dependencies to ensure all necessary components are included.
- **Validating Configurations**: Confirm that environment-specific configurations are accurate and meet the target environment's requirements.

Best Practice:

- Keep detailed records of migration processes and changes to facilitate troubleshooting and support future migrations.

Conclusion

Migrating applications across environments in Pega requires careful planning, testing, and monitoring to ensure a smooth transition. By following best practices and using tools like Product Rule, Deployment Manager, and dynamic system settings, administrators can minimize risks, maintain application stability, and ensure that updates are deployed efficiently.

Implementing Pega Deployment Manager

Pega Deployment Manager is a powerful tool designed to streamline the development and deployment process, facilitating continuous integration and delivery (CI/CD) within Pega environments. By automating the deployment pipeline, Deployment Manager enhances collaboration between development and operations teams, reducing deployment errors and speeding up the release cycle. This chapter provides a comprehensive overview of Pega Deployment Manager, its features, and a step-by-step guide for implementation.

1. Overview of Pega Deployment Manager

Deployment Manager offers a structured approach to managing application deployments, supporting DevOps practices within Pega. Key capabilities include:

- **Automated Pipelines**: Allows the setup of automated deployment pipelines for moving applications across development, staging, and production environments.
- **Continuous Integration and Delivery (CI/CD)**: Supports DevOps workflows, promoting frequent and reliable application releases.
- **Integrated Testing**: Enables automated testing at different stages of the pipeline, helping to identify issues early in the deployment process.
- **Visibility and Monitoring**: Provides real-time visibility into the deployment process, including success rates, failure points, and overall pipeline performance.

2. Key Components of Deployment Manager

Before implementing Deployment Manager, it's essential to understand its core components:

- **Pipeline**: A deployment pipeline consists of stages, tasks, and gates that define the process of moving an application from one environment to another.
- **Stages**: Each pipeline is divided into stages representing different environments, such as development, testing, staging, and production.
- **Tasks**: Within each stage, specific tasks define actions like unit testing, packaging, deployment, and validation.
- **Triggers and Gates**: Gates control the flow between stages, allowing for checks and validations, while triggers define the conditions that initiate specific tasks.

Best Practice:

- **Design pipelines to reflect your organization's release management process** by setting up appropriate stages and tasks for each phase of the application lifecycle.

3. Installing and Configuring Pega Deployment Manager

Pega Deployment Manager is available as an add-on, requiring installation and configuration before use:

1. **Install Deployment Manager**: Obtain Deployment Manager from the Pega Marketplace or directly from Pega support, and install it within your Pega environment.
2. **Configure the System**: Set up the Deployment Manager environment, ensuring the appropriate permissions, roles, and configurations are in place.
3. **Define Access and Security**: Grant access to users based on roles, typically including pipeline managers, developers, and release managers.

Best Practice:

- **Work with your DevOps and IT security teams** to ensure that Deployment Manager is configured securely and aligns with your organization's policies.

4. Setting Up a Deployment Pipeline

Once Deployment Manager is installed and configured, the next step is to create a deployment pipeline for your application:

1. **Define the Pipeline**: Start by naming the pipeline and selecting the application for which it will be used.
2. **Add Stages and Tasks**: Set up each stage, specifying the tasks that need to be completed in each environment.
3. **Configure Gates and Triggers**: Add gates to validate tasks before moving to the next stage and triggers to automate specific actions.
4. **Assign Approvers**: Designate users or teams responsible for approving stages, especially in critical environments like production.

Best Practice:

- **Use automated gates for non-critical environments** to speed up deployments, and manual approvals for high-stakes environments like production.

5. Automating Testing in Deployment Manager

Automated testing is a critical feature of Deployment Manager, ensuring that applications are thoroughly tested at each stage. Typical testing tasks include:

- **Unit Testing**: Automated unit tests verify the functionality of specific application components.
- **Functional Testing**: Validates that the application meets business requirements and functions as expected.
- **Performance Testing**: Measures application performance under load to identify potential issues.

By integrating testing within the pipeline, Deployment Manager helps detect issues early, reducing the risk of errors in production.

Best Practice:

- **Develop comprehensive test cases** for each stage of the pipeline, particularly for complex applications, to ensure stability across environments.

6. Managing Versions and Rollbacks

Deployment Manager supports version control and rollback procedures, allowing administrators to manage application versions effectively:

- **Version Control**: Each deployment is recorded as a new version, enabling administrators to track changes over time.
- **Rollback Capabilities**: If an issue arises in a new deployment, the previous stable version can be rolled back to restore functionality.

Best Practice:

- **Establish a rollback strategy** for critical applications and high-impact environments, including backups and contingency plans.

7. Monitoring and Troubleshooting the Deployment Pipeline

Deployment Manager provides real-time visibility into the deployment pipeline, allowing administrators to monitor the status and troubleshoot any issues:

- **Pipeline Dashboard**: View the current status of each pipeline, including completed, pending, and failed tasks.
- **Log Analysis**: Use Deployment Manager's log features to identify issues at specific stages, helping to diagnose and resolve problems quickly.
- **Alerts and Notifications**: Set up alerts for failed tasks or approval requests, ensuring that stakeholders are informed of critical events.

Best Practice:

- **Regularly review pipeline logs and performance metrics** to identify trends or recurring issues, optimizing the deployment process over time.

8. Best Practices for Using Deployment Manager in CI/CD

To maximize the benefits of Deployment Manager within a CI/CD framework, consider these best practices:

- **Frequent, Small Releases**: Deploy small, incremental updates to reduce the complexity of each deployment and simplify troubleshooting.
- **Automate as Much as Possible**: Automate testing, validation, and approval steps to streamline the pipeline and reduce the risk of human error.
- **Collaborate Across Teams**: Encourage collaboration between development, operations, and testing teams to ensure a seamless deployment process.

By following these practices, organizations can improve release efficiency, reduce deployment times, and enhance application reliability.

Conclusion

Pega Deployment Manager is a powerful tool for automating and managing the deployment process within a DevOps framework. By implementing Deployment Manager, organizations can achieve faster and more reliable releases, reduce deployment errors, and enhance collaboration across development and operations teams. This chapter provides the foundation for configuring, using, and optimizing Deployment Manager to support Pega applications and ensure streamlined deployment across environments.

Understanding Pega DevOps and CI/CD Pipelines

In today's fast-paced development environment, DevOps practices and Continuous Integration/Continuous Deployment (CI/CD) pipelines are critical for achieving efficient, reliable, and scalable application deployments. Within the Pega ecosystem, these practices are essential for managing frequent changes, enhancing collaboration between teams, and ensuring quick rollouts with minimal risk. This chapter delves into the principles of DevOps and CI/CD within Pega, the benefits of these practices, and how Pega's tools support them.

1. Overview of DevOps and CI/CD in Pega

DevOps is a set of practices that emphasizes collaboration between development and operations teams to automate the processes of software delivery and infrastructure changes. **CI/CD** is an essential component of DevOps, involving automated testing, integration, and deployment of applications. Together, DevOps and CI/CD aim to:

- **Increase Deployment Frequency**: Enable faster and more reliable release cycles.
- **Enhance Collaboration**: Break down silos between development and operations teams.
- **Reduce Risks**: Through automated testing and consistent integration, CI/CD reduces errors and improves the quality of deployments.
- **Automate Repetitive Tasks**: DevOps tools streamline tasks like testing, integration, and deployment, minimizing manual effort.

Pega supports these goals by providing tools like **Deployment Manager**, which integrates DevOps and CI/CD capabilities within the Pega environment, offering a cohesive framework for efficient application delivery.

2. Benefits of Implementing DevOps and CI/CD in Pega

Using DevOps and CI/CD pipelines within Pega brings several key advantages to organizations:

- **Faster Time to Market**: Automated deployments and testing processes accelerate the release cycle, enabling organizations to deliver features to end-users more quickly.
- **Improved Quality and Consistency**: Automated testing in CI/CD pipelines ensures that code quality is maintained, catching issues before they reach production.
- **Enhanced Flexibility and Scalability**: Pega's DevOps tools make it easier to scale development efforts and respond to changing business needs.
- **Greater Control and Visibility**: Real-time monitoring and reporting within the CI/CD pipeline provide visibility into the deployment status and health of applications.

3. Core Components of Pega's DevOps Toolset

Pega's DevOps ecosystem offers several tools and integrations designed to support continuous delivery, including:

- **Deployment Manager**: Automates CI/CD workflows, including packaging, testing, deployment, and monitoring.
- **Automated Unit Testing**: Allows developers to write and execute unit tests, which can be integrated into the CI/CD pipeline.
- **Version Control Integrations**: Enables integration with version control systems for managing code and change history.
- **Monitoring and Logging Tools**: Provides insights into the performance and reliability of applications throughout the pipeline.

Each of these tools plays a crucial role in implementing effective CI/CD pipelines within the Pega environment.

4. Setting Up a CI/CD Pipeline in Pega

Creating an efficient CI/CD pipeline involves setting up a series of automated stages that validate, package, and deploy applications. The general steps to configure a CI/CD pipeline in Pega are:

1. **Define the Pipeline Stages**: Establish stages that represent each phase of the application lifecycle, such as development, testing, staging, and production.
2. **Set Up Automated Tests**: Integrate unit tests and functional tests at each stage to validate code quality and functionality.
3. **Create Deployment Packages**: Automate the packaging process so that application artifacts can be easily deployed across environments.
4. **Establish Approval Gates**: For critical environments, set up approval gates that require manual verification before proceeding to production.
5. **Monitor the Pipeline**: Use Pega's monitoring tools to track the progress of each deployment, logging any errors or performance issues for quick resolution.

Best Practice:

- **Define custom stages for complex applications** to capture specific testing or validation needs, such as security checks, performance tests, or regression tests.

5. Continuous Integration in Pega

Continuous Integration (CI) is the practice of merging code changes into a shared repository frequently, allowing for automated testing to validate each change. In Pega, CI is achieved through:

- **Automated Testing**: Ensures that new code does not break existing functionality.
- **Real-Time Code Validation**: Provides immediate feedback to developers, helping to catch issues early in the development process.
- **Code Packaging**: Packages each code change into an artifact, which can then be deployed in the next stage of the pipeline.

Pega's Deployment Manager can trigger CI pipelines on a scheduled basis or upon specific actions, like code check-ins, ensuring that all code passes through automated checks before progressing.

6. Continuous Deployment and Delivery in Pega

Continuous Deployment (CD) is the practice of automatically deploying every change that passes automated tests into production, while **Continuous Delivery** involves staging approved changes for manual review before final deployment. In Pega, CD processes are set up as follows:

- **Automated Staging and Production Deployments**: Pega Deployment Manager supports automated deployment into staging and production environments.
- **Approval Workflows**: For mission-critical systems, approval workflows can be added as manual gates before deployment to production.
- **Rollback Mechanisms**: In case of errors, deployment manager allows rolling back to the previous stable version, reducing downtime.

Best Practice:

- **Use continuous deployment for low-risk environments** while enabling continuous delivery with approvals for critical environments to maintain control over the final release.

7. Monitoring and Managing the DevOps Pipeline

Monitoring is essential to ensure the CI/CD pipeline is running smoothly. Pega's monitoring capabilities include:

- **Pipeline Status Dashboard**: Provides a real-time view of the status of each pipeline, including ongoing tasks, successful deployments, and failed jobs.
- **Automated Alerts**: Notifications for failed tasks or issues enable immediate responses, minimizing delays.
- **Performance Metrics and Logs**: Detailed logs and performance metrics allow teams to diagnose issues quickly and optimize the pipeline over time.

Best Practice:

- **Regularly review and optimize pipeline metrics** to identify bottlenecks and improve deployment times.

8. Implementing Security and Compliance in CI/CD Pipelines

Security is paramount when deploying applications in production environments. Pega's DevOps tools support secure CI/CD processes through:

- **Role-Based Access Control (RBAC)**: Assigns permissions to users based on roles, ensuring only authorized personnel can modify or deploy applications.
- **Compliance Checks**: Integration of compliance checks in the pipeline to validate that all releases meet regulatory requirements.
- **Secure Artifact Storage**: Ensures deployment artifacts are securely stored and accessible only by authorized users.

Best Practice:

- **Integrate security testing tools** into the pipeline to identify vulnerabilities early, ensuring that only secure code is deployed.

9. Integrating Pega DevOps with Third-Party Tools

Pega DevOps integrates seamlessly with third-party DevOps tools, such as:

- **Jenkins**: For automated build and deployment workflows.
- **GitHub/GitLab**: For source code management and version control.
- **Splunk**: For enhanced monitoring and log analysis.

These integrations extend Pega's DevOps capabilities, allowing organizations to tailor the CI/CD pipeline to their specific workflows and technology stack.

Conclusion

Implementing DevOps and CI/CD pipelines within Pega enhances deployment efficiency, quality, and reliability. By leveraging Pega's Deployment Manager and related tools, organizations can achieve faster time to market, improved collaboration, and higher application quality.

Handling User Access and Permissions

Efficient and secure user access management is a cornerstone of any robust Pega implementation. Handling user access and permissions ensures that users have the appropriate level of access required to perform their tasks while maintaining the security and integrity of the application. This chapter explores Pega's tools and best practices for configuring and managing user access and permissions, from setting up roles to implementing role-based access control policies.

1. Importance of Access Control in Pega

Pega applications often deal with sensitive data and processes that require restricted access. Effective access control is essential to:

- **Protect Sensitive Information**: Restrict access to data based on user roles and responsibilities.
- **Maintain Data Integrity**: Ensure only authorized users can modify or interact with specific workflows or cases.
- **Compliance**: Meet industry-specific regulatory requirements by enforcing access policies.
- **Prevent Unauthorized Access**: Reduce the risk of internal and external security threats by managing permissions effectively.

2. Understanding Roles and Permissions in Pega

In Pega, access control is managed through **roles and permissions**:

- **Roles**: Define a user's access scope and determine which actions they can perform. Roles are usually assigned based on job functions.
- **Permissions**: Represent specific rights that a user has within the application, such as viewing or editing cases or accessing certain tools.

Access control in Pega relies on combining roles and permissions to enforce security policies and define user access accurately.

3. Configuring Access Groups

An **Access Group** in Pega specifies the roles, portals, and application versions a user can access. Access Groups are essential for managing user experiences and security:

- **Setting Up Access Groups**: Configure access groups based on user responsibilities and job roles. Each access group includes:
  - **Associated Roles**: Defines what the user can do.
  - **Default Portal**: Specifies the user interface presented to users in the group.
  - **Application Version**: Links users to a specific version of the application.

Best Practice:

- **Use descriptive names for Access Groups** to quickly identify their purpose, such as "Claims_Manager" or "Customer_Support_Rep."

4. Assigning Roles and Privileges

Roles in Pega grant access to specific actions and data within the application. When creating or assigning roles:

- **Define Role-Based Permissions**: Each role should include permissions tailored to specific functions, limiting actions based on job requirements.

- **Utilize Out-of-the-Box Roles**: Pega provides predefined roles that can be customized based on application needs. These roles include basic user and administrator roles.
- **Custom Roles for Special Use Cases**: When necessary, create custom roles for unique access needs, ensuring that they align with organizational security policies.

5. Leveraging Role-Based Access Control (RBAC)

Role-Based Access Control (RBAC) is a security model that assigns permissions based on user roles:

- **Creating an RBAC Framework**: Define user roles, permissions, and data access controls within Pega, mapping each role to specific permissions.
- **Assigning Users to Roles**: Assign each user to one or more roles based on their responsibilities, ensuring that permissions are restricted to what's necessary.
- **Defining Privileges**: Fine-tune permissions by associating privileges with certain activities or data classes, enhancing the flexibility of RBAC.

RBAC not only simplifies access management but also strengthens security by minimizing the number of individuals with elevated access.

6. Managing Access Control for Work Objects

Work objects are the core of any case management process in Pega. Access control for work objects determines who can create, view, edit, or resolve cases:

- **Configuring Access Control Policies for Cases**: Define which roles have permission to interact with work objects at various stages.
- **Setting Conditional Access Rules**: Use conditions to allow or restrict actions on cases based on the user's role or the case status.
- **Audit and Logging**: Enable logging for actions on sensitive work objects to maintain accountability and transparency.

Best Practice:

- **Implement role-based controls for high-risk actions** (e.g., case approval or data modification) to ensure only authorized users can perform these actions.

7. Customizing Access to Data Classes

In Pega, **Data Classes** store information relevant to cases, such as customer or product details. Managing access to data classes is critical to safeguarding sensitive information:

- **Defining Data Access Policies**: Set access policies to control read and write permissions for specific data classes.
- **Field-Level Access Control**: Restrict access to specific fields within data classes, especially for sensitive information like personal or financial data.
- **Setting Visibility Conditions**: Use visibility conditions to dynamically show or hide data fields based on the user's role.

Field-level access control is particularly beneficial in scenarios where certain data is restricted based on regulatory requirements.

8. Managing Access Through Authentication Mechanisms

Pega supports various authentication mechanisms to validate users before granting access:

- **Single Sign-On (SSO)**: Integrate Pega with SSO solutions to simplify login processes and enforce consistent access policies across platforms.

- **LDAP Integration**: Use LDAP directories for centralized user management, reducing the need for multiple accounts.
- **Multi-Factor Authentication (MFA)**: Add an extra layer of security for sensitive applications by requiring users to provide additional verification during login.

Best Practice:

- **Implement MFA for roles with elevated privileges** to add an extra layer of security against unauthorized access.

9. Auditing User Access and Activity

Auditing is an essential component of access management that enables administrators to track and monitor user activity:

- **Enable Access Logs**: Log access and activity data to track who is accessing the system, which actions they are performing, and when.
- **Generate Audit Reports**: Use Pega's reporting capabilities to create audit reports that summarize access patterns and highlight potential security concerns.
- **Monitor for Anomalies**: Regularly review audit logs and reports for any unusual patterns, such as failed login attempts or unauthorized data access.

Audit logs are invaluable for both security monitoring and compliance, providing a record of user actions for future reference.

10. Best Practices for Managing User Access and Permissions

To optimize user access management in Pega, consider the following best practices:

- **Principle of Least Privilege**: Grant users only the permissions they need to perform their tasks, reducing the risk of accidental or malicious actions.
- **Regularly Review Access Levels**: Periodically review roles and permissions to ensure they are still aligned with users' responsibilities.
- **Automate Role Assignments**: Use Pega's automation tools to manage role assignments dynamically based on changes in users' roles or responsibilities.
- **Implement Access Change Notifications**: Notify administrators when access levels are modified for critical roles or permissions to maintain transparency and oversight.

Following these practices can help prevent over-provisioning, improve compliance, and streamline the access management process.

Conclusion

Managing user access and permissions in Pega is essential for maintaining security, protecting sensitive data, and ensuring compliance. By leveraging Access Groups, RBAC, and authentication mechanisms, administrators can create a secure, role-based access control framework that aligns with organizational policies and regulations.

Section 10:
Case Studies and Real-World Applications

Successful Implementation Examples in Banking

Pega's application in the banking industry has been transformative, enabling institutions to automate processes, enhance customer experiences, and streamline regulatory compliance. This chapter provides real-world examples of successful Pega implementations in banking, illustrating how Pega's Business Process Management (BPM) and Case Management tools have contributed to increased efficiency and improved customer service in the financial sector.

1. Introduction to Pega in Banking

Banking is one of the most highly regulated industries, and it requires a blend of customer-centric and compliance-focused solutions. Pega's BPM software offers dynamic capabilities that align with these needs, empowering banks to:

- **Automate complex workflows** such as loan processing, fraud detection, and compliance checks.
- **Enhance customer interactions** by providing seamless, personalized service across multiple channels.
- **Ensure regulatory compliance** by automating risk management and reporting processes.

By leveraging Pega, banks have achieved operational improvements, cost savings, and enhanced customer satisfaction. Below are case studies illustrating Pega's successful deployment across various banking processes.

2. Case Study: Streamlining Loan Processing

Background: A large multinational bank faced challenges in managing its loan application process, which involved multiple departments, manual approvals, and significant paperwork. The bank needed a solution to reduce processing time and minimize human error.

Solution:

- **Pega's Case Management** framework was implemented to automate and streamline the loan application workflow.
- Pega's **Decision Rules** and **Business Rules Engine** (BRE) were configured to handle eligibility checks, credit assessments, and risk profiling.
- An **integration with third-party credit agencies** provided automated credit score retrievals.

Results:

- Loan processing time was reduced by **40%**, enabling quicker approvals and improved customer satisfaction.
- Error rates dropped due to the automated validation steps built into Pega's workflow.
- The bank experienced a **20% reduction in operational costs** attributed to decreased manual intervention and paperwork.

3. Case Study: Enhancing Customer Onboarding

Background: A regional bank wanted to improve its onboarding process for new customers, which previously required in-person visits and multiple forms. The objective was to digitize the onboarding journey, making it accessible and straightforward for customers.

Solution:

- Pega's **Digital Process Automation** tools were utilized to digitize the onboarding steps.
- A **self-service portal** was built on Pega, allowing customers to upload documents, verify identities, and complete forms online.
- Pega's **Real-Time Decisioning** enabled tailored offers and recommendations based on customer data collected during onboarding.

Results:

- The onboarding process time was reduced by **60%**, providing customers with a seamless experience.
- Customer engagement and conversion rates increased by **25%** due to the personalized onboarding experience.
- The bank reported higher satisfaction rates, with many customers appreciating the digital-first approach.

4. Case Study: Automating Compliance and Regulatory Reporting

Background: A major European bank needed a solution to manage the regulatory requirements introduced by GDPR and other international data privacy laws. Compliance was becoming time-consuming and expensive due to frequent regulatory changes.

Solution:

- **Pega's Compliance and Regulatory Reporting Module** was implemented to automate data privacy management and reporting.
- **Workflow automation** allowed the bank to track, record, and manage customer data requests (e.g., access or deletion requests) efficiently.
- Regular updates to Pega's rules and policies ensured that the bank stayed compliant with evolving regulations.

Results:

- Compliance task times were reduced by **50%**, freeing resources for other activities.
- Audit accuracy improved significantly due to the **automated data logging** and tracking capabilities.
- The bank reported increased regulatory satisfaction, reducing the risk of penalties and fines.

5. Case Study: Improving Fraud Detection and Prevention

Background: With rising fraud cases, a global bank wanted to bolster its fraud detection mechanisms, particularly around credit card transactions. Traditional detection methods were slow, leading to delayed fraud alerts and poor customer experiences.

Solution:

- **Pega's AI-driven Fraud Detection System** was introduced to monitor and flag suspicious transactions in real-time.
- Using **predictive analytics and machine learning**, the bank was able to profile transactions and identify potential fraud patterns.
- Integration with external data sources allowed Pega to cross-check flagged transactions with known fraud databases.

Results:

- Fraud detection speed increased by **80%**, enabling the bank to notify customers instantly and reduce fraudulent transactions.
- Customer trust and loyalty improved due to the enhanced security and rapid response times.
- The bank reported a **significant reduction in financial losses** attributed to fraud, validating the system's ROI.

6. Case Study: Optimizing Customer Service with Unified Case Management

Background: A prominent bank was experiencing customer service challenges due to disconnected systems across various channels (e.g., phone, online, in-branch). Customer inquiries often required multiple transfers, leading to dissatisfaction.

Solution:

- **Pega's Unified Case Management System** was implemented to provide a centralized platform for managing customer interactions across channels.
- The system offered a **360-degree view of customer profiles and histories**, allowing representatives to resolve inquiries more efficiently.
- Pega's **Dynamic Workflow Assignment** allowed cases to be routed to the most qualified agents based on the type of inquiry.

Results:

- First-call resolution rates increased by **30%**, as agents had full visibility into each customer's history and needs.
- Customer satisfaction scores improved, with customers reporting faster and more consistent service.
- The bank reduced costs associated with escalations and transfers by **20%**.

7. Lessons Learned from Banking Implementations

The following key lessons emerged from these Pega implementations in banking:

- **Automate and Optimize**: Automation of repetitive and compliance-heavy processes is essential in the banking industry. It reduces costs, minimizes errors, and improves response times.
- **Focus on the Customer Journey**: Pega's flexible platform allows banks to create customer-centric solutions, improving engagement and satisfaction.
- **Leverage Real-Time Analytics**: The integration of predictive analytics and machine learning enhances decision-making and risk management.
- **Ensure Agility and Compliance**: Pega's ability to adapt to regulatory changes without significant overhauls allows banks to stay compliant with less disruption.
- **Centralized Case Management**: A unified system for managing customer interactions streamlines service delivery and enhances the overall customer experience.

Conclusion

These case studies demonstrate the value of Pega's solutions in transforming banking operations. From fraud detection to regulatory compliance, Pega provides a versatile, scalable platform that addresses critical banking challenges while delivering measurable business benefits. Through these examples, it's evident that Pega's technology plays a crucial role in the modernization and digital transformation of banking, ultimately driving improved customer satisfaction, operational efficiency, and profitability.

Case Study: Pega for Healthcare Operations

Healthcare is an industry marked by complex workflows, stringent regulations, and the need for precise, patient-centered service delivery. Pega's platform has proven invaluable in healthcare, offering solutions that streamline administrative processes, improve patient engagement, and ensure compliance with regulatory requirements. This chapter provides an in-depth case study illustrating how Pega's Business Process Management (BPM) and Case Management capabilities can transform healthcare operations.

1. The Role of Pega in Healthcare

Healthcare organizations face numerous challenges, including:

- **Coordination of care** across departments and systems.
- **Compliance with healthcare regulations** such as HIPAA (Health Insurance Portability and Accountability Act).
- **Enhancing patient experience** through timely and personalized care.
- **Reducing operational costs** while maintaining high standards of service delivery.

Pega offers a unified platform that enables healthcare providers to automate, streamline, and optimize processes across the organization, providing a centralized view of patient data, workflows, and regulatory compliance.

2. Case Study: Improving Patient Enrollment and Eligibility Verification

Background: A large healthcare provider struggled with a manual, time-consuming patient enrollment and eligibility verification process. This delay led to longer wait times and frustration for patients, impacting overall satisfaction.

Solution:

- **Pega's Case Management** was used to automate the enrollment and eligibility verification process. Each patient's enrollment case was dynamically routed based on data inputs and requirements.
- Integration with external insurance databases and governmental systems enabled **real-time eligibility checks** for patients.
- Pega's **Business Rules Engine (BRE)** was configured to handle conditional checks, ensuring that eligibility and documentation were thoroughly verified.

Results:

- The enrollment process time was reduced by **70%**, significantly improving patient onboarding.
- Patient satisfaction scores improved as wait times for eligibility verification decreased.
- The healthcare provider achieved **20% cost savings** in administrative operations.

3. Case Study: Streamlining Claims Processing

Background: A healthcare insurer was experiencing inefficiencies in its claims processing system. Manual processing led to errors, extended processing times, and delayed reimbursements, affecting both patients and providers.

Solution:

- **Pega's Claims Management Solution** was deployed to automate the claims workflow, from submission to adjudication.
- **Predictive analytics** and **decision rules** were applied to evaluate claims, ensuring accurate and compliant processing.

- Claims were automatically prioritized and routed based on urgency and type, expediting high-priority cases.

Results:

- Claims processing time was reduced by **40%**, resulting in faster reimbursement for providers and patients.
- Error rates dropped due to automation, resulting in fewer claims being rejected or returned for correction.
- The organization experienced increased provider and patient satisfaction and reported a **15% reduction in claims-related costs**.

4. Case Study: Enhancing Patient Engagement through Personalized Communication

Background: A regional healthcare network aimed to improve patient engagement, focusing on preventive care reminders and appointment scheduling. The goal was to increase patient compliance with follow-up care and screenings.

Solution:

- Pega's **Customer Decision Hub** was implemented to deliver personalized communication based on each patient's medical history, preferences, and engagement patterns.
- **Automated reminders** for appointments, follow-up care, and preventive screenings were set up through Pega's workflow automation.
- Patient communication was tailored to individual needs, with multilingual and multichannel options to reach diverse patient demographics.

Results:

- Patient follow-up compliance increased by **25%**, with more patients attending scheduled appointments and screenings.
- The healthcare network experienced a **10% reduction in no-show rates**, contributing to improved resource utilization.
- Patients reported higher satisfaction due to personalized and timely communication, fostering a sense of proactive, patient-centered care.

5. Case Study: Ensuring Regulatory Compliance and Data Security

Background: Compliance with regulations like HIPAA is critical for healthcare providers. A large hospital system needed a solution to automate compliance checks and ensure data security across its digital workflows.

Solution:

- **Pega's Compliance Framework** was used to design workflows that enforced HIPAA-compliant data handling and storage practices.
- **Audit trails** were built into Pega's system to automatically track access, modifications, and transmission of sensitive patient data.
- Pega's **security features** were configured to include role-based access control, ensuring only authorized personnel could access specific data.

Results:

- The hospital system achieved **full HIPAA compliance**, with real-time monitoring for policy adherence.
- Data breaches and unauthorized access incidents were minimized, enhancing patient trust and institutional credibility.

- The automated compliance features reduced the administrative burden, allowing staff to focus more on patient care.

6. Case Study: Optimizing Staff Scheduling and Resource Allocation

Background: A healthcare provider faced challenges in efficiently managing staff schedules and resource allocation, leading to staff shortages and resource wastage.

Solution:

- Pega's **Workforce Management** tools were deployed to automate scheduling and shift management based on patient demand, staff availability, and skill sets.
- **Predictive analytics** were used to forecast patient volumes and staffing needs, optimizing resource allocation.
- Real-time dashboards allowed managers to make data-driven adjustments to scheduling, reducing overstaffing or understaffing situations.

Results:

- Staff scheduling efficiency improved by **35%**, reducing overtime and improving employee morale.
- Patient wait times were shortened due to better alignment of staff availability with demand.
- The healthcare provider saw a **15% reduction in labor costs** by eliminating inefficiencies in resource allocation.

7. Lessons Learned from Healthcare Implementations

Key takeaways from these case studies illustrate best practices and valuable insights for healthcare organizations using Pega:

- **Automate Repetitive and Time-Consuming Tasks**: By automating processes such as claims processing, patient enrollment, and compliance tracking, healthcare providers can achieve greater accuracy, reduce processing time, and cut costs.
- **Enhance Patient Engagement**: Personalized, timely communication improves patient satisfaction and compliance, positively impacting health outcomes and fostering stronger patient-provider relationships.
- **Ensure Robust Compliance and Security**: Leveraging Pega's compliance and security features enables healthcare providers to meet regulatory requirements, protecting patient data and maintaining trust.
- **Utilize Predictive Analytics for Resource Optimization**: By forecasting patient demand and staffing needs, healthcare providers can enhance resource utilization, reduce costs, and ensure adequate staffing levels.

Conclusion

Pega's role in healthcare goes beyond simple process automation; it serves as a powerful tool for improving patient care, ensuring compliance, and optimizing operations. These case studies highlight the versatility and impact of Pega's BPM and Case Management capabilities within the healthcare industry, demonstrating tangible benefits such as improved patient experiences, faster claims processing, streamlined compliance, and optimized workforce management. Through these real-world examples, it's clear that Pega provides the tools necessary for healthcare organizations to navigate their complex landscape while delivering high-quality care efficiently. The healthcare sector's unique needs and challenges align well with Pega's robust and adaptable solutions, making it a critical ally in achieving sustainable, patient-focused growth.

Automating Supply Chain Processes with Pega

The supply chain is a complex web of operations, demanding efficiency, flexibility, and visibility across all stages. Pega's powerful Business Process Management (BPM) and Case Management capabilities are instrumental in transforming supply chain management (SCM), helping organizations achieve streamlined workflows, enhanced visibility, and improved responsiveness to market demands. This chapter delves into how Pega can be used to automate and optimize various supply chain functions, with real-world examples demonstrating the impact of Pega in supply chain automation.

1. The Role of Automation in Supply Chain Management

Supply chain management involves multiple stages, from procurement and inventory management to distribution and customer fulfillment. The challenges often faced include:

- **Operational inefficiencies** due to manual processes and outdated systems.
- **Lack of visibility** into inventory and shipping stages, leading to stock-outs or overstock situations.
- **Communication delays** across stakeholders and departments, affecting the flow of goods.
- **High operational costs** due to inefficient logistics and resource management.

Pega's supply chain automation solutions provide end-to-end process visibility, integration, and automation, allowing organizations to manage complex supply chain functions with precision.

2. Case Study: Streamlining Procurement and Supplier Management

Background: A large manufacturing company faced challenges with its procurement process, which relied heavily on manual supplier communication and lacked efficient tracking for order approvals and updates. This led to delayed shipments, higher costs, and inconsistent supply availability.

Solution:

- **Pega Case Management** was employed to automate the procurement process, including request initiation, supplier selection, order placement, and shipment tracking.
- **Automated approvals** for purchase orders were set up, routing requests to the appropriate departments for swift action.
- Pega's **Supplier Management Module** provided a centralized dashboard for managing supplier interactions and contract adherence.

Results:

- The procurement cycle time was reduced by **50%**, enabling faster response to market demands.
- Supplier interactions became more transparent, with real-time updates available on order statuses.
- The organization reported a **15% reduction in procurement costs** due to better supplier relationship management and optimized order quantities.

3. Case Study: Inventory Optimization with Real-Time Visibility

Background: A retail company struggled with inventory inconsistencies, which often led to stockouts or excess inventory. Manual tracking across multiple warehouses and lack of real-time data visibility hampered their ability to meet demand efficiently.

Solution:

- Pega's **Inventory Management** capabilities were implemented to centralize inventory data, offering real-time visibility across warehouses and store locations.
- **Predictive analytics** were used to forecast demand based on seasonal patterns and sales history, aligning stock levels with projected requirements.

- Automated notifications and alerts were set up to prevent stockouts or overstock situations.

Results:

- Stock availability improved by **20%**, reducing the risk of lost sales due to out-of-stock items.
- Inventory holding costs decreased by **10%** through optimized stock levels and efficient warehouse management.
- Customer satisfaction improved as products were consistently available to meet demand.

4. Case Study: Enhancing Order Fulfillment and Shipping Efficiency

Background: A global logistics provider needed to streamline its order fulfillment and shipping operations. Manual processes and disjointed systems led to frequent delays, inaccurate order tracking, and customer dissatisfaction.

Solution:

- **Pega's Order Fulfillment Automation** was deployed to manage the entire order lifecycle, from order capture to delivery confirmation.
- Integration with third-party logistics providers enabled **real-time tracking** of shipments, providing customers with accurate updates.
- **Automated routing and dispatching** optimized shipment paths and reduced delivery time, particularly for high-priority orders.

Results:

- Order processing time was reduced by **40%**, allowing the company to fulfill more orders within shorter timeframes.
- Shipment errors were minimized, with accurate tracking information and order verification at each stage.
- The company achieved a **15% cost reduction** in logistics through optimized route planning and reduced dependency on manual tracking.

5. Case Study: Managing Returns and Reverse Logistics

Background: A consumer electronics retailer faced challenges with its return management, often resulting in delayed refunds and customer dissatisfaction. The lack of a streamlined process for handling returns and repairs led to operational inefficiencies and higher costs.

Solution:

- Pega's **Returns and Reverse Logistics** solution automated the return process, providing customers with a seamless experience from initiating a return to receiving a refund or replacement.
- **Case Management** enabled efficient tracking and routing of returns, with real-time status updates available to both customers and support teams.
- **Business Rules** were set up to classify returns based on criteria such as warranty status, product condition, and return reason, allowing quicker decision-making for refunds or repairs.

Results:

- The return processing time decreased by **60%**, leading to quicker resolutions and higher customer satisfaction.
- The cost of handling returns was reduced due to automation, freeing up resources to focus on more complex cases.
- The retailer reported a **25% increase in customer loyalty** due to improved return experience and reduced hassle for customers.

6. Case Study: Optimizing Demand Planning and Forecasting

Background: A large distribution company faced difficulties in aligning supply with demand, resulting in frequent stockouts or excess inventory. The absence of a predictive tool for demand planning often led to misaligned stock levels.

Solution:

- **Pega's Demand Forecasting** tools were implemented, allowing the company to use historical data, market trends, and seasonality to predict demand accurately.
- Automated alerts and adjustments helped the company adapt quickly to demand fluctuations, such as promotional periods or seasonal spikes.
- **Integration with sales and marketing data** allowed the company to refine forecasts and align supply chain activities with market demand.

Results:

- Demand forecast accuracy improved by **30%**, resulting in more balanced inventory levels and reduced waste.
- The organization reported a **20% reduction in stockout incidents**, improving customer satisfaction by ensuring product availability.
- Operational costs decreased as the company optimized resources based on anticipated demand.

7. Lessons Learned from Pega's Supply Chain Implementations

Pega's solutions for supply chain automation provide valuable insights and best practices for companies aiming to enhance their supply chain efficiency:

- **Automate Core Processes for Speed and Accuracy**: Automation minimizes delays and reduces human errors, enabling faster and more reliable supply chain operations.
- **Enhance Visibility for Better Decision-Making**: Real-time data visibility helps organizations make informed decisions, improving responsiveness to market dynamics.
- **Leverage Predictive Analytics for Demand Planning**: Forecasting and demand planning allow companies to align supply with demand, reducing costs associated with overstocking or stockouts.
- **Integrate with External Systems**: Seamless integration with external suppliers, logistics providers, and customers improves overall supply chain efficiency and transparency.
- **Customer-Centric Approach**: By automating order fulfillment, return management, and communication, organizations can enhance customer satisfaction, leading to higher retention rates.

Conclusion

The application of Pega in supply chain management is transformative, offering companies the tools to automate complex workflows, achieve operational efficiency, and enhance customer satisfaction. Through these real-world examples, we observe that Pega's platform provides a comprehensive approach to addressing the diverse needs of modern supply chains. Whether it's streamlining procurement, optimizing inventory, or enhancing order fulfillment, Pega enables organizations to stay agile and responsive in a competitive market.

Leveraging Pega for Customer Service Excellence

In today's competitive marketplace, delivering outstanding customer service is a top priority for businesses seeking to retain and grow their customer base. Pega's Customer Service application offers a comprehensive suite of tools and capabilities designed to streamline service processes, personalize interactions, and resolve customer issues efficiently. This chapter explores how Pega's platform transforms customer service operations, with examples from real-world implementations illustrating the benefits of Pega's capabilities in improving service quality and customer satisfaction.

1. The Importance of Customer Service in Modern Enterprises

Customer service has evolved from being a reactive support function to a proactive strategic asset. Key goals for customer service teams today include:

- **Reducing response times** to improve customer satisfaction.
- **Personalizing interactions** to build stronger customer relationships.
- **Automating common inquiries** to allow agents to focus on complex issues.
- **Improving first-contact resolution rates** to enhance service efficiency.

Pega's platform is designed to meet these needs by providing a unified approach to customer service that leverages automation, artificial intelligence (AI), and case management.

2. Core Capabilities of Pega's Customer Service Application

Pega's Customer Service application equips organizations with several features to enhance service excellence:

- **Intelligent Case Management**: Automates the end-to-end handling of customer inquiries, including categorization, prioritization, and resolution.
- **Next-Best-Action**: Provides recommendations for the most appropriate action based on real-time customer data, improving the personalization of interactions.
- **Unified Desktop**: Offers a single, consolidated interface for agents to access customer information, enabling quick responses.
- **Self-Service Options**: Enables customers to resolve issues independently through a self-service portal, reducing agent workload.
- **Omnichannel Support**: Integrates multiple communication channels, such as chat, email, phone, and social media, allowing seamless switching for customers.

3. Case Study: Improving Customer Resolution Time

Background: A large telecommunications provider struggled with lengthy call resolution times due to inefficient workflows and a fragmented agent interface. Customer satisfaction scores were declining as customers faced long wait times and inconsistent service experiences.

Solution:

- **Unified Desktop Integration**: Pega's unified desktop provided agents with a single interface for all customer data, reducing the time spent switching between applications.
- **Automated Inquiry Routing**: Pega's intelligent case management categorized and prioritized cases, routing them to the most appropriate agent based on expertise and availability.
- **Guided Interactions**: With Pega's Next-Best-Action recommendations, agents received contextual guidance during interactions, helping them resolve issues faster and with greater accuracy.

Results:

- The company reduced its average call handling time by **35%**, leading to a noticeable increase in customer satisfaction.
- Customer satisfaction scores improved by **20%**, with feedback highlighting the quicker and more effective service experience.
- Agent productivity increased as they spent less time navigating systems and more time focused on customer needs.

4. Case Study: Enhancing Self-Service for a Financial Services Firm

Background: A financial services organization received a high volume of routine inquiries, such as balance checks and transaction updates. These inquiries consumed significant agent time and prevented them from focusing on complex customer issues.

Solution:

- **Self-Service Portal**: Pega implemented a self-service portal where customers could access real-time account information, conduct routine transactions, and find answers to frequently asked questions.
- **Intelligent Chatbots**: Pega's AI-driven chatbot handled inquiries through the self-service portal, allowing customers to resolve issues without agent involvement.
- **Case Escalation Management**: If a customer's inquiry required agent intervention, the case was automatically escalated and routed to the right team, ensuring timely assistance.

Results:

- The self-service portal reduced call volume by **40%**, freeing agents to focus on more complex inquiries.
- Customers rated the self-service experience highly, with **85% of users** successfully resolving their issues without agent assistance.
- The organization reduced operational costs by minimizing the need for live agents to handle repetitive tasks.

5. Case Study: Driving Proactive Customer Engagement for a Retail Chain

Background: A retail company wanted to engage with its customers proactively to reduce churn and drive loyalty. The company's previous approach relied on generic marketing campaigns, which lacked personalization and did not effectively engage customers.

Solution:

- **Customer Data Insights**: Pega's analytics engine provided insights into customer behaviors, allowing the company to segment its customer base and tailor engagement strategies accordingly.
- **Proactive Next-Best-Action**: Leveraging Pega's Next-Best-Action feature, the company engaged customers with personalized offers, support messages, and reminders based on their purchase history and preferences.
- **Omnichannel Outreach**: Pega enabled seamless communication across channels, ensuring customers received relevant messages through their preferred medium, whether email, SMS, or in-app notifications.

Results:

- The personalized outreach efforts reduced customer churn by **15%**, as customers felt valued and engaged.
- Customer loyalty improved, with **30% more repeat purchases** among those who received personalized offers.

- The company observed a **25% increase in cross-sell and upsell opportunities**, enhancing revenue from existing customers.

6. Case Study: Streamlining Customer Onboarding in Banking

Background: A banking institution faced challenges with its customer onboarding process. The lengthy and complex procedure often led to delays, resulting in customer frustration and, at times, lost business opportunities.

Solution:

- **Automated Document Verification**: Pega automated the document verification process, reducing manual intervention and accelerating approval times.
- **Guided Onboarding Workflow**: Pega's guided workflow provided new customers with step-by-step assistance, simplifying the onboarding experience.
- **Real-Time Status Updates**: Customers received real-time updates on the progress of their onboarding application, reducing uncertainty and enhancing transparency.

Results:

- The average onboarding time was reduced by **50%**, allowing the bank to serve new customers faster and more efficiently.
- Customer satisfaction with the onboarding process improved significantly, with positive feedback emphasizing the speed and clarity of the experience.
- The bank reported a **10% increase in new account sign-ups**, attributed to the streamlined onboarding experience.

7. Best Practices for Achieving Customer Service Excellence with Pega

Through the above examples, key best practices emerge for leveraging Pega to drive customer service excellence:

- **Empower Customers through Self-Service**: Enabling self-service options, such as portals and chatbots, reduces agent workload and empowers customers to resolve routine issues independently.
- **Optimize Agent Workflows**: Pega's unified desktop and case management capabilities streamline workflows, allowing agents to focus on high-impact tasks.
- **Leverage AI for Personalization**: Pega's AI-driven Next-Best-Action recommendations enable personalized interactions, improving customer satisfaction and loyalty.
- **Ensure Omnichannel Support**: Providing seamless support across multiple channels allows customers to connect in their preferred way, enhancing their overall experience.
- **Adopt a Proactive Approach**: Use predictive insights to engage customers proactively, offering support or promotions before they need to reach out.

Conclusion

Pega's Customer Service application empowers organizations to elevate their service quality, meeting the modern demands of speed, personalization, and efficiency. By automating routine tasks, providing proactive support, and enabling self-service, businesses can transform their customer service operations from reactive to customer-centric.

Through these real-world examples, we see how Pega enables organizations to achieve customer service excellence, whether by reducing handling times, empowering self-service, or enhancing engagement. Adopting Pega's comprehensive customer service solutions can be a game-changer, helping businesses foster loyal customers and drive long-term success.

Pega's Role in Telecom Process Automation

In the telecommunications industry, where customer demand, operational efficiency, and service innovation drive competition, automation has become essential. Telecom companies face complex challenges, such as high volumes of customer requests, extensive service offerings, and frequent regulatory updates. Pega's Business Process Management (BPM) capabilities offer a comprehensive solution for automating workflows, enhancing customer service, and maintaining agility in a rapidly evolving sector.

This chapter explores how telecom companies can leverage Pega to streamline operations, from customer support to network management and compliance, using real-world applications that illustrate the platform's role in transforming telecom processes.

1. The Need for Automation in Telecom

The telecom industry operates in a high-demand environment where managing customer interactions, service activations, billing, and network maintenance must occur seamlessly. Common challenges include:

- **High Customer Volume**: Telecom companies manage large-scale customer interactions daily, requiring efficient processing of requests and issues.
- **Regulatory Compliance**: Frequent regulatory changes necessitate continuous adaptation and adherence.
- **Complex Service Offerings**: Telecom companies offer multiple services—mobile, internet, cable, and data solutions—adding complexity to their operations.
- **Data-Driven Decision Making**: Leveraging large volumes of data is crucial for understanding customer behavior, predicting demand, and optimizing network performance.

Pega's automation tools offer telecom companies a way to streamline these processes, reduce operational costs, and enhance customer experience by automating routine tasks and improving data management.

2. Key Capabilities of Pega for Telecom Automation

Pega's platform provides several critical functionalities that empower telecom companies to address industry-specific needs:

- **Case Management**: Manages end-to-end customer cases, automating the flow from initial request to resolution.
- **Robotic Process Automation (RPA)**: Automates repetitive, manual tasks within telecom operations, such as data entry and system updates.
- **AI-Driven Decisioning**: Utilizes predictive analytics to drive customer interactions, offering personalized responses and proactive solutions.
- **Omnichannel Support**: Ensures consistent customer support across channels, such as phone, chat, email, and social media.
- **Real-Time Analytics and Reporting**: Enables telecom companies to monitor performance, identify issues, and make data-driven decisions.

3. Case Study: Automating Customer Onboarding and Activation

Background: A major telecom provider faced delays in customer onboarding and service activation, impacting customer satisfaction and resulting in churn. Manual data entry, fragmented systems, and complex workflows contributed to delays and errors.

Solution:

- **Workflow Automation**: Pega's case management automated the onboarding process, integrating it with customer databases, billing, and service activation systems.
- **Real-Time Customer Communication**: Pega enabled the telecom provider to keep customers informed about the status of their service activation through automated notifications.
- **Error Reduction**: RPA bots were deployed to handle data entry, reducing errors and speeding up processing times.

Results:

- **Reduction in Activation Time**: Average activation time was reduced by **40%**, enabling quicker customer service initiation.
- **Enhanced Customer Satisfaction**: Customer feedback indicated higher satisfaction due to faster service activation and real-time updates.
- **Cost Savings**: By reducing manual errors and improving efficiency, the company decreased operational costs by **30%**.

4. Case Study: Proactive Customer Support with AI

Background: Another telecom provider wanted to improve customer retention by identifying and addressing service issues before they led to customer complaints. The company needed a proactive approach to monitoring service quality and predicting potential problems.

Solution:

- **Predictive Analytics**: Pega's AI-driven decisioning used historical data to predict which customers were likely to experience service disruptions or dissatisfaction.
- **Next-Best-Action**: The platform provided recommendations for preemptive support actions, such as reaching out to customers before issues escalated.
- **Automated Troubleshooting**: Pega's RPA automated troubleshooting steps, helping customers resolve issues without waiting for agent support.

Results:

- **Improved Retention Rates**: The company saw a **25% reduction in churn** as customers felt more valued and supported.
- **Increased First-Contact Resolution**: The proactive approach led to a **15% increase in first-contact resolution**, enhancing customer trust and satisfaction.
- **Efficiency Gains**: Automated troubleshooting freed agents to focus on more complex issues, improving overall support efficiency.

5. Case Study: Network Management and Compliance

Background: Managing network resources, compliance, and service outages are critical for telecom providers, especially those operating across regions with differing regulatory requirements. Manual processes and siloed data led to inefficiencies in network management for a large telecom organization.

Solution:

- **Centralized Case Management**: Pega's case management allowed the telecom company to track all network-related issues, compliance tasks, and maintenance schedules within a single, unified interface.
- **Compliance Automation**: Pega's automation tools monitored regulatory updates and adjusted network management workflows to ensure compliance.
- **Real-Time Analytics**: The platform provided real-time insights into network performance, helping the provider address outages proactively and maintain service quality.

Results:

- **Improved Compliance**: Automated compliance management reduced regulatory breaches, saving the company from costly fines.
- **Enhanced Network Uptime**: Real-time monitoring enabled faster response to network issues, achieving a **98% uptime rate**.
- **Operational Efficiency**: The centralized system decreased manual effort in network management tasks by **30%**, enhancing team productivity.

6. Case Study: Billing and Revenue Assurance Automation

Background: A telecom provider faced challenges with billing accuracy and revenue leakage due to manual processes and a lack of data integration between systems. Inconsistent billing led to customer complaints and impacted revenue collection.

Solution:

- **Automated Billing Workflows**: Pega's RPA and case management automated the billing process, ensuring timely and accurate invoicing.
- **Data Integration**: Pega integrated billing data with CRM, ERP, and customer management systems, reducing discrepancies.
- **Revenue Assurance Monitoring**: Pega's analytics monitored transactions for potential revenue leakage, alerting the company to discrepancies.

Results:

- **Increased Billing Accuracy**: Billing errors dropped by **60%**, leading to fewer customer disputes and a more streamlined revenue collection process.
- **Revenue Recovery**: The automation of revenue assurance monitoring helped the company identify and recover **5% in lost revenue**.
- **Customer Trust**: Accurate billing practices increased customer trust and reduced churn rates, strengthening the company's customer relationships.

7. Key Benefits of Pega for Telecom Process Automation

The case studies above illustrate the transformative impact of Pega in telecom operations. Key benefits include:

- **Operational Efficiency**: By automating manual workflows, telecom companies can handle larger volumes of transactions with reduced resources.
- **Enhanced Customer Experience**: Pega enables proactive support, real-time updates, and omnichannel engagement, leading to a superior customer experience.
- **Revenue Protection**: Through automated billing and revenue assurance processes, telecom providers can reduce revenue leakage and increase profitability.
- **Regulatory Compliance**: Pega's compliance automation tools help telecom companies stay up-to-date with changing regulations, reducing the risk of fines.

Conclusion

Telecom providers are increasingly turning to automation to stay competitive in a challenging market. Pega's comprehensive suite of BPM, RPA, and AI tools equips telecom companies to streamline operations, enhance service quality, and achieve operational agility.

By automating processes such as customer onboarding, support, network management, and billing, telecom providers can boost efficiency, reduce costs, and improve customer satisfaction. Pega's real-time insights and compliance features further empower telecom companies to adapt to regulatory changes and market demands seamlessly. As these case studies demonstrate, Pega's role in telecom process automation drives measurable results, transforming telecom companies into agile, customer-centric organizations.

Lessons Learned from Real-World Deployments

In the realm of digital transformation, real-world deployments of Pega Systems offer valuable insights into the complexities and best practices of implementing business process automation. This chapter examines lessons learned from various Pega deployments across industries, highlighting key takeaways for successful adoption, common challenges, and strategies to maximize the platform's value.

By studying these lessons, businesses can avoid common pitfalls, streamline their deployment processes, and leverage Pega's capabilities more effectively for operational excellence and customer satisfaction.

1. Understanding Stakeholder Needs

One of the primary lessons from successful Pega deployments is the importance of aligning stakeholder needs with project goals. Key takeaways include:

- **Identify Core Objectives Early**: Stakeholders, from executives to end-users, should have a shared understanding of the project's goals. Aligning early prevents scope creep and keeps the project focused.
- **Define Success Metrics**: Metrics such as efficiency gains, error reduction, and customer satisfaction should be defined at the outset to evaluate project impact and ROI accurately.

Case Example: In a banking deployment, project leaders conducted extensive stakeholder interviews to understand pain points in the loan processing workflow. This input directly shaped the application design, resulting in a solution tailored to user needs and significantly higher adoption rates.

2. Planning for Scalability and Flexibility

Deployments benefit significantly from planning for scalability, ensuring that the Pega solution can grow with the organization's needs. Lessons include:

- **Build for Future Growth**: Ensure the initial setup allows for adding new services, workflows, and departments with minimal changes.
- **Modular Design**: By creating modular components, businesses can reuse and expand functionalities, enabling flexibility in response to changing demands.

Case Example: A telecom company initially implemented Pega for customer service automation but later expanded it to network management and billing. The initial modular design allowed for seamless expansion, enabling a broader range of automated services without requiring significant reengineering.

3. Addressing Data Integration Challenges

Integrating Pega with legacy systems and disparate data sources can be challenging. Successful deployments illustrate how to overcome these barriers effectively:

- **Develop a Robust Integration Strategy**: Plan and test data integration paths to ensure compatibility with legacy systems.
- **Leverage API and Middleware Solutions**: Pega's API tools, along with middleware, simplify integration and facilitate real-time data flow between systems.

Case Example: In healthcare operations, Pega was integrated with multiple EHR (Electronic Health Record) systems. By using Pega's API and middleware tools, the healthcare provider created a unified platform that allowed seamless data sharing, reducing patient wait times and enhancing care coordination.

4. Prioritizing User Experience and Training

User experience (UX) is critical to successful adoption. Lessons from real-world deployments stress the importance of creating an intuitive UX and investing in comprehensive training:

- **Focus on Intuitive Interfaces**: Simplified interfaces and logical workflows improve user satisfaction and adoption rates.
- **Invest in Training Programs**: Training should be prioritized to ensure users feel confident in navigating the platform and understand its capabilities.

Case Example: A large retail organization used Pega to streamline its inventory management. The initial deployment faced resistance from employees unfamiliar with the software. After implementing an interactive training program and simplifying workflows, adoption rates increased significantly, leading to more efficient inventory management.

5. Ensuring Security and Compliance

Security is a critical aspect of any deployment, especially in highly regulated industries. Lessons emphasize that security and compliance should be integral to the implementation:

- **Integrate Security from the Outset**: Build compliance into the solution to avoid last-minute adjustments.
- **Stay Informed of Regulatory Requirements**: Regularly update security measures to remain compliant with industry standards and regulations.

Case Example: A financial services company used Pega for loan processing and compliance management. From the beginning, the solution was designed to meet stringent data privacy regulations, helping the company avoid costly compliance issues while maintaining customer trust.

6. Leveraging Analytics for Continuous Improvement

Successful deployments use analytics not only for monitoring but also for continuous process improvement. Key lessons include:

- **Monitor KPIs Actively**: Continuous tracking of key performance indicators (KPIs) allows businesses to identify and resolve issues promptly.
- **Use Analytics to Refine Workflows**: Analyze performance data to optimize workflows and improve service quality.

Case Example: An insurance company deployed Pega for claims processing and monitored KPIs like claim resolution time and customer satisfaction. By analyzing this data, they identified bottlenecks and implemented changes that reduced resolution time by 20%, resulting in higher customer satisfaction.

7. Preparing for Change Management

Change management is often a challenge in large-scale deployments. Effective change management strategies include:

- **Communicate the Vision**: Regularly update employees on the project's progress, benefits, and impact on their work.
- **Create a Support Network**: Establish a network of super-users or champions who can assist others and provide feedback to improve the solution.

Case Example: In a government deployment, a large-scale Pega application was rolled out to streamline citizen services. By designating change champions and providing ongoing support, resistance was minimized, and adoption was smooth across departments.

8. Avoiding Common Pitfalls

Real-world deployments reveal common pitfalls to avoid for successful implementation:

- **Underestimating Initial Planning Needs**: Insufficient planning can lead to unforeseen challenges. Allocate adequate time for planning before starting the deployment.
- **Neglecting Regular Updates**: Failing to update the system regularly can lead to performance degradation and security vulnerabilities.
- **Overlooking End-User Feedback**: Gathering ongoing feedback from users ensures that the system remains aligned with their needs.

Conclusion

Real-world Pega deployments offer invaluable lessons, from the importance of stakeholder alignment to planning for scalability and investing in user training. The most successful implementations prioritize continuous improvement and change management, creating a culture that embraces Pega's capabilities for ongoing innovation.

By applying these lessons, businesses can maximize the benefits of Pega, creating solutions that not only meet current operational needs but also prepare them for future growth and industry challenges.

Section 11:
Future Trends and Innovations

The Future of BPM with Pega

As businesses continue to evolve in response to rapid technological advancements, Business Process Management (BPM) remains a crucial component for sustaining efficient, customer-centric operations. Pega's BPM platform has already established itself as a leader in enabling business process automation, but the future promises even more exciting developments. This chapter explores the trends, innovations, and future directions for BPM with Pega, highlighting how the platform is positioned to support businesses in achieving greater flexibility, intelligence, and agility.

1. The Integration of AI and Machine Learning in BPM

One of the most transformative trends shaping the future of BPM is the integration of Artificial Intelligence (AI) and Machine Learning (ML). By embedding these technologies into Pega, businesses can expect:

- **Enhanced Decision-Making**: AI-powered decision engines will allow for more accurate, data-driven decision-making, improving customer experience and operational efficiency.
- **Predictive Process Automation**: ML algorithms can analyze historical data to predict future outcomes, proactively triggering automated responses to address potential bottlenecks before they impact performance.
- **Improved Customer Personalization**: Leveraging AI in Pega's BPM will enable deeper insights into customer behaviors, preferences, and trends, allowing organizations to provide personalized services at scale.

2. Embracing Hyperautomation

Hyperautomation, which refers to the combination of multiple technologies to automate as many processes as possible, is rapidly becoming a norm in BPM. In the context of Pega, hyperautomation will likely involve:

- **Advanced Workflow Automation**: By integrating robotic process automation (RPA), AI, and analytics, Pega can support end-to-end automation of complex workflows, minimizing manual intervention.
- **Unified Automation Tools**: Pega's low-code platform, combined with hyperautomation capabilities, will allow business users to design, manage, and optimize workflows with minimal IT dependency.
- **Seamless Integration with External Systems**: Pega's robust API capabilities make it an ideal platform for connecting with other enterprise systems, enabling a unified and comprehensive approach to process automation.

3. The Role of Low-Code Development in BPM Transformation

As businesses seek to innovate rapidly, low-code development platforms like Pega's are increasingly essential for agile BPM. The future of BPM will see:

- **Empowered Business Users**: Low-code will empower non-technical users to design, iterate, and implement processes, bringing development closer to those who best understand the business needs.

- **Accelerated Development Cycles**: The low-code approach will reduce time-to-market for new workflows and applications, allowing businesses to adapt quickly to changing demands.
- **Enhanced Collaboration**: By involving both IT and business teams in the development process, low-code facilitates better alignment between technology and business goals.

4. Pega's Expanding Role in Digital Transformation

As digital transformation becomes a key priority for organizations, Pega's BPM capabilities will play an increasingly critical role in enabling this shift. Future BPM implementations will focus on:

- **Cross-Functional Collaboration**: Pega's BPM solutions will facilitate collaboration across different business units, breaking down silos and encouraging holistic approaches to process management.
- **Agility and Resilience**: By centralizing process management on a robust platform like Pega, businesses can quickly pivot operations, allowing for greater resilience in times of disruption.
- **Data-Driven Transformation**: Pega's advanced analytics will help organizations harness data insights to drive transformation strategies, guiding decision-making and highlighting areas for improvement.

5. Adapting BPM for Remote and Hybrid Work Models

The shift towards remote and hybrid work models has transformed traditional business processes. The future of BPM with Pega will address these changes by:

- **Enabling Distributed Workflows**: Pega's cloud-based platform will support distributed teams, allowing users to access workflows and collaborate from any location.
- **Improving Collaboration Tools**: Future BPM applications will likely include enhanced tools for real-time collaboration and communication, helping remote teams stay connected.
- **Security for Distributed Access**: With employees accessing Pega from various locations, the platform's security features will evolve to ensure robust authentication, access control, and data protection.

6. Enhanced Compliance and Regulatory Support

As regulatory landscapes become more complex, Pega's BPM will adapt to provide stronger compliance tools, enabling businesses to navigate regulations efficiently:

- **Automated Compliance Monitoring**: Pega will offer automated compliance features that continuously monitor processes, ensuring they align with regulatory requirements.
- **Audit Trails and Reporting**: Advanced reporting capabilities will simplify audit processes, providing detailed insights into process history and modifications to meet compliance standards.
- **Proactive Regulatory Updates**: Pega will help businesses stay ahead of regulatory changes by offering tools to adapt workflows in response to new or updated compliance standards.

7. The Integration of IoT in BPM Processes

The Internet of Things (IoT) is transforming the way businesses operate, and Pega's BPM is expected to leverage IoT data to enable more dynamic and responsive processes:

- **Real-Time Process Adjustments**: IoT data can trigger automatic adjustments in Pega-managed processes, ensuring operations are continuously optimized based on real-world conditions.
- **Enhanced Supply Chain Management**: By integrating IoT data, Pega will enable real-time monitoring of supply chain processes, allowing for predictive maintenance, inventory management, and demand forecasting.
- **Customer Experience Enhancements**: IoT data will provide deeper insights into customer usage patterns, allowing Pega's BPM to deliver more tailored, context-aware customer interactions.

8. Leveraging Cloud and Edge Computing

As cloud and edge computing technologies advance, Pega's BPM will adapt to maximize the benefits of these infrastructures:

- **Scalability with Cloud-Native Applications**: Cloud-based BPM solutions on Pega's platform will offer businesses the scalability needed to support fluctuating workloads.
- **Reduced Latency with Edge Computing**: Pega can leverage edge computing to process data closer to the source, minimizing latency and improving process responsiveness.
- **Cost Optimization**: The combined use of cloud and edge computing allows organizations to manage data storage and processing more cost-effectively, optimizing BPM deployment costs.

9. Supporting a Culture of Continuous Improvement

The future of BPM with Pega involves not only technological innovation but also a shift towards a culture of continuous improvement:

- **Real-Time Feedback Loops**: By embedding analytics into workflows, Pega's BPM solutions will allow businesses to establish feedback loops, continuously refining and improving processes.
- **Agile Process Updates**: Pega's platform will support regular process updates, helping organizations respond quickly to changes in the business environment.
- **Employee Empowerment**: As BPM solutions become more user-friendly, employees at all levels will be empowered to contribute ideas for process optimization, fostering a culture of innovation.

Conclusion

The future of BPM with Pega is defined by innovation, adaptability, and integration. By embracing AI, hyperautomation, IoT, and cloud technology, Pega's BPM platform is poised to become a cornerstone of digital transformation efforts across industries. As organizations continue to seek ways to improve efficiency, drive customer satisfaction, and foster resilience, Pega's commitment to a robust and flexible BPM platform will be instrumental in helping them achieve these goals.

This transformative journey with Pega is not only about enhancing business processes but also about creating more agile, responsive, and future-ready organizations that can navigate the complexities of the modern business landscape.

Emerging Technologies in Process Automation

As the business landscape rapidly evolves, process automation technologies are advancing to meet new demands. The field of Business Process Management (BPM) is seeing substantial shifts as organizations strive to automate not just repetitive tasks but also complex decision-making processes. This chapter explores key emerging technologies shaping the future of process automation and how they integrate with Pega's BPM platform to enhance operational efficiency and innovation.

1. Artificial Intelligence (AI) and Machine Learning (ML)

AI and ML are transforming the BPM industry by enabling intelligent process automation that goes beyond predefined workflows. With Pega's AI capabilities, organizations can automate decision-making, understand patterns, and continuously optimize processes based on data insights. Key benefits include:

- **Predictive Analysis**: AI and ML models analyze past data to predict future outcomes, allowing Pega applications to make informed decisions and preemptively address issues.
- **Natural Language Processing (NLP)**: Pega uses NLP to process unstructured data like customer emails and chats, making it easier to understand customer intent and automate appropriate responses.
- **Continuous Learning and Improvement**: Machine learning models in Pega can evolve based on new data, enhancing their accuracy and relevance over time.

2. Robotic Process Automation (RPA)

RPA automates repetitive tasks by mimicking human actions in digital environments. Pega integrates RPA with BPM, creating a unified platform that handles both routine and complex tasks. This integration allows:

- **End-to-End Automation**: With Pega's RPA, organizations can fully automate workflows, combining rule-based processes with complex decision logic.
- **Cost Reduction**: RPA enables businesses to reduce operational costs by automating high-volume, low-value tasks.
- **Enhanced Accuracy**: RPA minimizes human errors in data entry and processing, increasing the accuracy of information in business processes.

3. Internet of Things (IoT)

IoT technology connects physical devices to the digital world, allowing data from sensors, machines, and devices to inform business processes. Integrating IoT data with Pega enables:

- **Real-Time Decision Making**: Pega can trigger processes based on IoT data, such as alerting maintenance teams when a machine's performance drops below a set threshold.
- **Enhanced Customer Experiences**: By using IoT data, Pega enables personalized services, such as automatically adjusting customer offerings based on their usage patterns.
- **Predictive Maintenance**: IoT data can help businesses predict equipment failure before it occurs, reducing downtime and maintenance costs.

4. Cloud Computing and Edge Computing

Cloud and edge computing technologies are reshaping how applications are deployed, scaled, and managed. Pega's cloud-native architecture and support for edge computing deliver advantages such as:

- **Scalability and Flexibility**: Cloud-based Pega applications can scale on-demand to accommodate fluctuating workloads, providing flexibility and cost savings.
- **Improved Data Processing**: Edge computing processes data closer to the source, reducing latency and enabling real-time decision-making in Pega applications.

- **Enhanced Data Security**: Cloud providers offer robust security controls, while edge computing minimizes data transfer, reducing exposure to cyber threats.

5. Blockchain for Secure Data Management

Blockchain offers a decentralized, secure ledger for managing transactional data, which can significantly benefit process automation. Although blockchain is not widely integrated into BPM yet, its potential use cases with Pega include:

- **Secure Data Storage**: Blockchain can enhance data security by storing records in an immutable ledger, reducing risks of tampering and fraud.
- **Transparency in Supply Chains**: Blockchain can record supply chain transactions, providing transparency and improving trust among stakeholders.
- **Smart Contracts**: By integrating blockchain with Pega, businesses can create automated contracts that self-execute when predefined conditions are met.

6. Intelligent Chatbots and Conversational AI

Chatbots and conversational AI allow businesses to automate customer interactions, improving service efficiency. Pega's support for intelligent chatbots enables:

- **24/7 Customer Support**: Chatbots can handle routine customer inquiries at any time, freeing up human agents for more complex issues.
- **Personalized Customer Experiences**: With AI-powered personalization, chatbots can provide tailored responses based on customer history and preferences.
- **Omnichannel Support**: Pega's chatbots work across multiple channels, including web, mobile, and social media, ensuring a consistent customer experience.

7. Augmented Reality (AR) and Virtual Reality (VR)

AR and VR are emerging technologies that can enrich customer experiences and employee training within automated workflows. While AR/VR use cases in BPM are still developing, future integrations with Pega may include:

- **Enhanced Training Programs**: VR can simulate complex workflows, providing immersive training experiences that help employees understand automated processes better.
- **Customer Engagement**: AR can be used to offer interactive product demonstrations, allowing customers to experience a product virtually before making a purchase.
- **Field Service Automation**: AR can assist field technicians by overlaying real-time information, helping them perform tasks more efficiently.

8. Hyperautomation

Hyperautomation combines multiple technologies—including AI, RPA, and BPM—to automate as many business processes as possible. Pega's platform is well-suited for hyperautomation initiatives due to its comprehensive capabilities:

- **Integrated Workflow Management**: Pega offers a unified platform for managing both automated and manual workflows, enabling end-to-end process automation.
- **Data-Driven Decision Making**: Hyperautomation relies on data insights, and Pega's analytics tools provide the necessary intelligence to drive continuous process improvement.
- **Adaptability to Business Needs**: With hyperautomation, Pega applications can quickly adapt to changing business needs, making them ideal for dynamic and complex environments.

9. Low-Code and No-Code Platforms

Low-code and no-code platforms empower users to design applications and workflows without extensive coding knowledge. Pega's low-code capabilities support this trend, enabling:

- **Rapid Development**: Business users can quickly create and modify workflows, reducing development time and costs.
- **Increased Collaboration**: Low-code platforms encourage collaboration between IT and business teams, ensuring that workflows align with business needs.
- **Enhanced Agility**: As business needs evolve, low-code tools allow for rapid adjustments to workflows, supporting agile operations.

10. Autonomous Process Optimization

Autonomous process optimization is an emerging trend in which AI-driven systems continuously monitor and optimize processes without human intervention. In the future, Pega may integrate this approach by:

- **Automatic Process Adjustments**: AI can monitor workflows and make real-time adjustments to optimize performance, reducing the need for manual oversight.
- **Self-Learning Processes**: By leveraging machine learning, Pega can enable processes to learn from outcomes, enhancing their effectiveness over time.
- **Reduced Operational Costs**: Autonomous optimization minimizes the resources required to monitor and refine workflows, delivering cost savings.

Conclusion

The future of process automation with Pega will be shaped by technologies that enhance intelligence, flexibility, and adaptability. As businesses adopt these emerging technologies, Pega's platform will continue to provide a robust foundation for deploying and managing automated processes. By leveraging AI, IoT, RPA, blockchain, and more, Pega will enable organizations to not only improve operational efficiency but also transform how they engage with customers, manage data, and respond to changes in the business environment.

Staying updated on these emerging technologies will be essential for organizations that wish to maximize the value of their Pega applications. Through continuous learning, strategic planning, and thoughtful integration, businesses can position themselves to benefit from the full potential of process automation in the years to come.

The Impact of AI and Automation on Business Strategies

In an era where artificial intelligence (AI) and automation are reshaping industries, the adoption of these technologies is no longer an option but a necessity for businesses seeking a competitive edge. With its robust BPM capabilities, Pega provides organizations with tools to harness AI and automation, transforming business strategies to meet evolving market demands. This chapter explores how AI and automation are influencing business strategies, the role of Pega in this transformation, and best practices for integrating these advancements into an organization's strategic planning.

1. AI and Automation: Catalysts for Business Transformation

AI and automation drive operational efficiencies, reduce costs, and enable data-driven decision-making. These technologies empower organizations to:

- **Streamline Processes**: Automation removes repetitive manual tasks, enhancing productivity and allowing employees to focus on more strategic activities.
- **Improve Decision-Making**: AI-powered analytics generate actionable insights from data, helping businesses make informed, timely decisions.
- **Enhance Customer Experience**: Personalized interactions and faster response times improve customer satisfaction and retention.
- **Drive Innovation**: By freeing up resources and providing deeper insights, AI and automation create an environment conducive to innovation.

2. Leveraging Pega AI and Automation for Strategic Advantage

Pega's platform combines BPM with AI capabilities, allowing organizations to streamline processes and optimize decision-making. Key features that enable strategic transformation include:

- **Predictive and Adaptive Analytics**: Pega's AI-driven analytics predict outcomes, allowing businesses to proactively address challenges and opportunities.
- **Intelligent Workflow Automation**: Pega automates complex workflows that involve decision-making and process management, aligning operations with strategic goals.
- **Customer Decision Hub**: This feature centralizes customer insights, allowing for real-time personalized interactions that drive customer loyalty and business growth.

By integrating these tools into their business strategies, organizations can adapt quickly to market changes, meet customer demands, and innovate more effectively.

3. AI in Strategic Decision-Making

The integration of AI into strategic decision-making transforms how organizations plan and execute initiatives. With AI-driven insights, businesses can:

- **Enhance Forecasting and Planning**: AI models analyze historical data to forecast trends, helping businesses make data-driven strategic decisions.
- **Optimize Resource Allocation**: Machine learning algorithms identify areas of high resource utilization, enabling organizations to allocate resources where they add the most value.
- **Identify New Revenue Streams**: AI uncovers hidden patterns in data, helping organizations discover untapped markets and opportunities for growth.

Pega's AI-powered capabilities provide real-time insights, allowing leaders to make decisions aligned with their strategic objectives.

4. Automation in Competitive Positioning

Automation enhances an organization's ability to respond to competitive pressures by improving speed, agility, and accuracy. Key benefits of incorporating automation in business strategies include:

- **Increased Speed to Market**: Automation accelerates product development and service delivery, allowing businesses to introduce new offerings quickly.
- **Cost Efficiency**: By automating repetitive tasks, businesses reduce operational costs, allowing them to price competitively.
- **Consistency and Quality**: Automated processes maintain high standards, reducing errors and improving quality, which strengthens brand reputation.

Pega's automation solutions support end-to-end process optimization, enabling organizations to gain a competitive edge by delivering high-quality products and services efficiently.

5. Enhancing Customer Engagement with AI-Driven Strategies

AI and automation enhance customer engagement by enabling personalized, responsive interactions. Pega's Customer Decision Hub and NLP capabilities allow businesses to:

- **Deliver Personalized Experiences**: AI analyzes customer data to provide tailored experiences, increasing customer satisfaction and loyalty.
- **Improve Responsiveness**: Automated chatbots and virtual assistants provide instant responses, enhancing customer support and engagement.
- **Anticipate Customer Needs**: Predictive analytics forecast customer behavior, enabling proactive engagement that fosters long-term relationships.

By integrating AI into customer strategies, businesses can differentiate themselves in the market and build stronger customer relationships.

6. Preparing for AI and Automation-Driven Business Models

As AI and automation reshape business landscapes, organizations need to adapt their business models to stay relevant. Strategies for future-proofing business models with AI and automation include:

- **Focusing on Agility**: Embrace flexible business models that can quickly adapt to technological advancements and changing customer expectations.
- **Emphasizing Continuous Learning**: Implement a culture of continuous learning and improvement to stay updated on AI and automation trends and maintain a skilled workforce.
- **Investing in Scalable Infrastructure**: Ensure that infrastructure can scale to accommodate AI-driven processes and automated workflows as they expand.

With Pega's scalable architecture and low-code development environment, organizations can implement agile, future-ready business models that leverage AI and automation.

7. Ethical and Governance Considerations

The increasing role of AI and automation in business strategies necessitates ethical considerations and governance. Key areas to address include:

- **Data Privacy and Security**: Establish protocols for handling sensitive data in compliance with regulations like GDPR and CCPA.
- **Algorithmic Transparency**: Ensure that AI algorithms are transparent, explainable, and free from biases that could affect decision-making.
- **Employee Transition and Upskilling**: Implement programs to help employees transition into roles that complement AI and automation, maintaining morale and job satisfaction.

Pega supports compliance with data privacy regulations, allowing organizations to responsibly integrate AI and automation into their operations.

8. Measuring the Success of AI and Automation-Driven Strategies

To determine the effectiveness of AI and automation in business strategies, organizations should track metrics such as:

- **Operational Efficiency**: Measure improvements in speed, cost reduction, and process accuracy.
- **Customer Satisfaction**: Track changes in customer satisfaction and retention rates, as these indicate the success of AI-driven personalization.
- **Return on Investment (ROI)**: Assess the ROI of AI and automation initiatives to ensure that investments align with business objectives.
- **Employee Productivity and Engagement**: Monitor how automation affects employee productivity and engagement, ensuring that automation complements the workforce.

Pega's reporting and analytics tools enable organizations to track these metrics, providing insights into the impact of AI and automation on business performance.

Conclusion

The integration of AI and automation into business strategies is essential for staying competitive in a dynamic marketplace. By leveraging Pega's AI-driven automation capabilities, organizations can streamline operations, enhance customer engagement, and drive sustainable growth. However, success depends on a thoughtful approach that considers ethical implications, aligns with organizational goals, and continuously measures performance.

As organizations navigate this transformation, adopting a strategic mindset that embraces AI and automation as tools for innovation, agility, and customer-centricity will be crucial. By embedding these technologies into the core of their business strategies, companies can thrive in the digital age and lead their industries into the future.

Preparing for the Next Generation of Pega Solutions

As digital transformation accelerates across industries, the evolution of Pega solutions is shaping how businesses can embrace the future of process automation and customer engagement. This chapter delves into key strategies for preparing your organization for the next generation of Pega solutions. By focusing on emerging trends, continuous learning, and robust implementation frameworks, businesses can harness Pega's capabilities to stay competitive and agile in an evolving landscape.

1. Anticipating Changes in the Pega Platform

Pega's development roadmap is centered around continuous innovation, adding new features and enhancing capabilities to support the changing needs of businesses. The following areas are anticipated to evolve:

- **AI-Powered Automation**: Advanced AI capabilities will enhance decision-making and streamline complex processes.
- **Low-Code and No-Code Development**: Pega's ongoing focus on low-code tools will make it even easier for non-technical users to build applications, expanding access to business users.
- **Cloud-Native Solutions**: Cloud functionality in Pega will continue to grow, with seamless integration for organizations leveraging multi-cloud environments.

By understanding these upcoming shifts, businesses can prepare to adopt new Pega features as they are introduced, ensuring a competitive advantage through advanced technology adoption.

2. Building an Agile Foundation for Future Pega Solutions

Preparing for future Pega advancements requires an agile foundation that allows for quick adaptation. Key aspects of an agile Pega environment include:

- **Modular Architectures**: Design applications with modularity in mind, allowing new components and technologies to be integrated easily as Pega evolves.
- **Flexible Data Models**: Use adaptable data models that can integrate new data sources, especially as Pega's AI and machine learning features require diverse data inputs.
- **Scalable Cloud Infrastructure**: Establish a cloud infrastructure that can handle increased demand and easily integrate with Pega's cloud-native enhancements.

By implementing these elements, organizations ensure they can swiftly incorporate new features and updates from Pega, staying at the forefront of process automation technology.

3. Embracing AI and Machine Learning for Advanced Automation

Pega's roadmap for AI and machine learning integration is designed to enhance decision-making, automation, and customer engagement. To prepare for these advancements, organizations should:

- **Invest in Data Management**: High-quality data is essential for AI-driven insights. Ensure your organization has robust data management practices to maximize the effectiveness of Pega's AI tools.
- **Train Teams on AI and Analytics**: Equip employees with foundational knowledge of AI concepts to effectively use Pega's predictive and adaptive analytics.
- **Adopt a Continuous Improvement Mindset**: AI and machine learning models improve with use. By iterating on processes and monitoring performance, your organization can fully leverage Pega's AI capabilities.

Preparing to utilize AI within Pega solutions can drive operational efficiency, enhance personalization, and facilitate smarter decision-making.

4. Implementing a Culture of Continuous Learning

To stay up-to-date with the next generation of Pega solutions, organizations must promote a culture of continuous learning:

- **Encourage Pega Certification**: Supporting team members in achieving Pega certification ensures a deep understanding of the platform and prepares them for future updates.
- **Create a Knowledge-Sharing Community**: Encourage collaboration through regular workshops, webinars, and discussion forums where team members can exchange insights and learn about the latest Pega developments.
- **Utilize Pega's Learning Resources**: Pega offers various learning resources, including documentation, tutorials, and user communities. Encouraging ongoing engagement with these resources keeps your team aligned with Pega's advancements.

A culture of continuous learning enables your team to rapidly adopt and excel in utilizing new features, maintaining a competitive edge as the platform evolves.

5. Leveraging Pega's DevOps Capabilities for Future Adaptability

Pega's integration of DevOps tools facilitates the continuous delivery of applications, enabling organizations to deploy updates efficiently. To prepare for future Pega solutions, focus on enhancing your DevOps practices:

- **Automate Testing and Deployment**: Automated testing and deployment reduce the time required to incorporate new Pega features, allowing your organization to adapt quickly.
- **Adopt CI/CD Pipelines**: Continuous Integration and Continuous Deployment (CI/CD) pipelines streamline application development, ensuring new Pega updates and features can be deployed without significant downtime.
- **Incorporate Feedback Loops**: Use feedback loops to gather user input on new features and improvements, aligning Pega application development with organizational goals.

With strong DevOps practices, your organization can maximize the benefits of new Pega solutions by facilitating quick adaptation and reducing time-to-market for new features.

6. Preparing for Enhanced User Experience Capabilities

As Pega continues to prioritize user experience (UX), organizations can expect new tools and enhancements aimed at improving the usability and accessibility of applications. Strategies to prepare for UX advancements in Pega include:

- **Adopt UX Best Practices**: Incorporate UX design principles into Pega development to create intuitive, user-friendly interfaces that meet evolving customer expectations.
- **Use Pega's Design System**: Pega offers a design system that provides pre-built UI components. By aligning with Pega's design system, your organization can seamlessly adopt new UX features as they are introduced.
- **Focus on Accessibility**: As UX trends increasingly emphasize accessibility, ensure that applications meet accessibility standards and provide inclusive experiences for all users.

By focusing on UX readiness, your organization can create applications that are both visually appealing and functionally robust, meeting the demands of next-generation users.

7. Monitoring and Adapting to Industry-Specific Innovations

Pega's next-generation solutions will be tailored to meet the specific needs of various industries, including finance, healthcare, telecommunications, and more. Prepare for industry-specific innovations by:

- **Staying Updated on Pega's Industry Offerings**: Follow Pega's updates on industry-focused solutions and evaluate how they align with your organization's needs.
- **Participating in Industry Events and Webinars**: Attend industry-specific Pega events to learn about use cases, best practices, and upcoming features tailored to your sector.
- **Collaborating with Industry Experts**: Engage with Pega consultants and industry experts to better understand how emerging Pega features can address unique challenges within your industry.

Keeping a close watch on industry-specific solutions enables your organization to leverage Pega innovations that align with your market and customer needs.

Conclusion

The future of Pega solutions promises to bring transformative advancements in AI, automation, DevOps, and user experience. By proactively preparing for these changes, your organization can leverage Pega to its fullest potential, maintaining a competitive edge in process automation and customer engagement.

To ensure a successful transition, build a flexible, agile foundation, invest in continuous learning, and embrace DevOps practices. Focusing on these areas will enable your organization to integrate Pega's new features seamlessly and capitalize on the strategic advantages they offer.

As Pega solutions continue to evolve, organizations that anticipate and prepare for these innovations will be well-positioned to lead in their respective industries, delivering value to customers and driving sustainable growth through advanced business process management.

How Pega Supports Agile Business Transformations

In today's fast-paced business environment, agility is crucial for organizations seeking to stay competitive and responsive to market changes. Pega Systems plays a pivotal role in enabling agile transformations by providing a flexible, scalable, and adaptive platform that supports the principles and practices of agility. In this chapter, we explore how Pega's tools, methodologies, and capabilities empower organizations to adopt agile practices and facilitate continual improvement across business processes.

1. The Essence of Agile in Business Transformations

Agile business transformation refers to the shift in organizational culture, processes, and technology to support adaptability, rapid response to change, and customer-centric practices. Key objectives of agile transformations include:

- **Enhanced Customer Satisfaction**: Delivering value consistently and responding quickly to changing customer needs.
- **Increased Flexibility**: Adjusting processes, products, and services in response to evolving market demands.
- **Cross-Functional Collaboration**: Promoting teamwork across departments for continuous improvement and innovation.

Pega's platform aligns with these objectives, offering a suite of tools that enable agile workflows, cross-departmental integration, and rapid development.

2. Leveraging Pega's Low-Code Development for Agile Initiatives

Pega's low-code development environment is a cornerstone for agile transformation, allowing both business and IT teams to collaboratively build, test, and deploy applications faster. Key benefits include:

- **Rapid Prototyping**: Pega's low-code tools enable teams to quickly create prototypes and gather feedback, essential for iterative development.
- **Reduced Development Time**: With visual interfaces and pre-configured templates, Pega speeds up development cycles, aligning with agile sprint timelines.
- **Empowerment of Business Users**: By enabling non-technical users to participate in app development, Pega fosters cross-functional collaboration and reduces dependency on IT for every change.

These capabilities make it easier for organizations to adapt to agile methodologies, bringing new solutions to market more efficiently.

3. Agile Case Management and Workflow Optimization

Pega's case management system is designed to manage complex workflows that adapt in real-time, an essential feature for agile operations. Key agile-supportive features in Pega's case management include:

- **Dynamic Case Types**: Pega supports creating case types that can evolve as requirements change, allowing workflows to remain flexible and adaptive.
- **Process Automation**: Pega's automation features reduce repetitive tasks and streamline operations, allowing teams to focus on high-value activities.
- **Real-Time Collaboration**: Case management in Pega fosters real-time collaboration across departments, supporting agile principles of teamwork and communication.

By using Pega's case management capabilities, organizations can design workflows that adapt to agile project needs, whether for customer support, project management, or internal operations.

4. Continuous Improvement through Real-Time Analytics and Feedback

A fundamental agile principle is continuous improvement, which requires ongoing feedback and the ability to make data-driven decisions. Pega's analytics and reporting tools enable organizations to:

- **Monitor Key Performance Indicators (KPIs)**: Pega's real-time analytics allow teams to track KPIs, ensuring alignment with business goals and agile objectives.
- **Gain Customer Insights**: Through detailed reporting on customer interactions, Pega helps teams understand customer needs and refine processes accordingly.
- **Adapt Based on Feedback**: Pega's analytics offer insights into user behavior, enabling organizations to adjust processes and improve service delivery based on real-time feedback.

These capabilities empower organizations to continuously assess their performance, make necessary adjustments, and ultimately enhance their ability to respond to changing conditions.

5. Supporting Agile DevOps and Continuous Delivery

Pega's DevOps capabilities align with agile principles, supporting continuous integration and continuous delivery (CI/CD) to streamline deployment and improve responsiveness. Key features include:

- **Automated Testing**: Pega's DevOps tools include automated testing capabilities, ensuring that changes can be deployed quickly and reliably.
- **CI/CD Pipelines**: Pega's CI/CD functionality enables frequent, small updates, reducing the risk associated with large-scale deployments and supporting agile development cycles.
- **Version Control**: Integrated version control within Pega facilitates rapid iteration, allowing teams to revert changes or deploy updates efficiently.

Pega's DevOps tools ensure that organizations can rapidly deploy updates without disrupting ongoing operations, aligning with the agile goals of continuous improvement and rapid response.

6. Enabling Cross-Functional Collaboration

Agile transformation relies on strong cross-functional collaboration, where teams work together to achieve shared goals. Pega's platform promotes collaboration through:

- **Unified Interfaces**: Pega's design encourages different teams to work within a unified interface, simplifying communication and reducing silos.
- **Shared Data and Insights**: Pega's data integration capabilities allow teams to access shared information, ensuring alignment and transparency across departments.
- **Role-Based Access Control (RBAC)**: By assigning permissions based on roles, Pega ensures that teams have access to the information they need without compromising data security.

This collaborative infrastructure helps organizations break down barriers between teams, fostering a more integrated, agile work environment.

7. Agile Compliance and Governance

In regulated industries, compliance remains a top priority, even in agile environments. Pega's compliance and governance features support agile practices while ensuring regulatory requirements are met:

- **Automated Compliance Checks**: Pega allows organizations to automate compliance checks, ensuring adherence to regulations without slowing down agile workflows.

- **Audit Trails and Reporting**: Pega's comprehensive reporting features provide audit trails, supporting transparency and accountability in agile projects.
- **Configurable Governance Frameworks**: Pega's governance frameworks can be customized to meet specific regulatory needs, helping organizations remain compliant even in fast-paced, agile environments.

These features help businesses maintain compliance while embracing agile practices, balancing the need for flexibility with regulatory demands.

8. Embracing a Culture of Agility with Pega

Beyond tools and technology, successful agile transformation requires a cultural shift toward continuous learning, innovation, and adaptation. Pega supports this cultural shift through:

- **Training and Certification Programs**: Pega offers extensive training and certification resources, helping employees stay up-to-date on agile practices and Pega's latest capabilities.
- **Agile Best Practices Resources**: Pega provides access to agile best practices and community resources, supporting organizations as they adopt and refine agile methodologies.
- **Community Collaboration**: Pega's user community offers a collaborative environment where organizations can share insights, troubleshoot challenges, and learn from other agile adopters.

This culture-building support ensures that organizations can sustain agile practices and continually evolve to meet future challenges.

Conclusion

In an era of rapid change and heightened customer expectations, agile business transformation has become essential. Pega's platform not only enables the adoption of agile practices but also fosters a culture of adaptability, collaboration, and innovation. By leveraging Pega's low-code capabilities, real-time analytics, DevOps tools, and cross-functional collaboration features, organizations can drive transformative change and remain competitive in an increasingly agile world.

Preparing for a successful agile transformation with Pega involves:

1. Embracing a modular, adaptive approach to application development.
2. Fostering a culture of continuous improvement and cross-functional collaboration.
3. Leveraging Pega's DevOps capabilities for streamlined deployment and rapid iteration.
4. Ensuring compliance within agile workflows, balancing regulatory needs with flexibility.

By following these strategies, businesses can leverage Pega as a catalyst for agile transformation, empowering them to meet market demands, improve customer satisfaction, and achieve long-term success in a dynamic business environment.

Section 12:
Learning and Certification Paths

Pega Training and Certification Overview

In a rapidly evolving technology landscape, ongoing training and certification are crucial for individuals seeking to stay competitive and deepen their expertise in Pega Systems. Pega offers a range of certification programs designed to validate technical skills and support professional growth within the Pega ecosystem. This chapter provides a comprehensive overview of Pega's training and certification pathways, highlighting how these resources empower learners and professionals to enhance their Pega skills and credentials.

1. Importance of Pega Training and Certification

Training and certification provide tangible benefits for both professionals and organizations:

- **Skill Enhancement**: Structured learning paths help professionals develop foundational and advanced skills within the Pega ecosystem.
- **Career Advancement**: Certifications validate expertise, often leading to better job prospects, promotions, and higher salaries.
- **Organizational Benefits**: Certified Pega professionals bring specialized knowledge to teams, improving project quality and efficiency.

By investing in Pega training, professionals and organizations can optimize performance and ensure alignment with best practices.

2. Pega's Certification Programs

Pega's certification framework offers multiple levels of certification across various roles, allowing individuals to specialize according to their career objectives. Key certification tracks include:

- **Pega Certified System Architect (PCSA)**: Ideal for beginners, this certification covers foundational knowledge of Pega's application development, configuration, and customization capabilities.
- **Pega Certified Senior System Architect (PCSSA)**: Designed for experienced system architects, this certification covers advanced topics, including data integration, performance, and troubleshooting.
- **Pega Certified Lead System Architect (PCLSA)**: The most advanced certification, aimed at senior architects and project leaders who oversee complex Pega projects. This track includes hands-on project work and comprehensive assessments.
- **Pega Certified Business Architect (PCBA)**: This certification focuses on business analysis and application design within the Pega environment, ideal for professionals involved in process modeling and requirement gathering.
- **Pega Certified Data Scientist (PCDS)**: For professionals working with Pega's AI and analytics features, this certification covers decisioning strategies, predictive analytics, and machine learning within Pega.

These certifications are structured to support skill progression, allowing professionals to start with foundational knowledge and advance through increasingly complex topics.

3. Preparation Resources for Pega Certification

To help candidates succeed in their certification exams, Pega offers a range of preparatory resources:

- **Pega Academy**: Pega Academy offers self-paced and instructor-led courses designed to cover key concepts, tools, and techniques. Courses are organized by role and skill level, enabling learners to focus on relevant material for their certification path.
- **Practice Exams**: Pega provides practice exams that simulate the actual certification exam experience. These tests allow candidates to assess their understanding, identify knowledge gaps, and get comfortable with exam formats.
- **Hands-On Exercises and Labs**: Pega Academy includes hands-on exercises and labs that reinforce learning through practical application. These resources provide guided practice to help learners build confidence with Pega's tools and features.
- **Study Groups and Forums**: Pega's online community includes study groups and forums where candidates can interact, share insights, and ask questions, fostering a supportive learning environment.

4. Navigating the Pega Academy Platform

Pega Academy is the central hub for Pega's training resources, and it is structured to provide a flexible and interactive learning experience:

- **Role-Based Learning Paths**: Pega Academy offers tailored learning paths based on the user's role, such as system architect, business architect, or data scientist, ensuring that learners focus on the most relevant material for their career goals.
- **Micro-Certifications and Badges**: In addition to full certifications, Pega Academy offers micro-certifications and badges that allow learners to demonstrate specific skills, such as API integration, UI design, or case management.
- **Interactive Learning Modules**: The courses on Pega Academy feature interactive elements, including quizzes, videos, and scenario-based exercises, making the learning process engaging and dynamic.
- **Progress Tracking and Reporting**: Pega Academy provides tools for tracking progress, allowing learners to visualize their progress toward certification and set milestones along the way.

These resources make Pega Academy an effective platform for both independent learners and teams pursuing professional development within Pega.

5. Preparing for Pega Certification Exams

Certification exams require thorough preparation to ensure success. Key preparation strategies include:

- **Focus on Key Topics**: Each certification exam has an exam blueprint, which outlines the specific topics and skills being assessed. Focusing on these areas ensures that candidates allocate their study time efficiently.
- **Review Hands-On Exercises**: Practical knowledge is essential for Pega exams, so reviewing hands-on exercises, labs, and real-world use cases is vital.
- **Utilize Pega Academy's Resources**: Make full use of Pega Academy's courses, quizzes, and practice exams to reinforce knowledge and build familiarity with exam content.
- **Join Study Groups**: Connecting with peers through Pega's forums or other online communities can provide insights, encouragement, and additional learning resources, making the preparation process more collaborative and comprehensive.

6. Benefits of Maintaining Certification

Pega certifications remain valid for a specified period, after which professionals are encouraged to renew their credentials. Key benefits of maintaining certification include:

- **Staying Current with Technology**: Pega's platform is continually evolving, and renewing certification ensures professionals stay up-to-date with the latest features and industry best practices.
- **Enhancing Career Opportunities**: Maintaining an active certification shows employers a commitment to professional growth and expertise in Pega, which can lead to increased job opportunities.
- **Access to Advanced Training**: Certified professionals often receive early access to new courses and advanced resources, allowing them to stay at the forefront of Pega's technological advancements.

Certification renewal typically involves completing updated courses and passing an assessment, allowing professionals to demonstrate their continued proficiency.

Conclusion: Advancing Your Career with Pega Certification

Pega's training and certification programs are designed to support the growth and success of professionals at all career stages. By investing in structured learning paths, practice resources, and ongoing certification, Pega enables professionals to develop essential skills and establish a competitive edge in process automation and business transformation.

To succeed with Pega certification:

1. **Identify Your Path**: Determine the certification track that aligns with your role and career goals, whether as a system architect, business analyst, or data scientist.
2. **Utilize Pega Academy**: Leverage Pega Academy's interactive courses, hands-on labs, and practice exams to build expertise and prepare for exams.
3. **Commit to Continuous Learning**: Stay updated with Pega's evolving capabilities by maintaining certification and participating in ongoing training.

By following these steps, professionals can maximize the benefits of Pega certification, positioning themselves as experts in process automation and driving successful business outcomes in their organizations.

Best Resources for Continued Learning

In the field of process automation and business transformation, continuous learning is essential for professionals to remain competitive and innovative. As Pega continues to evolve and introduce new features, professionals who stay current with these advancements gain a significant advantage. This chapter presents a curated list of resources and tools that will support your ongoing journey in mastering Pega, ensuring you stay updated with the latest in Pega systems, best practices, and industry developments.

1. Pega Academy: The Hub for Skill Development

Pega Academy serves as the primary resource for structured learning within the Pega ecosystem. It offers a variety of training courses, certification preparation materials, and role-based learning paths. Key benefits include:

- **Interactive Courses**: Pega Academy offers both foundational and advanced courses across various domains, such as system architecture, business analysis, and data science. Courses often include hands-on labs, interactive quizzes, and real-world scenarios.
- **Certification Preparation**: With dedicated resources for each certification track, Pega Academy provides exam blueprints, practice exams, and sample questions to help candidates confidently prepare for certifications.
- **Micro-Credentials and Badges**: Beyond full certifications, Pega Academy offers micro-credentials and badges that validate specific skills, such as API integration, user interface customization, or decisioning. These credentials allow professionals to gain recognition for specialized knowledge.

2. Pega Community: A Platform for Peer Support and Knowledge Sharing

The **Pega Community** is an online forum and resource center where Pega professionals can collaborate, share knowledge, and stay informed about the latest trends and features. Some key features include:

- **Community Forums**: These forums allow users to discuss specific challenges, share tips, and learn from experienced professionals. You can browse threads related to development, troubleshooting, best practices, and certification tips.
- **Community Blog**: Regular blog posts by Pega experts cover in-depth insights into new features, updates, and industry trends, providing valuable knowledge from the field.
- **Supportive Q&A Environment**: Pega Community also has a Q&A section, where users can ask questions, solve issues, and contribute answers, making it an excellent resource for practical problem-solving.

3. Pega Documentation and Developer Guides

Pega's official documentation serves as a reference for understanding platform capabilities, configurations, and development best practices. Pega offers:

- **Platform Documentation**: Comprehensive guides and manuals cover everything from system setup and deployment to specific module configurations, such as case management, integration, and automation.
- **How-To Guides and Tutorials**: For more specific tasks, Pega provides step-by-step guides that help developers implement features or troubleshoot issues. These guides cover both simple and complex scenarios.
- **Release Notes**: Each Pega release includes detailed notes that highlight new features, enhancements, and fixes. Staying updated on release notes is crucial for understanding the latest improvements and leveraging them effectively in your projects.

4. Pega Webinars and Events

Pega frequently hosts **webinars** and **live events** that allow professionals to engage with Pega experts and stay informed about the latest advancements. Types of events include:

- **Webinars**: Covering topics such as product releases, best practices, and industry applications, webinars provide insights directly from Pega's product and engineering teams.
- **PegaWorld iNspire**: This annual conference offers sessions, workshops, and networking opportunities with leaders in Pega development, innovation, and industry transformation. It is a valuable event for connecting with other professionals and learning about real-world applications.
- **On-Demand Webinars**: Pega's website offers an archive of past webinars, allowing users to learn about various topics on their own schedule.

5. Third-Party Learning Platforms and Courses

In addition to Pega's official resources, third-party learning platforms provide valuable resources for deepening your Pega expertise:

- **LinkedIn Learning**: With courses on process automation, case management, and business transformation, LinkedIn Learning offers general concepts that can complement your Pega-specific skills.
- **Udemy and Coursera**: These platforms offer courses in related fields, such as business process management, AI and machine learning, and software development. While not Pega-specific, these courses support broader knowledge and concepts.

6. Books and Publications

For those who prefer traditional learning materials, various books and publications provide deeper insights into topics related to BPM, automation, and case management:

- **Business Process Management: A Comprehensive Guide**: This book covers fundamental concepts and strategies in BPM, giving readers a solid foundation for applying BPM principles within Pega.
- **Artificial Intelligence and Machine Learning for Business**: Since Pega incorporates AI and machine learning, books on these topics provide additional knowledge to make the most of Pega's AI capabilities.
- **Case Management Frameworks and Best Practices**: Books on case management frameworks offer a solid understanding of workflow optimization and compliance, which are essential in Pega projects.

7. Staying Updated with Industry Trends

In a fast-paced technology landscape, staying informed about industry trends is essential for anticipating changes and innovations. Key resources include:

- **Tech News Outlets**: Websites such as TechCrunch, Wired, and InformationWeek regularly publish articles on AI, automation, and BPM developments.
- **Pega Partner Newsletters**: Many Pega partners, such as Accenture and Capgemini, release newsletters that cover trends, Pega implementations, and best practices in digital transformation and automation.
- **Social Media and Influencers**: Following Pega experts, trainers, and influencers on LinkedIn and Twitter can provide real-time insights, tips, and updates.

Conclusion

Staying updated in the field of Pega and BPM requires a proactive approach to learning. By utilizing resources such as Pega Academy, engaging with the Pega Community, reading key publications, and attending events, professionals can ensure they are well-equipped to handle evolving challenges and leverage new capabilities within Pega.

Steps for Continued Learning:

1. **Create a Learning Schedule**: Allocate dedicated time each month to engage with new materials, complete courses, or participate in community discussions.
2. **Engage with Peers**: Join forums, attend events, and collaborate with others to gain new perspectives and insights.
3. **Stay Curious**: Make a habit of exploring both Pega-specific and industry-wide developments, and adapt to emerging trends to keep your skills sharp.

By following these steps, professionals can not only advance their expertise in Pega but also remain valuable contributors to their organizations and the field of process automation.

Building a Career in Pega Development

In the evolving landscape of process automation and digital transformation, Pega development has become a highly sought-after skill. This chapter provides insights into building a successful career in Pega, including essential skills, certification pathways, job roles, and career advancement opportunities. Whether you're a beginner looking to break into the field or an experienced professional aiming to deepen your expertise, this guide will help you navigate the Pega development career path effectively.

1. Understanding the Core Skills for a Pega Developer

A successful career in Pega development requires a strong foundation in various skills and competencies, such as:

- **Technical Proficiency in Pega Platform**: Proficiency in core Pega modules, such as case management, decisioning, and integration, is essential. Developers must also be comfortable with the Pega design studio and rule-based development.
- **Business Process Management (BPM) Knowledge**: Since Pega is primarily a BPM tool, a solid understanding of BPM concepts is crucial. This includes workflow design, case lifecycle management, and business rules implementation.
- **Analytical and Problem-Solving Skills**: Pega developers often work on complex projects that require analyzing requirements, troubleshooting issues, and optimizing workflows. Analytical skills are essential to success.
- **Programming Knowledge**: While Pega is a low-code platform, familiarity with programming languages such as Java, SQL, and JavaScript can enhance a developer's capability, especially when working with integrations and data manipulation.
- **Soft Skills**: Effective communication, teamwork, and client engagement skills are vital for understanding business requirements and delivering solutions that align with client needs.

2. Exploring the Pega Certification Pathway

Certifications are a recognized way to validate your skills and improve job prospects in the Pega ecosystem. Pega offers a well-structured certification program with certifications targeted at different roles, including developers, business architects, and system architects.

- **Certified System Architect (CSA)**: The CSA certification is the entry-level certification for developers, focusing on core Pega functionalities and principles of application development.
- **Certified Senior System Architect (CSSA)**: The CSSA builds on the CSA and is ideal for developers seeking to deepen their knowledge. It covers advanced topics, such as integrations, performance tuning, and complex case management.
- **Certified Lead System Architect (CLSA)**: The CLSA is an expert-level certification and is designed for senior architects who lead complex projects. It covers architecture design, application governance, and Pega best practices.
- **Other Certifications**: Pega also offers role-specific certifications, such as Certified Business Architect (CBA), Certified Decisioning Consultant (CDC), and Certified Robotics System Architect (CRSA), allowing professionals to specialize in areas that align with their career goals.

3. Career Paths in Pega Development

A career in Pega development can lead to various roles with increasing levels of responsibility and specialization:

- **Pega Developer**: Entry-level role focused on implementing business solutions using Pega tools, working under the guidance of senior developers or architects.

- **Senior Pega Developer**: A more experienced role responsible for complex rule and workflow configurations, integrations, and troubleshooting.
- **Pega System Architect**: This role focuses on designing and architecting solutions within the Pega platform. Architects are responsible for ensuring applications align with best practices and project requirements.
- **Pega Lead System Architect**: Senior role responsible for overseeing the architecture of Pega applications across the organization, working closely with business stakeholders to align solutions with strategic goals.
- **Pega Business Architect**: Specializes in translating business requirements into Pega application configurations. Business architects play a critical role in designing workflows, user interfaces, and process flows that meet client needs.

4. Leveraging Job Opportunities and Building Experience

Breaking into the Pega development field often begins with entry-level positions. Here are strategies to build experience and progress in your career:

- **Internships and Junior Roles**: Starting with internships or junior developer positions provides hands-on experience in real-world projects, building foundational skills.
- **Freelancing and Contract Work**: Freelance projects in Pega development are available for those looking to build their portfolio. These roles provide exposure to diverse projects and industries, strengthening your expertise.
- **Networking and Mentorship**: Engaging with professionals in the Pega community through forums, user groups, or Pega events can open doors to job opportunities and mentorship.

5. Developing a Specialized Skill Set

Pega professionals can set themselves apart by specializing in specific areas of the platform. Some high-demand areas include:

- **Robotics Process Automation (RPA)**: As Pega RPA becomes integral to automation strategies, RPA skills are increasingly valued.
- **Decisioning and AI**: Pega's Customer Decision Hub and AI capabilities are widely used for customer engagement and marketing. Knowledge of decisioning logic, AI modeling, and predictive analytics is highly desirable.
- **Integration and API Management**: Pega applications often integrate with other systems. Mastery of API management, REST services, and data integration within Pega adds significant value.
- **Pega DevOps and CI/CD**: Pega's DevOps and CI/CD tools enable faster development cycles and better version control. Expertise in DevOps for Pega applications is an advantage for senior roles.

6. Building a Strong Professional Network

Networking is an invaluable part of career development. Connecting with other Pega professionals can provide insights, support, and job leads. Effective ways to network include:

- **Engaging with Pega Community**: Participate in the Pega Community forums, ask questions, and contribute your knowledge to build a presence within the community.
- **Attending Pega Events**: Events like PegaWorld and local user groups offer opportunities to meet other professionals, learn about industry trends, and showcase your skills.
- **Leveraging LinkedIn and Professional Groups**: Joining LinkedIn groups dedicated to Pega professionals and participating in discussions can help you connect with potential employers, mentors, and collaborators.

7. Career Advancement and Long-Term Growth

In addition to certifications and technical skills, developing leadership abilities and business acumen is critical for long-term growth. Here's how to progress through senior roles:

- **Transitioning to Lead Architect Roles**: Focus on gaining experience in solution architecture, cross-functional collaboration, and team leadership to transition into a Lead System Architect role.
- **Exploring Business-Oriented Roles**: For those interested in aligning technology with business strategy, roles like Business Architect or Decisioning Consultant offer pathways to merge technical and business expertise.
- **Continuous Learning**: Stay up-to-date with Pega's evolving features, participate in advanced courses, and read industry publications to maintain a competitive edge.

Conclusion

A career in Pega development offers a wide range of opportunities for growth and specialization. By focusing on certification, practical experience, and specialization in high-demand areas, professionals can build a fulfilling and dynamic career. Success in Pega development is not only about technical skills; it's about aligning with business goals, staying current with industry trends, and expanding your professional network.

By following these steps and building both technical and soft skills, you can advance through Pega's career paths and become an influential contributor to the field of process automation.

Tips for Passing Pega Certification Exams

Certification in Pega can be a valuable asset for advancing your career in process automation, equipping you with skills recognized by employers worldwide. This chapter provides strategies and tips to help you excel in Pega certification exams, whether you're working toward the Certified System Architect (CSA), Certified Senior System Architect (CSSA), or the expert-level Certified Lead System Architect (CLSA) credentials.

1. Understanding the Certification Pathway

Before starting preparation, it's essential to understand the structure and requirements of each certification:

- **CSA (Certified System Architect)**: Designed for beginners, this certification focuses on foundational Pega skills such as case management, user interfaces, and data handling.
- **CSSA (Certified Senior System Architect)**: Aimed at experienced developers, this level covers advanced topics like integration, performance optimization, and application debugging.
- **CLSA (Certified Lead System Architect)**: The highest level, requiring a deep understanding of Pega architecture, solution design, and best practices.

Each level builds upon the previous, so having a clear understanding of the prerequisites and exam content is crucial.

2. Utilize Pega Academy Resources

Pega Academy is a comprehensive platform offering resources tailored to certification exams. Key tips for using Pega Academy effectively include:

- **Complete the Relevant Courses**: Each certification has a corresponding course sequence in Pega Academy. Completing these courses is vital for covering all exam objectives.
- **Practice with Hands-On Exercises**: Pega Academy provides hands-on labs for practical experience. Take full advantage of these exercises to apply concepts in a real-world environment.
- **Review Lesson Summaries and Quizzes**: Each course module includes summaries and quizzes. Review these to solidify your understanding and identify areas needing further study.

3. Study Exam-Specific Topics

Each certification exam covers specific knowledge areas. Focus on mastering these core topics:

- **CSA Focus Areas**: Case design, user interface customization, decision rules, and data handling.
- **CSSA Focus Areas**: Integration techniques, debugging tools, performance management, and advanced case management.
- **CLSA Focus Areas**: Solution architecture, application governance, project best practices, and complex design patterns.

Pega's exam blueprints, available on Pega Academy, offer a detailed breakdown of topics. Reviewing these helps you understand the emphasis of each exam.

4. Practice Using Sample Questions and Mock Exams

Sample questions are invaluable for understanding the format and style of Pega certification exams. Here's how to leverage these effectively:

- **Identify Common Question Types**: Pega exams often include scenario-based questions. Practice identifying the best approach for each scenario, focusing on business requirements.

- **Use Mock Exams for Timing**: Time management is crucial during the exam. Use mock exams to simulate the test environment and gauge your pacing.
- **Review Answers Thoroughly**: For each incorrect answer, study the correct solution and understand the reasoning behind it. This approach helps improve your problem-solving skills and reinforces core concepts.

5. Build a Solid Foundation with Hands-On Practice

Practical experience is essential for success, especially for CSSA and CLSA exams that test advanced skills. Key hands-on tips include:

- **Develop Sample Applications**: Create small Pega applications to practice configurations and workflows. This exercise allows you to apply theoretical concepts and build a practical understanding.
- **Experiment with Different Use Cases**: Explore various business scenarios, focusing on how Pega's rules and features address specific needs. This practice improves adaptability and problem-solving.
- **Use Pega's Community Edition**: Pega offers a free Community Edition environment, ideal for practicing development tasks. Use this resource to get hands-on experience without any financial commitment.

6. Leverage the Pega Community for Insights and Advice

The Pega Community is a valuable resource for certification candidates. Tips for using the community effectively include:

- **Participate in Discussion Forums**: Join forums related to your certification level. Engaging in discussions with other candidates can provide insights and practical advice.
- **Read Blogs and Case Studies**: Many experienced professionals share tips, case studies, and best practices on the community portal. Reviewing these can help you understand real-world applications of Pega concepts.
- **Seek Guidance from Mentors**: If possible, connect with certified professionals willing to mentor you. Their experience can offer valuable guidance on difficult topics and effective study strategies.

7. Time Management and Exam Strategy

Effective time management and strategy during the exam can make a significant difference:

- **Read Questions Carefully**: Pega exams often contain scenario-based questions with intricate details. Take the time to read each question carefully to avoid missing essential information.
- **Eliminate Incorrect Answers**: For multiple-choice questions, use the process of elimination to narrow down your options. This technique can increase your chances of selecting the correct answer.
- **Don't Get Stuck**: If a question is challenging, mark it and move on. Answer all other questions first, then return to difficult questions if time permits.
- **Allocate Time Based on Question Difficulty**: Some questions may require more thought, while others are straightforward. Manage your time based on each question's complexity to ensure you complete the exam.

8. Preparing for Advanced Certifications: CSSA and CLSA

Preparation for CSSA and CLSA exams requires deeper knowledge and experience. Key tips for advanced certifications include:

- **Master Advanced Features**: For CSSA, focus on integrations, performance tuning, and error handling. For CLSA, study advanced architecture, best practices, and enterprise governance.

- **Work on Real Projects**: If possible, gain experience through real projects. The challenges faced in real-world projects are invaluable for advanced exams.
- **Focus on Solution Design**: CLSA, in particular, tests your ability to design comprehensive solutions. Study case studies and practice designing applications from scratch to refine these skills.

9. Staying Calm and Confident on Exam Day

Exam day can be stressful, but staying calm and focused is key to success. Here are strategies to ensure you're mentally prepared:

- **Rest and Eat Well**: A good night's sleep and a balanced meal can help improve concentration and reduce anxiety.
- **Practice Relaxation Techniques**: Techniques such as deep breathing can help you stay calm if you feel nervous.
- **Trust Your Preparation**: Remember the hard work you've put in and approach the exam with confidence in your abilities.

Conclusion

Earning a Pega certification is a commendable achievement that can open doors to new career opportunities. By following these study strategies, practicing consistently, and engaging with the Pega community, you'll be well-prepared to pass your certification exams and advance your career in Pega development.

Embrace the journey as an opportunity to deepen your knowledge and master Pega's powerful features. With dedication and effective preparation, you'll be well on your way to certification success and a fulfilling career in process automation.

Community and Support: Leveraging Pega Networks

Pega's community and network resources provide a powerful ecosystem for continuous learning, support, and career growth. From online forums and discussion groups to events and mentorship opportunities, Pega's networks enable professionals to connect, collaborate, and build expertise in BPM (Business Process Management) and process automation. This chapter explores how to make the most of Pega's community and support resources to advance your skills, stay updated with industry trends, and achieve your professional goals.

1. Introduction to the Pega Community

The Pega Community is a comprehensive online platform where users—from beginners to experts—can access resources, share knowledge, and discuss topics related to Pega's technology stack. Here's a brief overview of its core elements:

- **Forums and Discussion Boards**: A place for users to ask questions, share experiences, and troubleshoot issues.
- **Blogs and Articles**: Community members, including Pega experts, frequently share insights on best practices, technical tips, and real-world use cases.
- **Knowledgebase**: A curated collection of guides, articles, and tutorials that provide in-depth knowledge on various Pega topics.
- **Product Updates and Announcements**: Stay informed about new features, updates, and changes within the Pega ecosystem.

Joining and actively participating in the Pega Community allows you to stay connected with like-minded professionals and gain access to a wealth of knowledge that can supplement formal training.

2. Leveraging the Pega Community Forums

The forums in the Pega Community are a primary tool for connecting with other users, finding solutions to challenges, and exchanging knowledge:

- **Seek Answers to Technical Challenges**: Search for similar questions or post new inquiries to receive assistance from the community. Experienced users and Pega professionals frequently respond with solutions or advice.
- **Engage with Pega Experts**: Many Pega-certified professionals and developers are active in the forums, making it a valuable place to receive insights from experts in the field.
- **Share Your Knowledge**: By helping others with your expertise, you strengthen your understanding of Pega concepts and contribute to the community, potentially enhancing your professional reputation.

3. Attending Pega Events and Webinars

Pega hosts numerous events and webinars that provide deep dives into Pega tools, trends, and industry applications:

- **PegaWorld iNspire**: The annual PegaWorld conference offers insights into the latest trends and innovations in Pega technology, with sessions led by industry leaders and experts. Attending this event (in person or virtually) allows you to learn about Pega's future direction and how leading organizations are utilizing its technology.
- **Webinars and Virtual Events**: Pega regularly hosts webinars on technical topics, industry-specific applications, and emerging trends. Participating in these events helps you stay informed and learn new skills from Pega-certified professionals.

- **Meetups and Local Events**: Pega supports local community meetups where users can connect, network, and learn from one another in a more personal setting. These events are particularly useful for building relationships and sharing regional experiences.

4. Participating in Pega Certifications and User Groups (PCUGs)

Pega Certifications and User Groups (PCUGs) are specialized communities within the Pega network. By joining these groups, you gain access to targeted resources and events tailored to specific interests and certification levels:

- **Access Targeted Knowledge**: Each PCUG focuses on distinct areas (e.g., developers, business architects, etc.), providing targeted content and discussions relevant to your field.
- **Network with Peers and Mentors**: PCUGs bring together users at similar certification levels, allowing you to connect with peers who share your professional interests and can provide guidance.
- **Participate in Exclusive Events**: PCUGs often host exclusive events, webinars, and discussions that dive deep into advanced topics relevant to each user group.

5. Exploring Pega's Developer Communities on Social Platforms

In addition to the Pega Community, various online developer communities on social platforms provide further opportunities to learn, connect, and collaborate:

- **LinkedIn Pega Groups**: LinkedIn hosts several Pega-focused groups where professionals discuss trends, share insights, and post job opportunities. Joining these groups can provide valuable networking and career growth opportunities.
- **Stack Overflow**: While not Pega-specific, developers often discuss technical challenges related to Pega on Stack Overflow. Reviewing questions and answers on this platform can provide additional insights into common issues and solutions.
- **GitHub and Open Source Communities**: Some Pega developers share open-source tools and code on GitHub. Engaging with these resources is beneficial if you're interested in contributing to Pega-related projects or developing custom solutions.

6. Gaining Insights from Pega Blogs and Case Studies

The Pega Community features blogs, articles, and case studies that showcase practical applications and best practices. Reading these resources offers real-world insights into how Pega is used across various industries:

- **Best Practices and Tutorials**: Learn about process optimization, performance tuning, and best practices directly from Pega experts.
- **Case Studies**: Explore detailed case studies that highlight how organizations have leveraged Pega to achieve specific outcomes. These case studies can inspire your approach to similar challenges.
- **Industry Insights**: Articles often cover industry-specific applications of Pega, providing insights into how its tools are adapted across sectors like finance, healthcare, and telecommunications.

7. Mentorship and Guidance Through Pega Community Connections

Mentorship can significantly accelerate your learning and career growth within Pega's ecosystem. Here's how to connect with potential mentors and gain valuable guidance:

- **Reach Out to Pega Experts**: Engage with experienced professionals in forums and at events. Many are willing to provide advice or mentorship, especially if you demonstrate genuine interest.
- **Find Local Mentors in User Groups**: If you're part of a local user group, identify professionals who have advanced certification levels or specific expertise and approach them for mentorship.

- **Ask for Code Reviews and Feedback**: When working on Pega projects, ask experienced colleagues or mentors to review your work. Constructive feedback can help you improve and develop best practices.

8. Staying Updated with Product Releases and Community Announcements

Staying informed about new features and updates ensures you maximize Pega's capabilities in your role. Follow these tips to stay current:

- **Subscribe to Release Notes and Announcements**: Pega provides detailed release notes and update announcements, which include new features and enhancements.
- **Participate in Early Access Programs**: Pega occasionally offers early access to upcoming features. Participating in these programs allows you to learn about changes before they're widely implemented, giving you a head start.
- **Follow Key Pega Thought Leaders**: Many Pega professionals share insights about new features, best practices, and industry trends. Follow Pega thought leaders on platforms like LinkedIn to stay informed.

Conclusion

Leveraging Pega's community and support networks is essential for ongoing learning and career advancement. The resources, events, and connections available through Pega's networks provide invaluable support, whether you're preparing for certifications, seeking troubleshooting advice, or exploring advanced topics in BPM and process automation.

Embrace these resources as part of your professional journey, and actively participate in discussions, events, and knowledge-sharing activities. By integrating Pega's community resources into your learning path, you'll gain the support needed to excel in your role and unlock new career opportunities within the field of process automation.

Appendices

Appendix A: Glossary of Key Terms

This glossary provides definitions and explanations of key terms used throughout the book. Understanding these terms is essential for maximizing your grasp of Pega's process automation tools and BPM concepts.

Agile
A project management and software development approach that focuses on iterative progress, collaboration, and flexibility, often used within Pega implementations to adapt quickly to changing requirements.

Application
A software solution designed and built on the Pega Platform to meet specific business needs, typically involving workflows, rules, data models, and user interfaces.

Authentication
The process of verifying the identity of a user or system attempting to access Pega applications, ensuring security and data integrity.

Authorization
The process of granting access to certain features or data within Pega applications based on user roles and permissions.

BPM (Business Process Management)
A discipline that focuses on modeling, automating, and optimizing business processes, with Pega as a leading platform to achieve these goals.

Case Management
An approach to handling complex work in Pega, where each unit of work (a "case") has a defined lifecycle, from creation to resolution.

CI/CD (Continuous Integration/Continuous Deployment)
Practices in software development where code changes are automatically tested and deployed, ensuring rapid delivery and high-quality releases within Pega DevOps pipelines.

Data Model
The structure of data within a Pega application, defining how information is organized, stored, and accessed for use in business processes.

Decision Rules
Automated rules in Pega that guide the behavior of applications by determining outcomes based on specific conditions, often used to streamline decision-making processes.

DevOps
A set of practices that combines software development (Dev) and IT operations (Ops) to shorten the development lifecycle, increase deployment frequency, and improve application quality.

Digital Transformation
The integration of digital technologies, like Pega, into all areas of business to fundamentally change operations and deliver enhanced value to customers.

Flow
A model in Pega that defines the sequence of steps or tasks required to complete a business process, allowing applications to automate these workflows.

Interface
The point of interaction between Pega applications and users, external systems, or data sources, typically through APIs or user interfaces.

KPI (Key Performance Indicator)
A measurable value used to evaluate the effectiveness of a business process or workflow within a Pega application.

Low-Code Development
A visual approach to software development that enables users to build applications with minimal hand-coding, making Pega accessible to both technical and non-technical users.

Model-Driven Development
An approach in Pega where applications are built using predefined models, allowing rapid creation and adaptation of complex processes.

Node
An individual server or processing unit within a Pega environment, supporting distributed application processing and scalability.

Pega Deployment Manager
A tool within Pega that facilitates DevOps practices, allowing teams to automate and streamline application deployment processes.

RPA (Robotic Process Automation)
A technology within Pega that automates repetitive tasks by emulating human actions, enhancing process efficiency without altering underlying systems.

Rule
An individual configuration item in Pega that defines specific behaviors, actions, or outcomes in an application, such as decision rules, validation rules, and business logic.

RuleSet
A collection of rules within Pega, organized for specific application functions, that can be managed, versioned, and deployed as a unit.

SLAs (Service Level Agreements)
Predefined goals within Pega applications that establish time frames for completing tasks or cases, used to monitor and ensure timely performance.

UI (User Interface)
The design and layout through which users interact with Pega applications, including forms, screens, and navigation elements.

Workflow
The sequence of steps or activities within a Pega process, defining how tasks are completed from initiation to completion.

This glossary serves as a quick reference guide to help you understand the foundational concepts and terminologies in Pega Systems and process automation. Familiarity with these terms will empower you to navigate the Pega platform more effectively and apply BPM solutions confidently.

Appendix B: Pega Command and Syntax Reference

This appendix provides a concise reference guide to key Pega commands and syntax essentials, designed to support you as you develop and manage applications on the Pega platform. This guide is particularly useful for new and experienced developers alike, helping ensure accurate and efficient application configuration.

---

1. Creating Rules

- **Rule-Obj-Class**
  Defines a class within the Pega hierarchy. Syntax:
  `Class [Class Name] inherits [Parent Class]`
- **Rule-Obj-Activity**
  Defines a sequence of steps to automate processes. Syntax:
  `Activity [Activity Name] {Step [Step No]: [Action]}`

2. Data Pages

- **Data Page (D_ Prefix)**
  Used for loading and caching data within the application. Syntax:
  `D_[DataPageName].[Property]`
- **Loading Data Page**
  To refresh a data page manually:
  `DataPage.Load([DataPageName])`

3. Decision Rules

- **When Rules**
  Evaluate conditions within processes. Syntax:
  `When [Condition] Then [Outcome]`
- **Decision Table**
  Provides conditional branching based on input values. Syntax:
  `DecisionTable[TableName]`

4. Expressions and Calculations

- **Expressions**
  Used to calculate values dynamically. Common syntax:
  `[Property] = [Expression]`
- Examples:
  - `TotalAmount = Quantity * UnitPrice`
  - `DiscountedPrice = Price * 0.9`
- **Functions**
  Utilize built-in functions for data transformations, such as `toUpperCase`, `substring`, etc.
  `[Property] = toUpperCase([InputProperty])`

5. User Interface Configuration

- **Section Rules**
  Define UI sections within forms. Syntax:
  `Section [SectionName]`

- **Harness Rules**
  Configure page layouts and structure. Syntax:
  `Harness [HarnessName]`

6. Integrations

- **Connector Rule**
  Used to integrate with external systems. Syntax:
  `Connector [ConnectorType]:[Name]`
- **Service REST**
  Allows Pega applications to be accessed by external REST services. Syntax:
  `Service [ServiceType] URL: [BaseURL]`

7. Case Management

- **Create Case**
  Instantiate a new case type. Syntax:
  `Create Case [CaseTypeName]`
- **Worklist and Workbasket**
  Assigns tasks to users or groups. Syntax:
  `Assign [Worklist/Workbasket] [User/Group]`

8. Data Transform Rules

- **Setting Values**
  Assign values to properties within data transforms. Syntax:
  `Set [Property] = [Value]`
- **Copying Properties**
  Copy data from one property to another. Syntax:
  `Map [SourceProperty] to [TargetProperty]`

9. Error Handling

- **Error Messages**
  Set error messages on properties for validation. Syntax:
  `SetMessage [Property] = "[ErrorMessage]"`
- **Try-Catch in Activities**
  Handle errors gracefully within an activity by configuring error steps. Syntax:
  `Catch Exception {Action [ActionToPerform]}`

10. Flow Control

- **Flow Rule**
  Defines the stages of a process in Pega. Syntax:
  `Flow [FlowName]`
- **Decision Shape**
  Adds branching based on conditions in a flow. Syntax:
  `Decision [Condition]`

11. Performance Tools

- **Tracer**
  Traces the execution of rules to debug performance issues. Syntax:
  `Trace [Rule]`

- **Performance Profiler**
  Monitors application performance and identifies bottlenecks. Syntax:
  `Profile [Application]`

This command and syntax reference is intended to provide you with essential Pega commands and their structures. For more detailed examples or advanced configurations, refer to the official Pega documentation or community resources. Familiarity with these commands will significantly enhance your ability to build and troubleshoot Pega applications effectively.

Appendix C: FAQs on Pega Systems and BPM

This appendix addresses frequently asked questions about Pega Systems and Business Process Management (BPM). It provides clarifications on common inquiries to help deepen understanding and streamline application within Pega environments.

---

1. What is Pega Systems, and how does it relate to BPM?

Pega Systems is a technology company that offers a platform for BPM, customer engagement, and automation solutions. It enables businesses to design, implement, and manage processes that streamline operations and improve customer interactions. Through its BPM capabilities, Pega helps organizations automate workflows, enforce business rules, and enhance decision-making processes.

2. How does Pega BPM differ from traditional BPM software?

Pega BPM stands out by using a model-driven architecture, which allows users to design applications and processes visually without extensive coding. This approach speeds up development, reduces complexity, and promotes agility in adjusting processes to evolving business needs.

3. What is the Pega "no-code/low-code" approach?

Pega's no-code/low-code approach allows users to build applications through an intuitive, visual interface, using drag-and-drop tools and declarative rules rather than traditional programming. This method makes it easier for business users and non-developers to contribute to app creation, promoting collaboration between business and IT teams.

4. What are the core components of a Pega application?

The primary components of a Pega application include case types (for defining business cases), data types (for managing data entities), UI components (for designing interfaces), and rules (such as decision rules and data transforms). Together, these components define how applications function, respond to events, and interact with users.

5. How does Pega handle case management?

Pega supports case management by structuring complex processes into "cases," which represent specific business goals or work types. Within each case, tasks can be defined, assigned, and tracked as they progress through different stages. Pega's case lifecycle management tools allow organizations to monitor case status, handle escalations, and ensure compliance with business rules.

6. What are "rules" in Pega, and why are they important?

Rules in Pega are reusable components that define application behavior, such as decision-making logic, data handling, and UI layouts. By breaking down logic into individual rules, Pega enables easy customization, updates, and reuse of business logic across applications, which is a core strength of the platform.

7. How does Pega integrate with other systems?

Pega supports integration through various connectors, including REST, SOAP, and database connectors, allowing it to interact with external systems, databases, and APIs. Pega also offers tools for managing APIs and connecting with third-party applications, making it adaptable within diverse technology ecosystems.

8. What is Pega's Robotic Process Automation (RPA)?

Pega RPA automates repetitive, manual tasks by mimicking user actions within an application. RPA is particularly useful for integrating legacy systems where direct API connections aren't available, and it complements BPM by automating tasks within larger processes.

9. What are some typical use cases for Pega in different industries?

- **Banking**: Loan processing, customer onboarding, and regulatory compliance.
- **Healthcare**: Claims processing, patient engagement, and case management.
- **Telecom**: Service provisioning, billing, and customer support.
- **Insurance**: Policy underwriting, claims handling, and fraud detection.

10. How does Pega support decision-making within workflows?

Pega's decision management capabilities include tools for creating decision tables, decision trees, and predictive models. These tools help automate decisions based on data-driven insights, rules, and predictive analytics, allowing applications to adapt to real-time information and changing business conditions.

11. What is a data page in Pega, and how is it used?

Data pages in Pega are containers for loading and caching data required by the application, ensuring that data is readily available and reducing database calls. Data pages can be referenced dynamically and are central to efficient data handling within Pega applications.

12. How does Pega handle user access and security?

Pega implements user access control through role-based access control (RBAC), authentication mechanisms, and security policies that restrict access to application functions, data, and case types. Security features ensure that users can only access data relevant to their roles and maintain compliance with organizational and regulatory standards.

13. What types of certifications are available for Pega professionals?

Pega offers certifications for various roles, including System Architect, Senior System Architect, Lead System Architect, Decisioning Consultant, and Business Architect. These certifications validate expertise in building, managing, and optimizing Pega applications, and they support career advancement within the Pega ecosystem.

14. What tools does Pega provide for monitoring and troubleshooting?

Pega includes built-in tools such as the Tracer, Performance Analyzer, and Log Viewer for tracking system events, monitoring performance, and diagnosing issues. These tools are essential for maintaining application health, identifying bottlenecks, and ensuring smooth operation.

15. How is Pega evolving to meet future BPM and automation needs?

Pega continuously innovates with features like AI-driven decisioning, advanced analytics, and enhanced RPA capabilities. The platform aims to support agile digital transformations, enabling organizations to remain competitive in rapidly changing markets by automating increasingly complex business processes.

This FAQ appendix provides an accessible overview of common Pega and BPM concepts, helping users understand foundational elements and key functionalities that support Pega's effectiveness in automating business processes. For further information, refer to the recommended resources appendix or Pega's online community.

Appendix D: Recommended Further Reading & Resources

This appendix offers curated resources to expand your understanding of Pega Systems and Business Process Management (BPM). Each category includes books, online courses, communities, and official documentation that can enhance your skills and keep you informed on the latest developments in Pega and BPM.

---

1. Books on Pega Systems and BPM

- **"Pega Certified System Architect Exam Guide"** by Henry Fu – A comprehensive guide to help you prepare for the Pega Certified System Architect exam, covering foundational Pega knowledge and providing real-world examples.
- **"Business Process Management: Concepts, Languages, Architectures"** by Mathias Weske – This book offers a solid understanding of BPM concepts and architectures that are foundational for Pega's BPM applications.
- **"The Art of Business Process Management: The Missing Manual"** by Chris Taylor – Focuses on practical strategies for BPM implementation, aligning well with Pega's process-driven approach.

2. Official Pega Documentation and Knowledge Base

- **Pega Community** – Access tutorials, how-to guides, and the latest product updates. The community site offers a wide array of materials suited to different experience levels.
  - Website: [community.pega.com] (https://community.pega.com)
- **Pega Academy** – Pega's official learning platform provides a variety of self-paced courses, ranging from beginner to advanced, including preparation for Pega certifications.
  - Website: [academy.pega.com] (https://academy.pega.com)
- **Pega Documentation Portal** – The comprehensive portal with product guides, release notes, and technical documentation.
  - Website: [docs.pega.com] (https://docs.pega.com)

3. Online Courses and Tutorials

- **Pega Academy Certifications** – Courses geared toward certification, covering essential skills for roles such as System Architect, Decisioning Consultant, and Business Architect.
- **Udemy** – Look for courses related to "Pega Systems" and "Business Process Management," which often provide practical, hands-on exercises.
  - Website: [udemy.com] (https://www.udemy.com)
- **LinkedIn Learning** – Offers a variety of courses in BPM and automation fundamentals, with some courses covering topics relevant to Pega's core functionalities.

4. Industry Blogs and News

- **Pega Community Blog** – Contains insights, best practices, and success stories from Pega experts and users worldwide. The blog covers topics like product updates, use cases, and advanced techniques.
- **Pega DevOps and Agile Blog** – For those interested in DevOps practices with Pega, this blog highlights best practices for continuous integration, deployment, and agile development within Pega.
- **BPMInstitute.org** – This online community is dedicated to all things BPM and provides news, whitepapers, and webinars on BPM trends, which often intersect with Pega's core technologies.

5. Pega User Groups and Communities

- **Pega Collaboration Center** – Join forums, ask questions, and connect with other Pega users. This is an ideal place to troubleshoot and find advice on Pega-related challenges.
    - Website: [collaborate.pega.com] (https://collaborate.pega.com)
- **LinkedIn Groups (e.g., Pega Professionals and Pega Community)** – LinkedIn offers professional groups where Pega users and experts share knowledge, discuss industry trends, and post job openings.
- **Meetup Groups** – Explore Pega user groups in your area on [meetup.com] (https://www.meetup.com). Many cities host regular Pega meetups, where users can share insights and build professional connections.

6. Additional Technical Resources

- **Stack Overflow** – For troubleshooting specific issues, Stack Overflow hosts a growing library of Pega-related questions. Although unofficial, it's a valuable resource for developer support.
- **YouTube Channels** – Channels like Pega Academy's official channel offer video tutorials, updates, and walkthroughs for various Pega tools and capabilities.

These resources are designed to support ongoing learning and professional development within the Pega ecosystem. Whether you're a beginner or an experienced Pega professional, leveraging these resources will ensure you remain informed and adaptable in a rapidly evolving field.

Conclusion

As we conclude *Pega Systems: The Science Behind Process Automation*, it's essential to reflect on the transformative power of Pega Systems and Business Process Management (BPM) in today's dynamic business landscape. Throughout this book, we have delved into the core aspects of Pega's platform, exploring its architecture, tools, best practices, and advanced techniques. We've seen how Pega drives efficiency by automating processes, optimizing performance, and supporting seamless integration with other systems—all critical in empowering organizations to adapt and excel in a competitive market.

Pega Systems serves as a vital ally for organizations aiming to enhance customer experience, streamline workflows, and drive innovation through automation. From its foundational components to advanced capabilities like AI integration, robotics, and data analytics, Pega enables businesses to remain agile, optimize operations, and deliver customer-centric solutions. The real-world case studies included have demonstrated how organizations across various sectors have achieved remarkable success using Pega, offering practical insights into how these strategies can be applied across industries.

As you move forward, the skills and knowledge you have gained will serve as a solid foundation in your journey with Pega. Whether you're looking to advance your career, drive change within your organization, or stay at the forefront of technology and BPM innovations, your understanding of Pega Systems will be invaluable. Remember that learning and development in the Pega ecosystem is continuous, with opportunities to deepen your expertise through certifications, community support, and hands-on projects.

Stay connected with the Pega community, embrace new developments in BPM and process automation, and continue to explore emerging technologies that enhance Pega's potential. By doing so, you'll not only keep your skills sharp but also position yourself as a leader in the evolving field of process automation.

Thank you for choosing this book as your guide to mastering Pega Systems. Here's to your continued success in streamlining business operations and making a lasting impact through the power of process automation.

---

www.ingramcontent.com/pod-product-compliance
Lightning Source LLC
LaVergne TN
LVHW081754050326
832903LV00027B/1937

* 9 7 9 8 3 0 0 2 1 8 6 1 4 *